Praise for *Work-Based Learning*

"*Work-Based Learning* is a comprehensive effort to convey the rationale, application, and future value of continuous learning in the workplace. It is destined to become the de facto text on the topic."

> —Phillip DiChiara, managing director, the Boston Consortium for Higher Education

"When we designed our graduate programs to reflect the learning and development needs of young leaders, we began and ended our journey with *Work-Based Learning*. It has become the single source for anybody designing professional/management development programs in the workplace or in higher education."

> —Don Haggerty, associate provost, New Program Development and Graduate Studies, Champlain College

"This book truly hits the mark for corporate educators. It addresses the key learning issues for the workplace and is impressive in its breadth and depth. Joe Raelin is one of our country's experts in this area, and you'll see why through this book."

> —Robert F. Dischner, director, Learning and Development Solutions, National Grid US

Joseph A. Raelin

Foreword by T. J. Elliott

Work-Based Learning

Bridging Knowledge and Action in the Workplace

New and Revised Edition

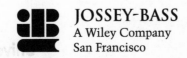

JOSSEY-BASS
A Wiley Company
San Francisco

Published by Jossey-Bass
A Wiley Imprint
989 Market Street, San Francisco, CA 94103-1741—www.josseybass.com

Jossey-Bass books and products are available through most bookstores. To contact Jossey-Bass
directly call our Customer Care Department within the U.S. at 800-956-7739, outside the
U.S. at 317-572-3986, or fax 317-572-4002.

Jossey-Bass also publishes its books in a variety of electronic formats. Some content that appears
in print may not be available in electronic books.

Library of Congress Cataloging-in-Publication Data
Raelin, Joseph A.
  Work-based learning : bridging knowledge and action in the workplace / Joseph A. Raelin ;
foreword by T. J. Elliott.—New and rev. ed.
      p. cm.—(The Jossey-Bass business & management series)
  Includes bibliographical references and index.
  ISBN-13: 978-0-470-18256-7 (pbk.)
  1. Executives—Training of. 2. Employees—Training of. 3. Organizational learning. I. Title.
  HD30.4.R33 2008
  658.4'07124—dc22

                                                                                2007051100

Printed in the United States of America
REVISED EDITION
PB Printing   10 9 8 7 6 5 4 3 2 1

The Jossey-Bass
Business & Management Series

Contents

Foreword

The goal of learning is performance, climbing from an unskilled present to a proficient future, from "cannot" to "can." The learner seeks to be more effective, to be able to act and produce a desired result. Whether the "performance" is purely physical, mostly mental, or a complex melding of domains, the learner wishes to effect a particular state, to secure a difference in the way that he or she inhabits the world. Performance at its best is a kept promise.

However, learning—the vessel to that promise—often remains elusive. It glances off us as podcasts, workshops, and lectures; it avoids our grasp as we chase mastery in the doing of some task. More importantly, when the learning is the hardier type that will alter who we are and make available a wider range of ever more valuable performances, it slips past us sometimes like a shadow, close but difficult to hold. This *transformative* learning, Jack Mezirow wrote, occurs when we make "a new or revised interpretation of the meaning of an experience, which guides subsequent understanding, appreciation, and action." We see the world in a different way and act more effectively. Such learning is consequential for individuals and institutions; it is the means by which change occurs and solutions emerge. Such learning comes hard.

That difficulty is one reason that *Work-Based Learning: Bridging Knowledge and Action in the Workplace (WBL)* by Joe Raelin is such an extraordinarily valuable book. With straightforward style, it unfolds the details of a method that renders the acquisition of such learning both more likely and more enduring. Raelin presents the reader with the possibility of a never-ending and always rewarding cycle of doing and reflecting that is rooted in work. As Joe points out early in this volume, "Work-based learning, then, differs from conventional training in that it involves conscious reflection on actual experience." This book excels because Joe provides direction on "how to set up various experiences that make use of the organic and reflective processes embedded in work-based learning."

That is not to suggest that *WBL* is a mere handbook. Rather each chapter is a *conversation* with the author that serves as a foundation for application of the ideas to a work-based learning instance. As someone lucky enough to have had conversations both real and literary with Joe Raelin, I appreciate the way in which he effortlessly enhances our ability to learn how to learn. Smoothly but substantially, he provides the "conceptual knowledge" on work-based learning that learners of that new discipline "need the opportunity to try out" so "it becomes contextual or grounded—in a word, that it becomes 'do-able.'"

In this case, what is being "done" is the design and administration of work-based learning, which though "new" as a formal discipline involves concepts as old as the practice of apprenticeship. However, the framework that Joe carefully and expansively constructs suits contemporary demands. The proportion of American workers doing jobs that call for complex skills has grown three times as fast as employment in general. Appropriately, work-based learning operates across many dimensions simultaneously—the team, the organization, the individual, the cognitive, the emotional, the social, and the project—and this book addresses each of them.

This kind of learning also entails risk for the learner. The process of work-based learning commences with trying, but then permits and perhaps even benefits from *failing*. As John Dewey wrote, "Failure is instructive. The person who really thinks learns quite as much from his failures as from his successes." (Or as Samuel Beckett opined: "Try again. Fail again. Fail better.") But a methodology that not only allows but even invites collapse because it might prove useful requires a book like this one, which provides an array of tools and the wisdom to make them understandable and coherent.

Joe fleshes out what the art of reflection comprises in a narrative that is both elegant and exhaustive. He ties Peter Vaill to Gregory Bateson, Brown and Duguid to Honey and Mumford so that this elusive practice becomes palpable to us. He reveals the almost ineffable qualities that are present in productive reflection. Writing deep in this volume that "experience solidifies the learning made tacit in experimentation but may lead to mastery more quickly when subjected to reflection," he gets to the heart of the matter. Experience and experimentation need reflection.

That has been my experience as I experimented on the concepts and then reflected upon the results for my learners—and for me. My appreciation for this book predates my arrival in my present job at ETS. I first read *WBL* soon after its original publication and was so delighted by its insights and resources that the university library supplying the book finally dispatched emissaries to hunt me down to ensure its return. (Okay, it was a work-study part-timer, but she was very tough.) After securing my own copy, I proceeded to use it as an organizational development consultant with many different clients, including ETS. In fact, I was hired in part because my CEO Kurt Landgraf wanted these very principles applied to leadership development. Our resulting *Learning for Business* program, now nearing its sixth anniversary, is sustained by the advice and ideas in the book. Next to the support of our CEO, this program co-created by Willa Thomas and myself has gained more from that source than any other element.

One of the characteristics that I appreciated instantly in Joe's 2000 version of the book was his matter-of-fact assertions of premises that are not the accepted wisdom or even common knowledge. When he states that learning should be viewed "as acquired in the midst of action and dedicated to the task at hand," I can simultaneously agree *and* note that much of the learning that is designed in workplaces fails to adhere to this view. Joe then proceeds over the next hundred pages to point out in a cordial way that much of what does transpire as training in work organizations is unsupported by what we know about learning.

The rewards of this new edition of *WBL* are significant. It sports an augmented compendium of resources expertly collected and contextualized. For practitioners like myself, a quick look in the index will allow me to grab a reminder on how to set up a journal or to see a deft graphic of the Ladder of Inference. More patient readers can discover how all of the different relevant theories of reflection fit together in a close reading of Chapter Six. This new edition delves further into dimensions forced by continued change in the organizational environment such as Virtual Team Learning and Experiments in the Developing World. The new edition of *WBL* is a mirror of its own premise: new learning widens and thus changes our entire conception of the learning process. The additions here are the products of Joe's own learning since 2000.

He writes with a confidence that I believe is a natural expression of the care that he has brought to the enterprise. As he has tested and talked and theorized, he researched and reviewed and reflected. This refinement strengthens this guide, making it even more valuable to the practitioner who uses its pages to frame and conduct experiments.

Why is an author's confidence so desirable—even necessary? Joe answers that question himself when he confesses that the practitioner "does not specify the methods of practice *in advance*. Rather, the methods of work-based learning are developed concurrently with work practices themselves." You are making it up as you go along, which is why work-based learning is so effective. It is learning that mirrors life.

Failure is not just a possibility for the learner; the session designer and facilitator face the same chance of befuddlement and frustration in this work. That possibility makes it all the more surprising and pleasing that the book espouses no overall approach by a practitioner or organization. It advises us to look constantly for opportunities for learning experiences for our colleagues. We are tempted to "hug the shore," and this book provides both the means and the impetus to get out into the open sea, which is where we must travel to reach our desired destination.

Such an approach is challenging to the potential user of this book. Who wants to be told that a recipe for success does not exist, that there are not ten steps or five tools that will solve all problems? To be warned that this learning is "messy" and midwived by real mistakes, that it requires and engenders humility, or that it will possibly threaten some in authority may prompt some to move to an easier text. In that sense, I believe this book calls for a robust audience: those who are no longer seduced by promises of easy and sure progress, who have themselves gained experience that tells them to beware of prescriptions, who want above all to be effective in their use of their own time and resources as well as those of their work organizations.

The people in that audience for this book make up a kind of community. One of their attributes is that they believe tacitly or explicitly that performance at its best *is* a kept promise. They frame it as a promise made between supervisor and employee, between teacher and student, between institution and individual, and even between facets of ourselves. This book fosters the keeping of all such promises.

Princeton, New Jersey   T. J. Elliott
December 2007   Chief Learning Officer
                                                    Educational Testing Service

Preface

Isn't it high time that we return learning to perhaps its most natural location—to the workplace? This book intends to do exactly that—to demonstrate how we can learn in the very midst of practice, as we dedicate ourselves to the task at hand. Yet, it also will show, in deference to theory, how we can successfully integrate such theory into our practice so that each informs the other. But it's time to get ourselves, at least in part, out of the classroom and take the step of learning to reflect both individually and collectively with others as we engage.

Is work-based learning not a most natural, even intuitive, process? If it were, we would not need a book of this nature. We would have already assembled the technologies to convert practice into learning. Unfortunately, some of us have forgotten how to learn in conjunction with our experience. We have separated theory from practice and have prematurely decided that our tacit actions cannot be brought into consciousness to shape our knowledge. There is a need, consequently, to catalogue in one place the many ideas and strategies available to us in order to demonstrate how we might recall that instinctive need to learn as we go. Yet, I am not prescribing a mere trial-and-error learning experience. Our work-based learning approaches, though elegantly simple and natural, have advanced to a point where they can accelerate our learning to learn. We now know how to learn collectively with others who too wish to develop their own capability. We now know how to engage our reflective powers to challenge those taken-for-granted assumptions that unwittingly hold us back from questioning standard ways of operating. We now know how to engage and then document the collective learning process to make it accessible to everyone and even contagious within the organizational environment.

The challenge of this book is to bring these ideas and strategies together to inspire a new generation of professional educators who will dare to experiment with this novel, yet age-old, natural approach. This book might thus serve as both a practical guide and a foundation to those who are ambitious enough to attempt work-based learning experiments in their own organization. In time, these experiments might turn into a continual process of growth at the individual level, development at the team level, renewal at the organizational level, and even reformation at the policy and cultural level.

Work-Based Learning: Bridging Knowledge and Action in the Workplace is a revision of the book first appearing as part of the *Addison Wesley OD Series* under the editorship of Ed Schein and Dick Beckhard. Since this original book came out in 2000, there has been a veritable explosion in interest in such work-based learning applications as action learning, action science, and communities of practice. Thus, I have updated the account to incorporate many of the innovations that have occurred in our field in the last decade, such as virtual team learning, critical studies, portfolios, multisource feedback, global action learning, and collaborative leadership.

I am grateful to the editorial and marketing staff at Jossey-Bass, especially Kathe Sweeney, Rob Brandt, Mary Garrett, and Brian Grimm, for placing their confidence in me and in this work to bring out a fresh edition in hopes of transforming the emphasis in learning from classroom to practice. There are also too many colleagues, students, and clients to name here, who have patiently allowed me to experiment with the ideas and practices-in-the-making covered in this book. If the approaches now read as coherent and tested, it is only because of your good will and encouragement.

Boston, Massachusetts   Joseph A. Raelin
December 2007

The Author

Joseph A. Raelin is an international authority in work-based learning and collaborative leadership development. He holds the Asa S. Knowles Chair of Practice-Oriented Education at Northeastern University and was formerly professor of management at the Wallace E. Carroll School of Management at Boston College. He received his Ph.D. from the State University of New York at Buffalo. His research has centered on human resource concerns, particularly the education and development of managers and professionals through the use of action learning. He is a prolific writer, with some one hundred articles appearing in leading management journals; among these articles are some frame-breaking works that are now heavily cited. An active speaker, he has given well over a hundred professional presentations and keynotes. Most recently, he has been a featured speaker and coach on the topic of shared or collective leadership—what he calls "leaderful practice"—and on the use of action learning methodology, a variant of work-based learning that encourages managers and executives to learn in the midst of their practice rather than only in the classroom.

Raelin is a recipient of the Management and Education Development Division Recognition Award for Contribution to the Field of Management Education, is a member of a number of boards, and is North American editor emeritus of the journal *Management Learning*, as well as associate editor of a new journal, *Action Learning: Research and Practice*. He is also a management consultant with over thirty years of experience working with a wide variety of organizational clients. Among his books are *The Clash of Cultures: Managers*

Managing Professionals, considered now to be a classic in the field of professionals and bureaucracy (Harvard Business School Press, 1991), and *Creating Leaderful Organizations: How to Bring Out Leadership in Everyone* (Berrett-Koehler, 2003).

Work-Based Learning

1

Introduction

I took a great deal o' pains with his education sir;
I let him run the streets when he was very young,
shift for his-self. It's the only way to make a boy
sharp, sir.

—Charles Dickens, *The Pickwick Papers*

What Is Work-Based Learning?

The sina qua non of organizational learning has become the need for learning to be ongoing. Only learning can keep up with change; in fact, recalling a familiar maxim of organization learning that has been attributed to both Reg Revans and Gregory Bateson, "The rate of learning must equal or exceed the rate of change."[1] Learning is what creates but also adapts, enlarges, and deepens knowledge. Without new or adapted knowledge, it is not possible to change either the meanings we attach to our actions or the actions themselves.

So, learning has to become a way of life in our organizational enterprises. As such, it has to be more than the sum of everyone's individual learning; it needs to become shared as part of an organizational ethic. That ethic requires the organization to deliberately unseat itself in order to cope with change, in order to "get smarter faster."

How can we introduce learning as an organizational property that extends to all managers? The answer lies in making learning arise from the work itself. Learning has to become natural, even fun. Unfortunately, we have become conditioned to a classroom model

1

that separates theory from practice, making learning seem impractical, irrelevant, and boring. But what if we make our work site a
perfectly acceptable location for learning?

This is where work-based learning comes in. Work-based learning expressly merges theory with practice, knowledge with experience. It recognizes that the workplace offers as many opportunities
for learning as the classroom. Such learning, however, needs to be
centered around reflection on work practices. Hence, it offers managers faced with the relentless pace of pervasive change an opportunity to overcome time pressures by reflecting upon and learning
from the artistry of their action. It is no longer acceptable to offer
the rationale, "We don't have a minute to think." Managers can no
longer react to change; they must anticipate and work with it. Reflection with others offers the key to competing successfully in the
twenty-first-century marketplace.

Work-based learning uses many diverse technologies, but prominent among them is the deployment of action projects, learning
teams, and other interpersonal experiences, such as mentorships,
that permit and encourage learning dialogues. Learning dialogues
are concerned with the surfacing, in the safe presence of trusting
peers, those social, political, and even emotional reactions that
might be blocking operating effectiveness.

There are three critical elements in the work-based learning
process:

1. It views learning as acquired in the midst of action and dedicated to the task at hand.
2. It sees knowledge creation and utilization as collective activities, wherein learning becomes everyone's job.
3. Its users demonstrate a learning-to-learn aptitude, which frees
   them to question underlying assumptions of practice.

Work-based learning, then, differs from conventional education
in that it involves conscious reflection on actual experience. Fun-

damental to the process is the concept of *metacognition*, which means that one constantly thinks about one's problem-solving processes.[2] It is not enough just to ask, "What did we learn?" but also to ask, "What does it mean or how does it square with what we already know?" Hence, learning can be more than just the acquisition of technical skills. It also constitutes the reframing necessary to create new knowledge. Smith refers to programs of work-based learning as "throwing a net around slippery experience and capturing it as learning."[3] Ohmae adds that learning of this type requires a combination of rational analysis and imagination and intuition.[4] Using both hemispheres of the brain, one reintegrates information into new patterns.

Although I shall detail many examples of work-based learning experience in the chapters to follow, finishing with a prototype model in Chapter Eleven, it might be useful to get an early glimpse of what elements are normally incorporated into work-based learning programs. Adapting the prior work of Kolb on learning styles,[5] Honey and Mumford provide a glimpse of what a work-based learning experience might look like (see Figure 1.1).[6] Within a work setting, the process might start by having a manager undertake an experience that is new or unique and attempt to learn what that experience meant and what it achieved for the organization. For example, a human resource (HR) manager might benchmark her hiring practices against a number of companies participating in a regional trade association. This is acting in what Honey and Mumford refer to as an *activist* role. However, they also recommend that the manager become a *reflector*, which entails some deep reflection about the unique experience, brought about normally through public dialogue with some like-minded colleagues. For example, the HR manager might assemble a small group of colleagues from the association to meet both in-person and online to react to each other's practices, including their recruitment and selection procedures.

In the next role, the *theorist* role, the manager, continuing the public dialogue, interprets what the experience meant in context,

Figure 1.1. Honey and Mumford's Learning Cycle and Learning Styles

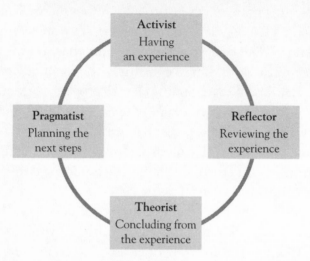

Source: Adapted with permission from *Capitalizing on Your Learning Style* ©1983, 1985, 1986, 1989 Peter Honey and Alan Mumford. Published by Organization Design and Development, 610-279-2002, www.hrdq.com.

perhaps by comparing it with other actions, checking it against other theories, and so forth. Finally, in the last stage of the learning process, the manager in a *pragmatic* role plans what steps might be taken next to extend the experience, keeping in mind how the learning that has already been acquired might be applied. Completing our example, the HR manager would use the ongoing dialogue with her colleagues, in addition to other written sources, as a means of adding to her knowledge base. She would attempt to implement some of these new ideas into her work setting while continuing to reflect on these initiatives on her own as well as with her learning team and her work site colleagues.

Work-based learning, then, is mindful and situated learning in the sense that it does not view preexisting knowledge as fixed but rather as provisional until tried out in a given context or in practice.[7] Further, it recognizes that learning can occur spontaneously in a given situation. It is not akin to learning a set of facts to be stored and used later but rather to bringing new tools to bear in order to figure out how to cope with instant challenges arising from the practice field. Learning is thus tied to practice, arising as people attempt to solve new and interesting problems, often improvising as they go.[8] Lévi-Strauss referred to this spontaneous improvisation as "bricolage," or the practice of using the materials of the situation in creative and resourceful ways.[9]

Note that the role of language changes under work-based learning conditions. It is not just a means to transmit information from one mind to another, from those who know to those who do not. It can become the means for creating and expressing new knowledge in the making.

Derived from action itself, work-based learning may be thought of as a natural process tied to the human instinct to grow. In this sense, it is very much a part of our being. Accordingly, we might match it against seven unique criteria proposed by Peter Vaill for making learning a *way of being*.[10]

- *It is self-directed.* The learner has substantial control over the purpose, content, form, pace, and evaluation of the learning.
- *It is creative.* There is no pre-set goal, nor are there pre-set methods in work-based learning. The learner is asked to create on the spot to find and solve problems.
- *It is expressive.* Learning occurs in the process of doing it and expressing it. All nuances of the experience, especially one's tacit performance, are engaged. Unlike in the instance of classroom learning and even in some experiential learning, we do not know what will happen at the conclusion of our practice. Learning occurs in conjunction with experience, potentially beforehand, as long as we theorize about what we are about to do and compare our experience with it. Learning also occurs during and after the experience as we attempt to improve our often tacit behavior by reflecting on what we did, through peer advisement, or from instruction.

- *It involves feeling.* Work-based learning entails emotional involvement in the context itself. We care about what we do and what we have accomplished. We feel the learning as well as possess it intellectually.

- *It is real-time.* We do not learn in an artificial, sheltered environment; we learn within the fray of practice itself, within genuine operating environments. Our learning is purposeful, dedicated to helping us solve the challenges that confront us in the moment.

- *It is continual.* Once work-based learning becomes natural to the learner, it becomes a never-ending process. We are always open to surprises, to new ways of doing things. Change is accepted as a given in life; hence, learning becomes part of our very being.

- *It is reflective.* We become not just more aware of our own learning processes but also more aware of (and more interested in publicly commenting on) the processes of others.

Uniqueness of This Book

Having read this far, you may begin to wonder what is unique about this book. How does it differ from the myriad of works out there on organizational learning? First, the field of work-based learning is still new, although it has been recognized in the past through other labels, such as adult learning, vocational education, cooperative education, school-to-work, and so forth. Books in these fields typically come from the generic fields of education and higher education and thus do not focus on the action dimension in management and organizations. Further, although this book is about learning in organizations and how that learning is managed, it adopts a unique approach. Most methods designed to help people develop their organization to be more effective and more humane or to help them develop themselves come in the form of a recipe. The recipe is like a tool that has been devised by someone else but that can be successfully applied within the user's organizational or team culture. For example, we have reengineering and quality tools, we have access to talent management platforms, and the like. This book presents very few such tools. Why? It is because the philosophy of work-based learning does not specify the methods of practice *in advance*. Rather, the methods of work-based learning are developed concurrently with work practices themselves. If there is a recipe to be afforded here, it is one that merely prescribes how to set up various experiences that make use of the organic and reflective processes embedded in work-based learning.

In this way, this book parallels some of the recent work in organizational learning and the learning organization; yet, here too there is an important difference. Organizational learning characterizes a set of activities that allow organizations to grow and learn in order to sustain themselves and improve. The learning organization characterizes the type of organization whose internal structure and process allow organizational learning—in other words, that allow it to grow and learn. Work-based learning characterizes those developmental activities and educational efforts within the organization to help it establish a culture of organizational learning.

The closest parallel to work-based learning is of course *action learning* and a close second would be *action science*. However, these "action strategies" have developed along distinct epistemological traditions, as have such interrelated methods as mentorship, journaling, or developmental experiences. As yet, there has not been any attempt to distinguish the commonalities across these approaches and to bring them together as part of a new, yet comprehensive, tradition, which we can now refer to as *work-based learning*.

The Plan for the Book

Before we plunge immediately into the applied world, it is important that we first consider the theoretical and practical context of work-based learning in order to understand its rationale. We shall start, then, in Chapter Two by considering what I am calling the *new learning*, a work-based process that is based on reflective principles and that may be the one way to successfully overcome the frenetic pace of our corporate world. In Chapter Three, the emerging tradition of work-based learning will be compared with other familiar and closely allied management and organizational learning approaches. Chapter Four is my theory chapter and hence may be one that some of my less-sympathetic readers may choose to skip. It develops a comprehensive conceptual model that integrates the learning styles embedded in work-based learning.

Three of the most popular learning styles or strategies of work-based learning, which evolve out of my conceptual model, will be detailed in Chapter Five; namely, *action learning, community of practice,* and *action science*. In Chapter Six, I pay special attention to the fundamental basis for work-based learning—*public reflection*. It is only through public reflection that we can create a collective identity as a community of inquiry. From there, we embark in Chapter Seven on a discovery of four specific reflective practices known to be quite representative of work-based learning experience: *learning teams, journals and portfolios, developmental planning,* and *developmental relationships*. Chapter Eight is devoted to the art of facilitation in work-based learning, especially as applied to learning teams. In Chapter Nine, the most popular of all work-based learning techniques, the *action project,* is discussed at length. Chapter Ten is devoted to those organizational officials who—having sold the concept of work-based learning in their organization—now have to prove it by sound management practices and reliable measurement techniques. Finally, the last chapter, Chapter Eleven, displays a prototype work-based learning program and incorporates some thorough examples of such programs in use today, locally and globally.

2

The Grounds for
Work-Based Learning

What one knows is, in youth, of little moment;
they know enough who know how to learn.

—Henry Adams

The World of the Busy Executive

Executives live in a world of frenetic activity. They tend to see the
world around them as hostile and dependent but for their intervention. Action is required. Delaying decisions is seen as a sign of
weakness, even if the delay may subsequently produce a better decision. Yet, is it possible that the frenetic activity of executives is a
drug against the emptiness of their organizational lives? Constant
action serves as a substitute for thought.

Meanwhile, reflection and its counterpart, listening, receive
short shrift in society. We don't seem to be interested in the whole
story, in the data. We even perfect the art of interruption so that we
can show our "*pro*-activity" and gain the boss's attention. There was
a time before instant replay when humans had to get the whole
message or it would be lost forever. We seem to have lost the art of
listening, and we seem to be unwilling to perfect the art of public
reflection, in which we show a willingness to inquire about our own
assumptions and meanings and those of our friends.

One rationale for this action obsession is that in our current
global economic system, we face the imperative of "grow or die."
According to John Adams, the growth mantra has become an ad-
diction, along with deadlines.[1] It produces a mass denial that we

can continue on as we are, with no ill effects. Its essence is an inner need to prevent awareness of the connection between our behavior and its consequences. As with all addictions, recovery requires a willingness to confront the pain that's being avoided. However, as long as we continue to operate on narrow, short-term growth cycles, we will continue to think about life as *having,* not as *being.* We will continue to go for what is tried and true, not what is unknown or risky. We will continue to live in a myth of "positive thinking," which externalizes, which sees the good life as a matter of outer arrangements, not as a balance of both success and inner well-being. Caught in our own insecurity, we will feel that we have to be the hero, to create rather than co-create with others.

Under the constant stress of the office, few permit themselves the time for introspection or self-assessment, let alone public reflection. But if we are to make learning a response to the pace of our world and yet a natural extension of ourselves, we will need to slow down. And in that slowing down, we might find the grace and self-assurance to perform more meaningfully, even more effectively. This is because in speed, we often overlook the fruits of our labor, not to mention that we tend to produce unintended byproducts, such as exhaustion and pollution.[2] Think about some of the champion runners that we have witnessed in person or on television. They seem to be moving in slow motion, their stride almost effortless, yet they are running at great speeds due to a concentrated and efficient cadence. Perhaps no one exemplified this effortless movement more famously than Michael Johnson, a five-time Olympic gold medal winner. Johnson was known for his unique running style, which consisted of an upright stance, short steps, straightness of his back, and minimal arm drive, defying the perceived wisdom that a high knee lift was essential for maximum speed.

In an emotionally charged exercise that my colleague Robert Leaver and I orchestrate, called Actors and Reflectors, corporate participants demonstrate to themselves the contradictions of a pure action orientation (at all costs) at work. People are asked to volunteer to sit in either a chair marked *action* or one marked *reflection.*

Sitting opposite each other, taking opposite positions, they debate from their respective frames. The actors demonstrate how the workplace is going at warp speed. The reflectors demonstrate what can be done to slow down the pace of the workplace. At the conclusion of the exercise, participants reflect upon the factors in their lives that compel them to think about the following:

- The quality of their work and personal experience
- What others at work are saying about the intense pace of the workplace
- Their desire for personal reflection time
- Their desire for more genuine conversation in a group or with a colleague
- What the community is saying it needs from business

The New Learning

Who among the readers of this book has not experienced at least one of the following organizational changes: top management transition, restructuring, sudden competitive threat, technological transformation, downsizing, merger, spin-off, divestiture? The list could go on and on, but the pace of change will not let up. Twenty-first-century organizations will need to be highly nimble, capable of deploying spontaneous teams of employees within ever-changing organizational configurations in response to shifting market conditions. What can practitioners do about these changes? Survival itself will consist of absorbing the forces of change and responding with the correctly forecast organizational response. In other words, it requires learning, for only learning can keep up with change; in fact, recalling again the maxim of Gregory Bateson and Reg Revans: *the rate of learning must equal or exceed the rate of change*.

The learning we are talking about will need to differ markedly from our age-old conceptions. The skills we "learned" in school typically become obsolete by the time we find a job or develop a career.

It is thought that most young people now preparing themselves for the job market will experience some six or seven different careers in their lifetime, each requiring new skills. In fact, the whole notion of skills as a set of technical abilities to perform a job has itself become obsolete. Replacing skills is the new idea of learning, which will be commingled with the notion of work itself. The most valuable employee will be the updated one, the one who can shift with the organizational environment.

In a similar vein, the notion of apprenticeship, though fundamental to learning, needs a reinterpretation to be viable for twenty-first-century careers. A workplace learning process that dates as far back as the history of work itself, apprenticeship inducts trainees into a community of practice. What makes it distinctive from classroom education is that the master's or teacher's practices constitute the standards of performance for the apprentice.[3] In addition, apprenticeship offers a number of advantages over classroom learning:[4]

- The activities to which the apprentice is a witness are organized around work to be done; hence, the mastering of tasks is appreciated for its immediate use value.
- There is a temporal ordering of skill acquisition from the easy to the more complex.
- Skill acquisition derives from the ability *to do* rather than the ability *to talk about what to do*.
- Standards of performance are built right into the work environment in which the novice participates.
- Teachers and teaching are largely invisible. To a large extent, the person who judges the apprentice's performance is the apprentice.

Yet apprenticeship cannot be a proper metaphor for the new learning in modern society unless it is modified in two critical ways. First, work in the twenty-first century, be it management, machine repair, systems engineering, or law, entails more cognitive or implicit knowledge than physical or observable knowledge. Therefore, apprenticeship requires the talent of externalizing processes symbolically. For example, fixing machines equipped with microprocessors requires technicians to represent structures and processes. Second, traditional apprenticeship presumed relative constancy in the activities being learned. However, modern work activities often hold few constants or routines. We need learning processes that can entertain volatility in the work environment.

Consequently, to be vocationally successful, people will need to replace the idea of skill or competence with the *metacompetence* of learning. By metacompetence, I am referring to competence that transcends itself. It is not any particular skill that is critical but the *change* of that skill to adapt to the environment. Another way of putting this is to say that the most important skill or metacompetence is that of *learning to learn*. Rather than learning job-specific skills, workers will be asked more and more to learn situation-specific principles attending to a given work domain. By mastering these principles, they can be expected to handle ongoing variability in work demands.

The learning I am addressing here, the "new" learning, will also have a personal, even spiritual, side, as it will be based on the self-reflective principle of becoming. Personal learning of this character (which I will refer to in this book as the practice of reflection) allows us to investigate our precarious nature. It also invites others to review our nature under the assumption that exposure is oftentimes preferable to concealment. None of us wish to make our lives an open book. The T-group movement of the 1960s proved that total disclosure doesn't really free us any more than utter stoicism. Yet we need to err on the side of more disclosure as we attempt to develop ourselves and try out new roles. Our growth is measured not just in quantitative terms but also in qualitative terms. We are as concerned about the human qualities of dignity and integrity as with our competitor's market share. In this sense, our obligation is that we do the only thing that we ultimately can contribute of ourselves, that we grow and become who we want to be.

The Basis for the New Learning

Consider how the new learning widens and therefore changes our entire conception of the learning process. Keep in mind that work-based learning—compared with conventional learning modalities, such as training—is designed to be consistent with the new approach. First of all, let's recall that *to learn* is a verb—an action verb that is associated with a phenomenon in motion. Learning is thus continuous—like the shark, if it stops, it dies. I am always puzzled by corporate educators who depict knowledge as a competitive advantage. Learning is what creates and also adapts, deepens, and transfers knowledge. Since learning is ongoing, knowledge by itself cannot constitute a competitive advantage, for once it is acquired, it will become stale if not continually renewed. It is learning, then, in its active sense that constitutes the competitive advantage.

Learning is both a cognitive and a behavioral process, although it is cognition that is both the sufficient and necessary condition for learning to occur. On the other hand, a behavioral manifestation may be necessary to distinguish learning from knowing. Consider an example from the domain of wellness. Most of us know that our bodies need exercise, and we also know what foods make for a healthy diet. Learning may not become apparent, although it may have occurred, until we process that knowledge in a way that leads us to exercise regularly and eat healthy foods consistently.

How does learning evolve? Learning begins when we attend to information. At that instant, information from the environment or from within the self is compared to cognitive frames that we already hold. For example, we may come in contact with data that challenge existing patterns or meanings. As this process of comparing meanings unfolds, we may or may not change our behavior. This is why behavioral change is elective insofar as learning is concerned. We may choose not to change after having experienced a cognitive reinforcement of what we already know. We may also use the new information to change our frames or patterns of relationships but we may not change behavior or even need to change behavior at that moment. However, the new meanings now stored in memory could eventually produce new behavior.

Learning can take place at three levels, though we tend to associate it most with the first.[5] In *first-order*, or *single-loop*, learning, new data produce a direct challenge to current actions. As we question our prior actions produced from reliable frames, we may choose to try new actions. In this way, *first-order learning* resembles what we commonly think of as "trial-and-error." We are essentially moving from using preexisting habitual responses (*zero-order learning*) to learning about such responses.

In *second-order*, or *double-loop*, learning, we learn about contexts sufficiently to challenge the standard meanings underlying our habitual responses. Thus, using second-order learning, we find ourselves capable of transferring our learning from one context to the other. By the time we can move to *third-order learning*, we become aware that our whole way of perceiving the world may have been based on questionable premises. We learn about the context of contexts, such that our entire assumptive frame of reference can be challenged. Indeed, it is conceivable that without third-order learning, the potential for transfer of learning characterized by second-order learning may be limited, as practitioner actions and even adjustments become habitual and unwittingly inflexible.[6] For example, in the midst of action, we may begin to rely on preconceived criteria for appropriate action. Unfortunately, this tendency limits our innovation in working through irregularities in certain contexts. Using third-order learning, one holds a reflective conversation with one's situation. In this way, we attempt to uncover the underlying assumptions guiding our work and readjust our practice.

Consider an example: the executive staff of a large company determines that in order to stay lean, the company will need to reduce head count. So they appoint a task force to "learn" how to proceed with a rational restructuring of the company. Should they lay off workers across-the-board? Should they concentrate on weak operating units? Should they rely on natural attrition? Or should they make specific cuts? Working thus far at the first order of learning, perhaps someone on the task force might pose a second-order thought or question: "I'm wondering whether we have a real productivity problem." "On what basis has the decision been made to make us more lean?" "What evidence is there that restructuring through layoffs is the correct solution to begin with?" "Maybe there's another way to attack the problem." "Maybe we don't even have a problem to begin with, but we are on the verge of creating one."

In third-order, or *triple-loop learning,* or what Russ Ackoff termed *dissolution*, basic premises are questioned.[7] In this case, someone might ask why it is that reductions-in-force or restructuring constitutes the set of usual alternatives proposed whenever there's concern about productivity. Someone might also ask why the organization permits disquiet at the top of the company to lead to knee-jerk implementation efforts or what prevents individuals from raising these types of questions to the executive staff to begin with.

Just-in-Time Learning

Work-based learning, then, is concerned with learning at each of these three levels but is particularly interested in providing a setting for third-order, or triple-loop, learning to emerge. As such, learning-to-learn will become more critical than learning specific topics. Second, as we acknowledge that individuals learn in different ways, we will need to accommodate diverse learning styles and contexts. Third, and perhaps most important, learning will gradually become separated from a pedagogical place.

The classroom need no longer be the sanctuary for learning. Indeed, consistent with the orientation of this book, the workplace can be viewed as a prime location for learning. In fact, we are even moving away from an old presumption that one has to travel to a place in order to obtain one's learning. Learning can occur; indeed, it can be created in the very work that we do in our own organization. Peter Francis, president and chief executive officer of J. M. Huber, a $2.3 billion industrial materials and natural resource-products company based in Edison, New Jersey, offered the following perspective:[8]

Many people equate organizational learning with school, and they respond, "Yuck!" Yet everybody I know has something they love to do, whether it's crocheting, playing the banjo, reading, or traveling. They must feel the joy of learning when they're doing it. The challenge is creating—and perpetuating—that love of learning in your organization.

In this way, learning can be viewed as responding to the individual's needs and preferences and being delivered just-in-time to be of use to one's work, to one's thinking, and to one's feelings. Note that the role of teacher must also be reconceptualized. Teachers are not necessarily instructors who provide information to captive audiences. In the new learning described here, teachers are just as likely to be mentors, group project leaders, learning team facilitators, and designers of learning experiences.[9]

I am not suggesting, however, that the instructional role of teaching should disappear in work-based learning. Especially at the early stages of skill acquisition, there needs to be instruction, often best provided as closely to the work in time and space as possible. When tied to a specific set of tasks, this form of instruction can also be referred to as *on-the-job training*. Instruction in this setting should vary in response to the needs of the job and of the worker. For example, at times the instruction will be *front-loaded*, provided prior to the performance. At other times, the instruction can be *back-loaded*, whereby instruction follows an initial attempt to perform on one's own. Instruction may also proceed "just-in-time" to assist workers as they confront challenges that they cannot overcome.[10]

Meanwhile, instructors can use any number of techniques to enhance instruction, such as modeling and demonstrating, storytelling, and coaching. A particularly effective method connected with on-the-job training is Bruner's concept of *scaffolding*, through which the supports provided for the neophyte may be gradually removed as he or she gains proficiency and knowledge.[11]

In due course, learners are expected to develop the confidence to learn on their own or collectively with other co-learners.[12] Thus, teachers need to seek a balance between scheduled answers and unscheduled inquiry in order to help learners develop their critical thinking skills. In particular, metacognition can be especially valuable to help workers learn how to construct new knowledge when faced with workplace problems for which there is no commonly accepted solution. Under such unpredictable circumstances, teachers can encourage learners to engage in *reflection-in-action*, incorporating such behaviors as on-the-spot reframing, re-evaluation of past experiences, or spontaneous testing of available knowledge to arrive at a solution to the immediate problem.[13]

With the new learning comes the realization that learning involves active engagement in the action at hand. One doesn't become "learned" by simply spouting formulas or proofs. Citing prepared answers to standard questions will do little to establish one's expertise. Learning occurs not only within the classroom but also within a community of practitioners who are involved in contested interaction about the real questions of practice. In fact, knowing only the explicit formulas is what gives the outsider away. Those on the inside know more. Brown and Duguid characterize this action form of learning in this way:[14]

> People don't become physicists by learning formulas any more than they become football players by learning plays. In learning how to be a physicist or a football player—how to act as one, talk as one, be recognized as one—it's not the explicit statements, but the implicit practices that count.

In the domain of executive education, organizations are gradually turning toward pedagogical approaches that address immediate corporate issues rather than those that subject their executives to lengthy and lofty theoretical lectures or even worn-out case studies.[15] Such organizations believe that general management principles are best illustrated by weaving real-life corporate strategies and problems into the curriculum. The thinking behind this approach is in fact the classic business formulation of return on investment

(ROI). Participants in programs derive personal learning while simultaneously working out creative solutions to current corporate dilemmas. The classroom is increasingly being seen as just a temporary station for illustrating a concept or tool that must then be applied to a current challenge or issue on a real-time basis to complete the developmental experience. Otherwise, the classroom concept risks at best being lodged in memory, incapable of seeing the light of day. As Art Hill, former director of the Carlson Consulting Enterprise, a real-world experiential component of the MBA program at the University of Minnesota, says, "Not all esoteric ideas pass the test of practicality."[16]

How Managers and Professionals Have Traditionally Learned

Up to now, I have made references to the conventional management and professional development approach, but let's give it a closer look. First, I'd like to consider training. We spend literally billions of dollars on management training throughout the world. At the same time, there is growing concern that we are not netting a sufficient return from this considerable investment. In particular, while most trainees enjoy their training classes, any performance effects tend to be at best short-lived.[17] Transfer of learning on the job can be quite low; in fact, in some cases, fewer than 5 percent of trainees are reported to have used their training within the work environment. According to Sveiby, after five days, most people remember less than 10 percent of what they heard during a lecture.[18] When activities are used involving seeing and hearing, the retention climbs to about 20 percent. But when trainees learn from doing, they remember 60 to 70 percent of what they practice.

The problem with classroom training is that it tries to make neat an activity that is normally messy—be it technical work that is found in the trenches or the very practice of managing others. Neatness and order derive in turn from control, so it is no surprise that most training activities are under the fairly precise control and pacing of the trainer, not the trainee. Such knowledge work as management, furthermore, is a complex practice since problems change from one setting to the next. It is no wonder that practitioners who travel off to residential training experiences, though personally transformed by the training, find it almost impossible to influence their organizations in the "transformed" way when they get back. The problem is that the transformation is individual in scope. The individual may have been transformed, but the organization and its departments and divisions have remained in their familiar patterns while the executive was away. Clearly, we need an educational approach that appreciates the contextual variety in management and professional practice.

According to Brinkerhoff and Gill, there are five scenarios out of six that could make the typical training program not only ineffective but also highly inefficient.[19] The sixth successful scenario centers on employees receiving the right training when they need it. The other, less-propitious scenarios, which the authors feel are unfortunately common, are the following:

1. Employees receive the right training but it is too late to use.
2. Employees receive training that is irrelevant to their work environment.
3. Employees are forced to wait for training that they need.
4. Employees wait for training that they do not need.
5. Employees attend training to escape a punishing work environment.

Items 1, 3, and 4 address the issue of learning being just-in-time, as noted earlier. In other words, learning must occur as one encounters a problem. Knowledge or skills provided after they are needed may be wasted, forgotten, or worse, poorly transferred, if they are no longer relevant. The fifth item needs no explanation, but the second suggests that training resources may be wasted if they are not tailored to the situation confronting the employee.

When courses are provided off-site by trainers not familiar with the organizational environment, further waste may occur if the training content is delivered without knowledge of the firm's or unit's cultural and political idiosyncrasies.

A fairly typical account of a training department's response to a managerial need was reported by Stamps as he described how Xerox initially attempted to integrate three of its separate customer service departments at its Texas customer service center.[20] The consolidation was expected to take two years because the corporate training department, which is in Leesburg, Virginia, would have to craft separate curricula—each involving weeks or months of design—for each aspect of the various customer service jobs. The reason for requiring this much time at the outset was due to the need to place training department officials on-site to determine training requirements, which would then, in turn, be handed off to the curriculum designers back in Leesburg. Once the curriculum was written, there would be the training itself, which was expected to take fifty-two weeks.

Unfortunately, once the training was delivered, the trainees reported that they spent too much time on tasks that they never or seldom performed and far too little time on some of the most crucial aspects of the job. Their trainers, although good platform presenters, were not themselves customer service reps, so they trained on the basis of a carefully crafted curriculum, not on the basis of actual experience. There was also no time for trainees to practice what they were taught during the three to four weeks of training. As a result, when they finally got back to their job, they had forgotten most of what they had been taught. For example, trainees were put through eleven weeks of lectures on credit procedures before they were allowed to take their first call.

Having considered the pitfalls of training, let's look at the other principal method of developing managers and executives—through experience per se; that is, by rotating them through a wide range of experiences so they can learn the broad task of managing the whole organization.[21] In practice, managers are often given a variety of "stretch" assignments to season them and to expose them to various operating areas to help them learn "general management" skills. Unfortunately, these assignments, though often challenging, do not necessarily come with any consistent form of mentorship; nor is the assignee given much chance to reflect with others on the skills presumably being learned. Experience, in other words, tends to teach in private, reinforcing the notion that learning is done individually, not collectively, in organizations.

Nevertheless, experience can be a very effective learning vehicle and has some clear advantages over formal courses:[22]

- It is not a scare commodity. It occurs naturally on an everyday basis.
- It is not artificial or isolated from the actual work itself. It occurs simultaneously with the actions of people as they carry out their regular work roles.
- It is unquestionably relevant. Any learning that results from the experience is highly likely to be applicable to the work situation from which it arose.

There are ample lessons available to practitioners in their everyday experience; all they have to do is take advantage of them. Gerber points out, for example, that workers can learn from such practices as making mistakes and learning not to repeat them, solving problems, interacting with others, being an advocate for one's colleagues, offering leadership to others, or practicing quality assurance.[23] Unfortunately, unless these practices are brought out into collective consciousness, much of what is learned may not be generalizable or transferable. From cognitive research, for example, we know that experience—though producing formal and informal knowledge of one's organization—may not necessarily help practitioners learn from the tacit skills that they may be actually using in accomplishing their tasks effectively.

Consider the common use of job rotation, which is thought by many human resource managers to be the most effective route into general management. Job rotation assignments expose "high-potential" managers to a cross-section of operating departments in both line and staff roles. After completing the assignments, the cream supposedly rises to the top. Yet why is it that many of these aspiring managers fail in their first general management assignment? Unfortunately, though they may have exhibited effective skills in their job rotation experiences, there is typically little opportunity for them to reflect on and process these skills and competencies, *even when they were performed effectively*. But when confronted with new situations calling for the use of these same skills, they haven't learned sufficiently to know that these implicit skills can be applied (or not applied, as the case may be) in the new context.

As an example, perhaps one of the assignments given to a trainee is to work with a management negotiating team to hammer out a labor agreement with one of the company's powerful unions. During the course of the negotiations, the trainee may have picked up some valuable bargaining skills. When placed in his first general management job, the former trainee faces the challenge of staffing a new project group within a matrix structure. Unaware that he is in a negotiating environment, he selects people from the various functional organizations—accounting and control, operations, market research, quality—to staff the new project team, only to find resistance from each appointee and often from the appointee's boss. He attempts to circumvent the resistance by asking his boss to intervene on his behalf, only to find his boss astonished that he hadn't solved the problem already.

What happened here is that our trainee hadn't learned sufficiently about contexts to apply techniques that he had in fact learned. His learning, however, was at a technical first-order level, which did not translate into the new environment. Was our trainee learning-disabled? I would contend that it was not necessarily an intellectual gap that caused this trainee's downfall. Rather, the organization itself may have set him up for failure by disregarding the need for ongoing reflective practices throughout his training, which was based only on experience.

In addition to experience per se, some training departments like to use "experiential" activities to attempt to simulate real life experience. As I shall point out in Chapter Four, these simulated endeavors, often referred to as *experiential* or *active learning*, can be quite effective in giving trainees a taste for the use of concepts in action. However, simulated experience is just that—simulated, not real. Simulation is not designed to be real but in fact to simulate reality as a way to give trainees a taste of what might ensue in real experience. Experiential learning thus has a valid role to play as a precursor to real work-based experience; however, it cannot be a substitute. Ultimately, we need to move from having learners think about how others would act in certain situations, to having them think about how they themselves would act, to having them act. Simulated experience often makes reality appear to be tidy or logical. Trainee actions seem to generate their desired effect. Yet trainees do not obtain necessary reflection in how their plans and actions get misinterpreted once placed in the woolly world of action. Likewise, human contacts often seem to lead to agreements in simulations, even in those that involve tough negotiations. Real experiences seem to lead to a higher degree of disagreements and failures and require reflective practices to help practitioners overcome these unplanned disturbances.

A More Radical View

There is another set of reasons that formal training may not be working as well as we might like, especially in our management development programs, but they have more to do with psychology and politics than with pedagogy. Let's start with the proposition that although educators, whether in formal university classrooms or in corporate training facilities, have every good intention of teaching about their subject, quite often their students—as practitioners—go to great lengths not to learn what is taught. This contradiction by no means suggests incompetence on the part of university or corporate instructors. In fact, both make every effort to make their sessions active and practical. For example, classes tend to be packed with a variety of hands-on activities, cases, and exercises. There is maximal emphasis on practical techniques and normally minimal coverage of theoretical concepts.

Unfortunately, an implicit theory guides the foregoing pedagogical approach: Practitioners themselves are actually passive learners under the assumption that they cannot take charge of their own learning and cannot use conceptual knowledge unless it is reinterpreted for them and delivered using carefully reconstructed methods.[24]

The passivity of learners is reinforced by the long-standing assumption that the role of the teacher is to rescue learners from their state of "not knowing." Teachers collude in allaying learner anxiety by structuring the curriculum to minimize unexpected or anxiety-provoking occurrences and by controlling the class to prevent destabilizing dynamics, be they irrelevant discourses from students, emotional outbursts, or even silences. The last thing expected from teachers is to confront students with their own state of not knowing and to help them face the fears that such not knowing can produce. Otherwise, such a practice would be akin to abdication of one's responsibility as a teacher to meet the students' dependency needs.[25]

Further disjunction between this implicit theory of teaching and actual practice evolves when the knowledge presented does not jibe with organizational realities. Although the delivery of courses may cover leading-edge content, it often presents perspectives that might not yet be embraced by the organizational hierarchy. Hence, although well-presented by instructors and consequently well-understood by students, the new knowledge may be strategically tucked away by these students for fear that its use would be punished if practiced in that same hierarchy. This very condition was acknowledged by former chief learning officer at GE and at Goldman Sachs, Steve Kerr, who once quipped, "It's Organization Development 101. You never send a changed person back to an unchanged environment."

We might also propose a more sinister view, explaining why students may purposely not learn from their courses. In the instance of management development, the adoption of formal programs is normally planned by the top of our knowledge dissemination industry. Top managers discuss with trainers in advance the apparent content to be covered in training sessions. Department chairs and their faculty review the course curriculum to decide what should be included. The knowledge that gets produced and disseminated conforms to a worldview that is often disparate from the locus of its implementation—operating management. Meanwhile, there is a well-known tendency on the part of operating managers, at various levels within the hierarchy and representing different subunits that compete for resources, to intentionally distort information passed down from the top.[26] Coming back from courses, they know too well which knowledge they can put into effect and which is better left aside or even intelligently rejected.

An Integrative View

The previous, radical view notwithstanding, there are many effective development programs that are legitimately and responsively offered to very eager consumers of the knowledge and skills provided. In such programs, practitioners may be given ample opportunity both to try out and to implement any new methods directly into their workplace. In such instances, work-based learning can and should be allied with traditional methods of educational delivery. At the same time, work-based learning can correct some of the limitations of classical training methods. In closing this chapter, I will depict nine flaws that I believe to be associated with conventional training and show how work-based learning addresses each of these weaknesses.[27] To bolster some of my arguments, I will refer to a research study I conducted at Lancaster University in the United Kingdom of three graduate-level programs, each of which used the form of work-based learning known as action learning.

1. *Lack of opportunity to practice and transfer training experiences.* As I have depicted, in conventional training, trainees attend a course or workshop and then are expected to practice or put into effect the training principles or skills as soon as they return to their job. In distributed training models, sessions are spaced apart; hence, time is occasionally allotted in subsequent classes to discuss the impact of any personal or professional changes. Although the latter approach addresses the issue of transference, it is normally not a key component of the training experience, as most courses require students to move on in order to cover new content. In work-based learning, the application of course principles and skills is fundamental to the experience inasmuch as students are expected to use them in their project work. The issue of transference is directly tackled in learning teams as participants debate their successes and disappointments in implementing course-based ideas. Furthermore, as they encounter resistance to their plans and actions, compared with general training programs, they now have the opportunity to bring back their experiences to their colleagues for further reflection. After completing a program, students have not only studied theory but have also tried it out in practice and have reflected on its utility as well. The workplace is the classroom.

2. *Paucity of leadership and other related competencies.* The evolving global marketplace has increased competition and subsequently has increased the demand for flexible and experienced professionals and managers. Consequently, in-house training is shifting its focus to competencies such as leadership, strategic thinking, visioning, ethical judgment, and versatility. Unlike traditional development programs, work-based learning can have a positive and noticeable impact on a practitioner's development in such areas. In project work, for example, participants could be required to employ resources throughout the organization, using all the people skills and political acuity they can muster; take the risk of making a major decision; and then present and defend that decision in a professional, yet convincing, manner to upper management. The leadership and behavioral

strengths and weaknesses of participants soon become apparent, providing them with the opportunity to learn from experience. In my research study, colleagues of the participants mentioned that they had noted some significant behavioral changes as a direct result of their participation in work-based learning.[28] In particular, participants were noted to have markedly changed in the area of questioning behavior, especially at the strategic organizational level, although within the work unit as well. Participants were also reported to have developed a renewed openness to new experiences and greater sensitivity to others. These behaviors would appear to signify leadership competencies that are unlikely to be learned from passive educational experiences. Indeed, being able to question and learn from new experiences and from other people represent hallmarks in the search for quality management.

3. *Lack of business and organizational relevance.* Human resource development staff frequently attempt to make coursework relevant to their organization's function and to its culture by tailoring their offerings. Nevertheless, at times it is more economical to use "off-the-shelf" programs. A familiar criticism of such offerings is that though well presented, they may not relate well to one's specific culture. When work-based learning programs deploy projects in the participants' own organizations, it is unlikely that business or organizational relevance would even crop up as an issue since the focus is on real problems.

4. *Absence of a learning-to-learn orientation.* Many practitioners attend courses out of necessity or obligation. They obtain their credits or certificates and then move on to do their job perhaps slightly better prepared than they were prior to the training. More often than not, they are not inspired to continue learning on their own; if a deficiency arises, there's always another course. Since work-based learning often just whets the participants' appetite in relevant theory, they almost automatically seek more information as they embark on their projects. The search process becomes fundamental to learning since past experience may not suffice as a guide. It teaches a fundamental proclivity of learning-to-learn that tends not

to be disregarded once the training is over. Indeed, in the earlier cited research study, 87 percent of the participants committed themselves to continue the learning process after completing the program. The experience seemed to have stimulated some genuine intellectual curiosity such that business books would now compete with trashy novels for reading "at those holidays in Spain" (as one respondent wryly commented).

5. *Insufficient time for interaction.* We know that one of the most favorable side benefits from training is the opportunity that participants get to share experiences and trade tips and build their networks. Yet, this is normally considered a secondary objective, not a primary goal of the experience. Work-based learning makes collegial interaction and conversation a fundamental component of the program. Participants are not only encouraged but also obliged to discuss their project experiences with one another. Naturally, during this time, they also engage in informal networking and sharing. Often their exchanges entail a fair amount of self-examination and candid feedback, which tend to lead to more realistic self-perceptions.

6. *Cynicism.* As I pointed out previously, if training outcomes are not considered a normal part of operating behavior, participants may sense a disjunction between course content and everyday organizational life and become cynical about course attendance.[29] Although this kind of thinking can never be eradicated totally, it is less likely to arise in work-based learning settings since managerial legwork is required to launch the program in the first place. If executive sponsors do not want certain practices performed in their organization, then they won't sanction the respective projects. However, once they endorse a work-based learning effort, they tend to be prepared for double- and triple-loop learning challenges. Hence, program participants are likely to know early on whether their learning will be considered valuable and legitimate and appropriately rewarded.

7. *Avoidance of diversity issues.* We have heard so much about the changing demographics of the workforce. Because their opportunities to acquire sophisticated skills are sometimes limited by circumstance, language, or even bias, historically underrepresented

workers present a special training dimension. Work-based learning promotes adaptive behavior as well as the more traditional technical skills, encouraging employees to face the challenge of working within a diverse workgroup head-on. For example, learning teams expect members to engage in free and open exchanges, leading in many instances to disclosure about feelings toward one another. It is natural in this setting to inquire about diversity in cultural viewpoints.

8. *Excessive costs*. Often traditional programs are held off-site and require enormous outlays to pay for high-overhead vendors. While the instructional component of work-based learning may be held off-site, projects and learning teams are often assembled on-site. Facilitators and mentors can be recruited from within the company. Material costs such as for books, videos, or podcasts tend to be modest. Although participants may spend time away from their regular jobs as in traditional courses, they typically work on significant projects that could reap substantial benefits for the organization. In Chapter Ten, I will devote an entire section to how the returns on work-based learning compare with its costs.

9. *Sidestepping critical reflection*. Compared with conventional learning, practitioners in work-based learning can rely on their own theories to guide their knowledge as much as on academic theories presented to them. Therefore, they can begin to focus explicitly on the generation of their own knowledge. They are in a position as much to invent new practice theories as to adopt those already devised. However, they need to ensure that their knowledge be dynamic and thus subject to critical reflection by both themselves and their immediate peers, as well as by others in different settings. The latter instance suggests that practitioners become active researchers in their own right through ongoing sharing with colleagues in alternative work and professional sites. They enact interventions that recursively produce learning for themselves, for their organizations, and for the wider community.[30] In this way, they subject their evolving theories to constant scrutiny and revision.

3

The Distinctiveness of
Work-Based Learning

It is what we think we know already that often
prevents us from learning.
—Claude Bernard

Having established the grounds for work-based learning, we now
need to examine its distinctiveness compared with other familiar
and closely allied organizational learning approaches. Most affiliated with work-based learning is organizational learning itself. I
have already suggested in the Introduction that work-based learning might be considered the engine of organizational learning in
that it furnishes the developmental activities and educational efforts to help an organization establish a culture of organizational
learning. I hope to demonstrate how work-based learning relates to
the competencies movement and how it might alter educational
policy. In a similar way, though less extensively, I also consider in
this chapter the characteristics of individuals and organizations that
might predispose them to work-based learning. I devote a special
section on the relationship between work-based learning and leadership and conclude with one of the newest traditions in work-
based learning: its relationship to critical theory.

Work-Based Learning and
Organizational Learning

Just as individuals need to learn in order to actualize their being, to
engage with their environment, to grow and become, organizations
need to learn to maintain themselves and of course to improve.

Any organization that has survived within our current turbulent global environment is likely to already be a learning organization in one form or another. Some pundits sell "organizational learning" as another recipe for competitive advantage, but in fact it is more than that. It is a way of organizational life that will keep the organization intact, that will allow it to be ever adaptable to its surrounding environment. It may even be considered a survival ethos: those organizations that will survive are those that can absorb what is going on in their environment and act on that information appropriately.[1] Essentially, such organizations "learn their way out" of environmental challenges.

So, organizational learning can characterize a set of activities that go on in a learning organization. And what is a learning organization? According to Vaill, it is a type of organization whose internal structure and process are marked by imaginative flexibility of style in its leadership and by empowered contributions from its membership.[2] It is constituted to learn and grow and change. Its members engage in a continual process of discovery and experimentation. In such organizations, learning becomes a way of life. Members feel free to challenge the governing values of their practice. Structures and standards can change to accommodate new information. These organizations tend to be involved in a continual process of discovery and experimentation. Perhaps Al Flood, former chairman of the Canadian Imperial Bank of Commerce, said it best when he noted that in a learning organization, the company doesn't "force employees to learn, but creates a context in which they will want to learn."[3]

Learning organizations also work to maintain a fit within their environment. Their members diagnose their organization's predicament, integrate this information into a shared mental model, and then use that mental model to modify as required the rules that guide decision making and action.[4] Learning is thus the critical link between plans and operations, between our thinking and our doing. We learn what worked and what didn't work. Further, if the process is continuous, if we can challenge the organization to deliberately engage in a steady diet of reflection, we can learn constantly. Trial-

and-error learning occurs only after failures. True organizational learning should just as likely occur after breakthroughs or after successes. We shouldn't need a crisis to point out the gap between our plans and our execution. We are just as interested in learning what went right as what went wrong.

There is a natural tie between organizational learning and the popular practice of knowledge management that encompasses generating, disseminating, and assimilating the intellectual assets within the organization. As I noted, the learning organization, with its emphasis on organizational learning, engages in activities that stress the generation of new knowledge through free exchange of information, experimentation, and the sharing of existing knowledge. The main difference between organizational learning and knowledge management seems to reside in the relative emphasis on technical versus behavioral explanations. Some knowledge management practitioners tend to focus on improving accessibility to information through such technical means as networking technology. Others, more aligned with the organizational learning school, are concerned with cultural and behavioral processes inside the organization that can induce or impede creativity and learning.

In this book, I am not as much concerned with differentiating these approaches as with showing how work-based learning can serve as an engine for transforming an organization to be receptive to learning. First, we need to understand the process of organizational learning, for which some familiar knowledge management concepts can be instructive. Consider the three-step approach proposed by DiBella, Nevis, and Gould:[5]

1. Knowledge acquisition: This is the development or creation of skills, insights, and relationships.

2. Knowledge sharing: This involves the dissemination to others of what has been acquired.

3. Knowledge utilization: This entails the integration of knowledge so that it can be assimilated, made broadly available, and generalized to new situations.

Let me describe these three steps in a little more depth. In *knowledge acquisition*, new knowledge is created through the development of new ideas, made available through internal or external sources. If the knowledge in question is formal, then acquisition entails the provision of documents, reports, or online information from personal or institutional repositories either inside or outside the organization. If the knowledge is tacit, then the creation of new knowledge requires a formal elicitation of this less-structured information into a usable format.

Sensemaking is thought to be a key driver of knowledge acquisition.[6] Changes in the environment of an organization create internal discontinuities.[7] People begin to challenge their usual interpretations of phenomena. They may find that "doing things the way we always have" may no longer work, causing a rethinking of how to manage new contingencies. A case of effective sensemaking was reported by Meyer, at a San Francisco community hospital that had suffered a major physician strike due to an abrupt cancellation of the group's malpractice insurance.[8] The administration of the hospital anticipated the strike two months before it happened. They collectively developed a scenario that projected the consequences of the strike, distributed it to all department heads, and then asked each to develop new knowledge to cope with the contingency of a major work stoppage. When the strike hit and occupancy sank to 40 percent, the hospital was ready. In fact, cost cutting was so effective that the hospital actually made money during the strike!

Knowledge-sharing means getting the information into the hands of the people who might need it, though they may not even realize the need. Hence, the knowledge carrier has to be aware of and learn how to work through a good deal of organizational interference, such as local language idiosyncrasies or inattentiveness. In fact, Dixon recommends that carriers may need to spend some time in another person's space before there is a willingness to accept the new knowledge.[9] The organizational culture itself may also present a barrier to knowledge dissemination since it often exerts conformity, exercises control, and otherwise deters learning except for what is delivered according to accepted norms.[10] Since new knowledge may be disruptive, users have to be prepared to reframe their problems or to confront dilemmas between their espoused beliefs and their actual practices. Further, the organizational culture needs to be shaped to encourage everyone to share their knowledge. For example, compensation and performance evaluation can be linked for purposes of sharing knowledge.

The knowledge infrastructure within the firm should be user-friendly; in other words, employees should find it easy to connect with one another, be it through internal e-mail or Intranet platforms, so that they can swap information with one another. Some organizations may wish to take the step of appointing a chief knowledge officer, whose role it is to set knowledge policies and procedures and to champion and shepherd them through the organization. In addition, people can be appointed at the department level to ensure that everyone knows how to contribute to the knowledge database.

Knowledge utilization continues the dissemination process to the level where knowledge can be widely integrated throughout the organization. Grant refers to this process as "knowledge capability."[11] It is one thing to have new knowledge lodged within the specialties that directly use it; it is another to integrate this knowledge throughout the organization. Perhaps Chris Argyris has been most instrumental in providing organizations with methods to circumvent the barriers to knowledge utilization in his advocacy for what is called Model II behavior.[12] In a Model II world, organizational members make free and informed choices about change based upon valid information, and they maintain as a consequence a high internal commitment to any new behavior that they adopt. Therefore, they feel free to make their reasoning explicit and to reveal their inferences, knowing that their colleagues and peers will do the same. They regard assertions as hypotheses to be tested, challenge errors in the reasoning of others, and openly explore differences even to the point of bringing up the "undiscussables."

A good example of knowledge utilization comes from the U.S. Army at its Center for Army Lessons Learned (CALL) at Fort Leavenworth. CALL sends teams of experts into the field to observe missions firsthand—collecting, analyzing, and integrating insights from dispersed sources—and then works with both line and staff organizations to disseminate the knowledge in various forms.[13] CALL's knowledge management system has been put to the test on many occasions, when it has been called upon to prepare troops for both combat and peacekeeping operations. For example, using observation and analysis of prior engagements as well as actual deployments of troops, CALL developed twenty-six scenarios likely to be faced by the troops in a Haitian operation, complete with video footage, virtual simulations, and scripted responses. In actuality, the troops in Haiti ultimately faced twenty-three of the twenty-six scenarios developed.

Knowledge Transfer

Integral to the organizational learning processes described in the previous section is the notion of *knowledge transfer*. Learning organizations make it their business to see that knowledge is freely transferred throughout their organization from department to department. This has to be done in such a way, however, that one unit can make sense of the data received from another. In many instances, more than a database is needed. A representative from a unit, say manufacturing, might be made available to a design unit to help interpret a particular transferable process. Sharing resources in this way might even be required across similar functions that are located in different regions of the country or the world. Buckman Laboratories, a Memphis-based specialty chemicals company with business in over seventy countries, has an unusual but highly successful knowledge-sharing practice.[14] The company asks its salespersons to write up a unique case history of how one of its customers developed an application of a Buckman product, most likely one that had not been suggested in product manuals or training programs. As these case histories make their way around the company, salespeople in different regions begin adding these applications to their sales calls. Access to the cases is as simple as logging on to the company's knowledge network. Besides maintaining a library of case studies, Buckman's network provides employees with a set of interactive forums through which employees can dialogue with others, no matter where they might be in the company, to get answers to their operating questions.

Learning-oriented companies are beginning to deploy *knowledge shepherds*, whose job it is to collect and diffuse learning throughout the organization. These shepherds do not have to be subject matter experts; rather, they know how to lead inquisitive parties to the appropriate sources of information. Moreover, they tend to be an important fount of institutional memory in their own right. The World Bank uses an often overlooked resource: shepherds-retirees. These shepherds register their skills and experience, providing bank employees the opportunity to "shop on-line" for their institutional knowledge. Michele Egan reports how one such retiree, a former country director, helped facilitate a network of current country directors, who, though in diverse geographical locations around the globe, wanted to learn from each other.[15]

Shell's Learning Center employs ten subject matter specialists, who comb both internal and external sources for leading-edge practices, which are then contributed to the company's knowledge management system (KMS) repository. Similarly, at Monsanto, topic experts are appointed to sift through and contribute material on particular topics. Shepherds are also assigned to ensure that dialogues are carried out among different departments.[16] At Pricewaterhouse-Coopers, *knowledge concierges* maintain some twenty-five internal databases. They regularly purge, add, and reorder information such that any consultant in the firm can tap another's knowledge by accessing the relevant database.[17]

Knowledge shepherds often operate in conjunction with internal benchmarking or best practice teams. Benchmarking teams are typically formed to export and adapt outside practices for the organization. Best practice teams tend to be part of the ongoing networking structure of the organization, charged with identifying and transferring existing internal or notable external practices. At Chevron, the best practice teams are coordinated by functional experts called *process masters*, who act as internal consultants assisting with the transfer.[18]

The Use of Experts

The most basic form of knowledge transfer is the familiar master-apprentice relationship.[19] The master shows how things are done, the apprentice imitates the process, and the master evaluates the effort. As apprentices begin to apply the rules inherent in the work process, they begin to look elsewhere for inspiration, perhaps from explicit written sources or from other experts and their peers. Once they become very skillful, they might become experts themselves. What is it that characterizes expertise?

We know that experts are able to revise their cognitive patterns or frames quite flexibly in response to changes in environmental cues.[20] Indeed, they do not as much stop and think (of which theory and procedure should be used next) as keep alive, in the midst of action, a multiplicity of views of the situation.[21] For the master, the consideration of the rules of inquiry become sufficiently tacit so as to allow improvisation, and in so doing build heuristic knowledge.[22]

Expert practitioners are thus able to enrich their inquiry by examining competing frames of reference of particular situations in order not to reduce their perception to a single, all-inclusive perspective.[23] Experts possess wisdom, which is far more than knowledge, for it characterizes what you are rather than what you have. Wise people consider what *needs* to be explained.

The novice and even the learned craftsperson typically know in advance the job that needs to be done. Their task is akin to a jigsaw puzzle: they must merely put the pieces together in an organized manner. The master, or what in Anglo-American societies is often referred to as the wise "professional," does not view the task as a jigsaw puzzle, recognizing that the task is not set in advance. The master, therefore, develops new tools or new ways of thinking about the job before being able to complete it satisfactorily. Invented on the spot, these new tools are designed to fit the requirements of the job at hand. Using wisdom, the master is able from time to time to make something that was never dreamed of before, rather than solving something that was already there. Masters do not see truth as "out there" but for their temporary incapacity. Rather, they perceive the need to develop new ways, or new language, to solve new problems. To recall Nietzsche, their ability is founded on self-knowledge, or self-overcoming, rather than on discovering the truth.[24]

Although we treasure our masters as a basis of knowledge transfer, at the same time we also need to reduce our dependency on experts. All experts are not necessarily competent in or even interested in teaching. Many prefer, in fact, to work on their own, except for occasional professional exchanges with peers outside the organization.[25] So, it becomes critical to spread expertise around the unit or organization as much as possible. This can be accomplished by allowing cross-functional deployment of staff, which allows workers to do more than one job. Piggybacking can also be used. According to Sveiby, *piggybacking* is a structure in which senior professionals display their skills for juniors to imitate.[26] For example, at *Affärsvärlden*, a Swedish magazine, junior writers accompany senior journalists to interviews and press conferences in order to learn some of the tricks of the trade. Sveiby also recommends making more use of open-space offices to promote more face-to-face open communication of tacit knowledge. Professionals and individual contributors who wish to share their expertise can participate in work-based learning experiences through informal mentorships.

Expertise may be available from sources not only inside but also outside one's organization. Novices can learn a great deal from merely observing interactions between experts. Once they get their feet wet, they might be able to draw lessons from stories or anecdotes shared between other workers in their presence. In time, they might also be able to learn the "tricks of the trade" from members of the community outside their particular specialty. In one study in the construction industry, novice site managers were reported to have learned the most from both observing and talking with bricklayers, architects, machine operators, technicians, dealers, and commercial representatives and officials.[27]

The Engine of Change

Work-based learning can be the format of preference to establish a culture of organizational learning. First, work-based learning arms the organization with the proper skills to establish a community characterized by inquiry. In particular, participants in work-based learning programs, by being asked to reflect regularly on their practice experience, develop the confidence to challenge fundamental assumptions about their actions and those of others. Work-based learning also breeds teamwork, characterized not just by mutual task work but by consideration of others. The reflective orientation of work-based learning supports the simple yet overlooked practice of giving time to one's work colleagues.[28] As members of a learning team prosper from the support of their colleagues, they become inclined to extend the culture of learning to others. Once a critical mass of people have experienced work-based learning, the organization as a whole may develop the necessary will to embark on a mission of learning. Finally, work-based learning provides the necessary structure or platform for organizational learning to occur. For example, executives will begin to notice the impact of action learning project teams, the emergence of communities of practice, the development of informal mentoring relationships, and other manifestations that enable the process of organizational learning.

Work-based learning can also be a complement to or even a substitute for expertise in a work unit or in the organization as a whole. It can create a shift in the organizational culture from dependence on expertise to learning with and from fellow learners. The knowledge made available arises not from a treasury of available expertise but naturally from the collaborative inquiry of fellow learners deciding through experience what to do next. Work-based learning, then, calls for a partnership in learning wherein different people with different ideas engage wholeheartedly with each other in order to resolve each other's problems as partners-in-adversity, so to speak.[29] To be effective, the partnership needs to be supportive and at the same time challenging, deeply caring yet questioning. Those participating find that they have not only addressed a pressing problem but have also engaged in a continuing process of professional and personal development.

Hence, consistent with my view regarding the need to update the concept of apprenticeship, expertise in work-based learning is not so much an instruction as a tacit guidance.[30] In fact, the responsibility for structuring the learning process is shared between master and apprentice. The dialogue between the two helps both to interpret and articulate experience. Without the inquiry of the apprentice, the craft knowledge of the master—largely a knowing-in-action—remains for the most part unarticulated.

Knowledge transfer does not occur naturally in conventional training. Unless the instructor makes provisions for trainees to share with one another, the learning that takes place tends to be passive and individual. Any knowledge transfer that does occur goes on in the interstices of the training experience. In lauding the knowledge transfer properties of management development at Shell, for example, Arie de Geus admitted that course attendees evaluating their experience tended to give explanations such as this: "It was not so much what I learned in the official sessions but what I picked up from my colleagues during the breaks that was important."[31]

Work-based learning attempts to bring these "off-line" conversations, often considered by trainees to be the most useful segment of their training, into the learning experience itself. Classroom training tends to segment the formal learning from the informal, and in many cases, it doesn't even acknowledge the value of the latter. In work-based learning, the informal learning that transpires in learning teams, in significant developmental relationships, in unplanned crises that erupt in project experiences, and so on is made a centerpiece of the experience. Formal learning is as much developed to support the inquiry process on behalf of ongoing problem solving as it is for its own sake.

The initiation of work-based learning processes can begin quite modestly, perhaps with some experiments in remote parts of the organization, to build credibility for the idea that learning and work can be synonymous. In organizations already attuned to a climate of risk, work-based learning projects can take place at the highest strategic levels of the organization. In a collaborative action learning program organized through the National Action Learning Program (NALP) in Ireland, twenty small Irish companies were recruited and organized into four action learning networks.[32] Each network team included the chief executive or general manager of the participating companies plus one additional member of their senior management group. The NALP experiment chose to focus its work on world-class manufacturing. In one of the networks, a provider of geographical information services, upon re-characterizing its focus to be more production- than customer-oriented, found its processes to be wanting in the area of production planning. The team identified the need to focus their improvement efforts on their organizational structure and on the process of work allocation. Another firm, an Irish subsidiary of a major financial services firm, was experiencing poor process management, poor service recovery, and underdeveloped measures of performance, leading to several areas for improvement, such as more efficient handover of orders-in-process across departments.

A consortium, called the Global Executive Learning Network (GEL), under the direction of Dr. Yury Boshyk, channels action learning interventions to the highest ranks of its participating corporations in the belief that the strategic objectives of the organization and the developmental needs of the organization's top and emerging leadership should be linked.[33] Using what is referred to as *business-driven action learning*, it seeks to achieve practical and transformational results for its client organizations while providing executive development at the same time. The head of human resources at one of GEL's clients, Siemens AG, noted, "The speed at which a corporation can learn and employ new knowledge is a decisive factor in competition. It is not enough to learn and work. Learning and working must be integrated. Only then can a corporation be a learning organization."[34]

Work-Based Learning and Competencies

Another tradition in organizational learning—the *competency movement*—has a number of parallels to work-based learning. In brief, the intent of the competency movement is to identify and develop competencies or behavioral characteristics of practitioners that are specific, observable, and verifiable.[35] Once in practice, competencies are thought to lead to superior managerial and professional performance if performed well.[36] Although some competency endorsers, such as Boyatzis, understand that these competencies need to be adjusted for contextual factors, such as environmental and internal organizational conditions,[37] most competency writers believe that there are certain tasks required of all position leaders in any organization. Competencies labeled *generic* are thought to be applicable to an entire class of practitioners across organizations and positions.[38] On the other hand, *organic* competencies constitute those that apply to particular jobs and are specific to the context and language of the organization.[39] It is my view that only organic competencies can have the specificity and fluidity to represent meaningful categories of work.

The generic competency movement seems to be operating, unfortunately, under the methodological flaw known as multiple causality. As has already been purported, managers and professionals need to respond to an unpredictable environment through an abiding commitment to learn. Rather than emphasize predictability, they need to look for patterns that lurk beneath seemingly random behavior. Hence, causal links, such as the one proposed between competencies and performance, are unlikely to be tenable. Although some competencies might contribute to effective performance, surely there are other attributes, tangible and intangible, controllable and uncontrollable, that also cause effectiveness.

The real issue at the heart of the generic competencies debate is whether competency attainment is necessary to be a good practitioner. Competencies that might lead to effective behavior for one job in one organization may not translate into effectiveness for that job in a different organization or even for a similar job in the same organization.

Assuming one could identify relevant competencies for a given managerial job, the applications within human resources (HR) management are legion. Competency models have been used in all phases of human resource strategy, including recruitment, selection, performance management, team development, process improvement, and compensation, as well as development and training. Indeed, competencies are thought by some HR managers to represent the language of their strategic human resource policy, allowing the organization to match its available human resources against its strategic needs.[40] The HR development function in particular benefits from tailoring competencies to one's own environment. Development here does not refer merely to positioning oneself for a rapid ascent up the managerial hierarchy. It refers to learning those skills that will inspire both individual and team performance. Competencies used for development, however, need to take context into consideration. They should be *organic*, arising from the specific context of the individual, job, and organization, rather than from an artificial list. Organic competencies offer a language for purposes of feedback discussions. By preserving the local idiom, practitioners can recognize identifiable categories of performance.

Pedler, Burgoyne, and Boydell identified three overarching categories of competencies, each of which incorporated generic as well as situational components.[41] The first category represents basic knowledge used in decision making and action. Besides mastery of problem-solving techniques and functional competence, basic knowledge also requires working knowledge of the organization and its policies.

The second category constitutes specific skills and attributes that directly affect behavior. Here again, generic competencies—be they interpersonal sensitivity, leadership, team development, or initiative—are combined with contextual attributes, such as awareness of organizational politics. The third category constitutes meta-qualities, such as ingenuity, open-mindedness, and self-awareness, which allow practitioners to develop the situation-specific skills that they may need.

Work-based learning operates at all three levels identified by this seminal work. In their project work, participants are challenged to work within and then stretch the boundaries of their local operating context. They are in essence prevented from being effective if they plunge ahead unaware of their surrounding organizational culture. To the extent the program also furnishes conceptual foundations in functional domains, these ideas or theories can find immediate application in the everyday working environment. The utility of these theories, however, is tested against their actionable relevance. How do participants recognize the effectiveness of their knowledge and competencies? They not only obtain feedback from milestones in their project work, but their workplace peers and their learning team peers are always present to offer a reading of their ongoing performance.

Meanwhile, the skills and attributes brought out in the workplace, whether in their project work or in their regular operating responsibilities, are also placed under constant scrutiny. Participants in the safe environment of the learning team actually look forward to bringing out examples of their practices for examination within the group. Where the program also institutes self-assessment vehicles, participants match their performances both in the job and within the group against assessed strengths and weaknesses.

Finally, the meta-competencies receive special consideration in work-based learning. This is no more apparent than in the public reflection called for in learning teams and in other development relationships built into the program. Participants are asked to challenge their fundamental assumptions about their practices, even when such challenge can precipitate some uncomfortable behavioral change and soul-searching. In order to proceed in this kind of learning environment, the development of such meta-qualities as open-mindedness, ingenuity, and interest in self-development is encouraged.

Work-Based Learning and Educational Policy

The expression, *work-based learning,* has made its way into educational policy at the secondary, postsecondary, and adult education levels. For example, the 1994 U.S. legislation called The School-to-Work Opportunities Act, though now phased out, set in motion activities that were classified as *work-based* compared with those termed *school-based* learning. Although there have been many ways of referring to work-based learning as a component of educational policy, most definitions consider it to be constituted of relatively structured activities occurring in the workplace that equip students with the knowledge, skills, and attitudes to succeed at work and in society. Students learn by doing real work that is often designed to support learning in the classroom and also to promote the acquisition of broad transferable skills. By equipping young adults with work-related skills, work-based learning promotes a high level of work role identification, which in turn positively influences their successful transition into the work environment.[42]

There is a rich diversity of delivery options in work-based learning within schools that tend to involve partnerships between the school, the organization providing the work opportunity, and of course the student. Often referred to as *experiential education activities,* they may come in the form of service learning, cooperative education, internships, clinical practice, international experiences, undergraduate research, and fine arts studio. Although each activity may have a different functional orientation—for example, clinical practice is usually sanctioned through explicit pedagogical guidelines specified within the allied health professions—they tend to subscribe to particular quality standards. For example, students and employers mutually plan for successful experiences through orientations that seek to maximize learning. The students' participation is actively monitored and assessed both by the school authorities and through supervision within the work site. There is attention paid to safety and of course to compliance with state and federal labor laws. Most of these modalities provide opportunities for reflection. Students either are paid for their services or receive academic credit, and in some cases, they receive accreditation for prior learning and experience.[43]

An interesting example of the application of work-based learning within the adult education arena is the Jobs to Careers program supported by the Robert Wood Johnson Foundation in collaboration with the Hitachi Foundation. It seeks to advance the skill and career development of incumbent workers providing care and services on the front lines of the health care system. These workers represent a diverse group, such as medical assistants, health educators, laboratory technicians, substance abuse counselors, and home health aides, practicing in such settings as acute care hospitals, long-term care institutions, behavioral and community health clinics, and public and community health organizations. They constitute a vast population of some 4.7 million people in the United States alone, and though they perform work critical to the viability of our nation's health care system, their learning opportunities and career advancement are currently limited, leading to their short supply and rapid turnover. The Jobs to Careers initiative seeks to address the career plight of these workers through a number of human resource approaches, prominent among which is the use of work-based learning strategies. The program requires partnerships between employers and educational institutions to develop learning opportunities through work and within the workday. By capturing, documenting, and rewarding learning that occurs on the job, it hopes to establish academic credit or industry-recognized credentials for achievement.

As an example, mental health technicians in one community residence refined their case management skills while earning a certification in Drug and Alcohol Rehabilitation. Their supervisors were also trained to codevelop and observe the technicians' learning objectives. The program incorporated some didactic instruction and fieldwork and articulated with bachelor's and master's level degrees.[44] Comparable experiments have been reported elsewhere. For example, a collaborative project between Newcastle Hospital Trust and the University of Northumbria, in the United Kingdom, was undertaken to prepare twenty-one experienced nurses to practice independently in minor injury units while receiving accreditation of their learning.[45] The framework was referred to as *accredited work based learning* and incorporated such features as professional and academic profiling of each participant; development of learning contracts between the participant, a clinical manager, and academic staff; clinical shadowing and skill development; collection of evidence of achievement of learning outcomes; clinical skill assessment in the workplace; and internal and external examination.

With work-based learning now in the twenty-first century playing an increasing role in educational policy, what lessons have we learned to ensure it makes a valuable contribution to both youth and adult education? First, early assessments of school-to-work programs have reinforced the now familiar logic that work-based learning activities be well-coordinated with the classroom. Work-based and school-based learning should not be segmented. In other words, work-based activities are not meant to be accomplished once students have learned their lessons. Rather, they offer an opportunity for students to apply their classroom principles immediately into work as well as to reflect on their work practices.

Another lesson for educational policy is that, as Hamilton and Hamilton once warned, "Simply placing young people in workplaces does not guarantee that they will learn."[46] There needs to be dedicated attention to reflection on their work activities as close as possible to such activities. It is unfortunately often too late to begin the process of reflection after the experience is over. Any learning cannot otherwise be tested against the real world of practice. As I shall often point out in this book, the reflection should also be collective as well as concurrent. Participants can learn as much from sharing their incidents and stories with others as from their own introspection.

As in the Schools to Career program, it is important that all parties to the learning—the school, the placement organization, and the student—commit to this form of education.[47] For example, just providing courses within the workplace is not the same as learning from real work experience. Work-based learning does not subscribe to the perspective that knowledge is permanent; that it can be acquired through protracted study or mental acquisition and thus only through reason and intellect not through emotion and reflection.[48] Contextualized learning is just as viable a form of learning as classroom learning. Just appreciating this transformation in thought as regards the basis of epistemology—how people learn—is as good a starting place as any in establishing the value of work-based learning.

Readers may ask why a pronouncement regarding the value of practice in learning is necessary, especially when it comes to preparation for knowledge work, such as the professions, which are embedded in practice itself. From a historical point of view, in the United States, it appears that our state universities and colleges and second-tier private universities, in order to gain respectability, attempted to emulate their first-tier cousins, which were meanwhile still teaching using tried-and-true classroom methodologies that relied on cognitive development rather than field-learning approaches.[49] Furthermore, to sustain prestige, these institutions encouraged their faculty to continue to develop their research at the expense of more time-consuming teaching strategies, which afford greater intersection with the practice world that their students would someday face on their own. The scholarship chosen by the faculty would also rarely scrutinize their own practice—rather, it would be used to explore the content of their discipline.[50]

It is no wonder that critics in nearly all the professions have formed a chorus denouncing our universities for preparing students with the wrong competencies, rather than those required to become successful in their fields.[51] In particular, the critics have ultimately detected that our professional education has emphasized the technical skills over the interpersonal, the accumulation of facts over wisdom, and a focus on individual accomplishment over intersubjective appreciation. At the same time, it is not surprising that a hierarchical, decontextualized, and cognitive form of education would emerge in a provision that became detached from the world of practice. Even in contemporary liberal arts education, although there is interest in developing autonomous lifelong learners, only recently have curricular models emphasized the value of real-world and interdisciplinary connections.[52]

Predisposition Toward Work-Based Learning

Are there certain types of individuals and organizations that are predisposed to work-based learning? I have found that in terms of individuals, those likely to derive useful benefits from these programs tend to be looking for a challenge, to be committed to their organization, to be consistent in their beliefs and actions, and to be risk-oriented.[53] Bunning adds that such individuals need to be curious in their outlook, creative and innovative, and collaborative.[54] They are also likely to be opportunistic (in their learning) and collectivist. An *opportunistic learner* is someone who is committed to learning in life from whatever source is available—reading a novel, being engaged in conversation, observing an interesting display. Such a learner doesn't need proof that learning can occur as much from experience itself as from the formal discipline of teaching. Opportunistic learners also are curious about which circumstances seem to produce the most efficient and effective learning for themselves.[55]

Individuals with a *collectivist orientation* are those who have a general propensity to cooperate with others in group endeavors.[56] Whether it be in project work involving others or in learning teams, work-based learning tends to require a commitment to work and learn in the company of compatriots. Those with individualistic orientations, who prefer to work and learn on their own, tend to object to the group work contingent in successful work-based learning programs.

Elena Antonacopoulou's work, though not concerned specifically with work-based learning, can be quite instructive regarding the predispositions of individuals toward company-based educational efforts.[57] She distinguishes between *philomathic* and *mathophobic* learners. *Philomathia* describes individuals who maintain positive attitudes toward learning and a readiness to explore and improve through learning. *Mathophobia* describes individuals who are reluctant to or lack confidence in their ability to learn. Mathophobics often refuse to take personal responsibility to develop themselves, have little sense of direction, and are typically unwilling to explore different learning avenues. What makes someone mathophobic? In her study of a major bank in the United Kingdom, Antonacopoulou found that these anti-learning managers were not just passive in the face of learning opportunities but in some cases were actually fearful of admitting their ignorance because it might be disclosed in a public setting. They also felt that they were unable to influence the learning environment in the organization.

Besides these internal factors, Antonacopoulou also found that organizational norms and policies could affect individuals' predisposition to learn. Most dampening to personal learning habits was the company's inconsistency between its espoused support of development activities and its actual implementation of this policy. A manager in human resources politely noted, "When people at the top pay lip service to aspects they breach, they do not give the example for others to follow." Other organizational factors revealed in the research were incompatibility of learning style between company and individual, lack of support from one's boss and from one's other colleagues, and discontinuity and lack of clarity concerning the organization's expectations.

Krystyna Weinstein suggests that work-based learning seems to be most effective with individuals who can release an "inner learning cycle."[58] They do more than merely recall experience; through internal processes, they make themselves open to personal transformation. These processes incorporate an awareness of, a desire to, and the personal courage to change on the basis of personal insight.

Another personal construct that has high promise of serving as both an antecedent to as well as a resultant of work-based learning success is *work self-efficacy*. The concept of self-efficacy has been widely established in the literature as a critical construct within Albert Bandura's social learning theory.[59] It constitutes a judgment about one's ability to perform a particular behavior pattern. Self-efficacy expectations are considered the primary cognitive determinant of whether or not an individual will attempt a given behavior. While self-efficacy, in general, refers to one's confidence in executing courses of action in managing a wide array of situations, work self-efficacy assesses workers' confidence in managing workplace experiences. A new work self-efficacy inventory under development at the Center for Work and Learning at Northeastern University, for example, measures a range of behaviors and practices—for example, exhibiting teamwork, expressing sensitivity, managing politics, handling pressure—attending to one's beliefs in his or her command of the social requirements necessary for success in the workplace.[60] Because efficacy is a malleable property, employees may achieve relative success in their jobs as well as learning within the workplace by increasing their confidence in performing many of these work-related behaviors.

In terms of the organizational qualities that facilitate work-based learning, I found that cultures that value collaboration over individualism and organizations that are clear on their mission and goals seem to produce better work-based learners. Bunning also contributes some additional qualities in the organizational domain.[61] In particular, work-based learning outcomes are enhanced in organizational cultures that value:

- Organizational nondefensiveness
- Learning as a basic norm

- Process-oriented leadership in addition to a focus on content
- Reflective self-examination by individuals and teams
- Commitment to change

Finally, Honey also defines a series of behaviors on the part of managers and staff that he feels need to be present if the culture is to support work-based learning.[62] Among these behaviors, three stand out beyond those already mentioned. In particular, in learning-oriented cultures, people tend to (1) ask a lot of questions, (2) explicitly talk about learning, and (3) freely admit their inadequacies and mistakes.

Work-Based Learning and Leadership

This chapter, which has been showing how the tradition of work-based learning connects to other management and organizational development approaches, would not be complete without reference to the critical topic of leadership. Work-based learning, as we have established, supports a different form of organization than classic bureaucracy. Bureaucracy, by definition, is concerned with rules and regulations that are devised to impose order on an organization. The learning organization, on the other hand, though recognizing the value of some order, at the same time reassesses it by challenging its closely held assumptions and structures. It upends standard ways of doing things by encouraging independent thinking from the factory floor to the executive suite. It recognizes that knowledge becomes stale as soon as it is used and requires learning to adapt, deepen, and transfer it.

If work-based learning contributes to turning the structure of bureaucracy upside down, then it should come as no surprise that it also tends to disrupt the classic definition of the leader as the one "who stands out in front." Over time, the especially dialogic approaches of work-based learning appear to surface a different form of leadership, one denoted by a collective form of leadership, which I refer to as *leaderful*.[63] This is a new term, but it is required because the idea of involving everyone in leadership and seeing leadership as a collective property is quite distinctive from its familiar heroic archetype. Leaderful practice also falls in some respects into the domain of *shared leadership*, which has roots in empowerment, self-directed work teams, and self-leadership.[64] However, unlike some traditions in shared leadership, it is collective rather than sequential or serial.[65]

Leaderful practice is based on four critical tenets, referred to as "The Four C's." The leadership of teams and organizations can be *concurrent, collective, collaborative* and *compassionate*.

Concurrent leadership means that not only can many members serve as leaders, but they can also do so at the same time. No one, not even the supervisor, has to stand down when someone is making a contribution as a leader. *Collective leadership* means that everyone in the group can serve as a leader; the team is not dependent on one individual to take over. *Collaborative leadership* means that everyone is in control of and can speak for the entire team. All members pitch in to accomplish the work of the team. Together they engage in a mutual dialogue to determine what needs to be done and how to do it. Finally, in *compassionate leadership*, members commit to preserving the dignity of every single member of the team, meaning that they consider each individual whenever any decision is made or any action taken.

The link between work-based learning and leaderful practice can be established across all four tenets, but I would like to point out two principles that stand out. First, a spirit of organizational learning at the macro level provides a critical condition for the effects of work-based learning to be fully experienced. If everyone participates in leadership, then no one needs to stand by in a dependent capacity. Everyone is primed for learning. In such an organization, members surface their insights, become comfortable questioning their suppositions, and exhibit a humility that recognizes the limits of their knowledge.

The second principle that underlies the link between work-based learning and leaderful practice is that the culture of the organization endorse a spirit of free inquiry. Because the root of many of our organizational problems may not be known in advance, there is a need for inquirers to be nonjudgmental and to be relatively equal in status. Certainly, on given topics, individuals will have different degrees of expertise. But expertise is rarely exclusive and can also be ephemeral as problems become increasingly complex and multifunctional.[66] Although it is possible for one or a few persons to come into prominence in the search for solutions to our problems, generations of group process research suggest that these solutions will be far more robust as other members variably get involved in the process and participate as part of a collaborative venture.[67]

Let's consider now how work-based learning can elicit each of the tenets of leaderful practice.

Concurrent Leadership

Because it professes that leadership can be exhibited by more than one person in the group at the same time, concurrent leadership is arguably the most radical proposition in leaderful practice. At the early stages of the life cycle of any team or organization, it is unlikely that inexperienced members will agree cognitively or behaviorally with this proposition. Hence, they may need encouragement, evidence, and practice to arrive at this form of participation. Work-based learning requires team members and facilitators to work through critical developmental issues. How prepared are its members to share leadership with one another? Do they need to rely on one person to assume standard leadership responsibilities? Who will see to it that the best use will be made of the team's resources, that the strengths and weaknesses of the team members will be recognized? Who will provide support to team members in need? Who will be concerned with fostering team spirit? Who will explore and report on opportunities outside the group?

These issues are learning issues. Work-based learning does not insist that they be lodged within any one person; rather, they become the knowledge responsibilities of the entire team. In other words, what is critical is that the key responsibilities of the team to ensure its integrity and performance get done.[68] There is no advance specification as to which person or role occupant accomplishes them. They are learning requirements that the team as a whole must attend to. As they are learned, involving practice and gradual mastery, concurrent leadership becomes more than an aspiration. It becomes a reality.

Among the skills afforded through work-based learning that contribute to concurrent leadership are those that fall under the general domain of group dynamics. Understanding how groups develop and the specific interpersonal skills that members need to use is part of the "curriculum" in any work-based learning experience. Participants are placed into project teams and learning teams to work and reflect together on their collective processes and accomplishments. They need to learn how to divide up the work fairly, how to support one another for the good of the team, how to decide what they need to do to function as an effective unit, and how to develop a sufficient level of trust to commit to one another.[69] It is only when teams become prepared to take control of their own tasks that they no longer need managerial control. It is at this point that they become self-managed without the need for a dominant leader.[70] Each member can exert requisite control when needed. This may include the critical boundary function of the group, the function that gains access to and screens information for the team and helps it obtain outside resources.[71] Although this function typically resides with the position leader, it need not, especially when the outside resource is a professional body or stakeholder more known to specialists within the team than to the named supervisor.

Herb Kelleher, former CEO of Southwest Airlines, went as far as to say that lodging control within a single supervisor or executive would not only be a form of learning deprivation but also a strategic blunder:

> A financial analyst once asked me if I was afraid of losing control of our organization. I told him I've never had control and I never wanted it. We're not looking for blind obedience. We're looking for people who on their own initiative want to be doing what they're doing because they consider it to be a worthy objective. That I can-

not possibly know everything that goes on in our operation—and don't pretend to—is a source of competitive advantage. The freedom, informality, and interplay that people enjoy allow them to act in the best interests of the company.[72]

Collective Leadership

Having considered the concurrent perspective of leadership—that it can be practiced by members of a team at the same time—it is not a leap of faith to view leadership as something that the entire community does together. In such a setting, everyone is challenged to learn; no one needs to stand by in a dependent capacity. Accordingly, organizational members willingly seek feedback, openly discuss errors, experiment optimistically with new behaviors, reflect mutually on their operating assumptions, and demonstrably support one another.[73]

Work-based learning sustains collective leadership through the discipline of reflective practice. Participants assemble into learning teams, where they begin to question one another about their project experiences. In due course, they also extend their inquiry to each other's professional and personal experiences. They develop a peripheral awareness of others. They come to know learning as a collective process that extends beyond the individual. In the learning team, the inquirer learns as much as the focal person; indeed, the entire group *learns to learn together* as all members become mutually responsible for the decisions and actions of the team.

Learning can be accomplished, then, just-in-time and in the right dose to be helpful to practice.[74] Furthermore, it does not have to become disassociated from the notion of place. It can be designed to assist leaders in navigating through the cultural and political landmines of their own organization. It can be dedicated to solving actual problems faced by the business in question. As we shall see, work-based learning also endorses the practice of double-loop learning—learning that probes to the underlying assumptions and even premises behind planned strategies.[75] People learn to question what might even be considered sacred.[76]

Consider the use of a targeted action learning process at mammoth Johnson & Johnson, a broad-based health care company, composed of nearly two hundred distinct operating companies. Former CEO Ralph Larsen introduced its FrameworkS strategic process, the capital S signifying the multiple frames through which a strategic team could view its project mission. According to the process, the company would invite ten to twelve people from its various operating divisions to join the executive committee in a significant strategic undertaking. The new team members would be chosen for the geographical, technical, or organizational perspective they could bring to bear on the issue at hand. They were not necessarily high-ranking executives as much as people with various talents to add value to the project deliberations. The team typically would go off to a remote location for a week to work on the project. Meetings were run democratically, with no one imposing rank or exerting privileged status. After the initial gathering, additional subcommittees and task forces were organized to continue to research the issues and take the necessary actions. FrameworkS teams have accordingly steered the company into new markets, new technologies, new businesses, and even new values (such as their "What's New" Program, focusing the company on innovative practices). FrameworkS was viewed as successful because of its collective learning, which widened Johnson & Johnson's reach into strategic avenues previously unexplored.[77]

Collaborative Leadership

Work-based learning models collaborative leadership through three explicit principles. First, it models dialogic processes that take a stance of nonjudgmental inquiry. Participants are encouraged to express genuine curiosity about the suggestions of others and to avoid maintaining hidden interests. The principal interest is in a salutary outcome across individual, group, and organizational levels of performance. Second, they are encouraged to submit their own ideas and views to the critical scrutiny of others. In this way, they become receptive to challenges to their own ways of thinking, even to discovering the limitations of how they think and act. Third, they entertain the view that something new or unique might arise from a mutual inquiry that could reconstruct everyone's view of reality in an entirely new way. They are willing to disturb their own preconceived worldviews on behalf of a common good.

So, mutual inquiry invites all members of a community to come into the circle and fully advocate their views but also to be prepared to listen to and deeply consider those of others. As such, it recognizes that the contribution of all members of the community, no matter what their social standing, can only arise from civil dialogue, which permits open disclosure of each person's beliefs, feelings, and assumptions.[78] As a leadership development approach, it teaches humility at the outset because it is practitioner-centered, not trainer-centered.[79] No one has all the answers. Indeed, even the questions need to be mutually rediscovered. The speaking referred to here is thus reciprocal, leading to the production of new and lived realities.[80]

Work-based learning is also concerned with collaborative inquiry since it calls for engagement by participants in action projects that often involve challenges to the status quo, in particular to the operating conditions in the participants' own organizations. As such, projects may end up questioning familiar political and social relationships in the organization. Indeed, work-based learning participants typically become avid questioners, not only of their own local culture but also of conditions outside their operating purview.[81] Projects tend to take on a life of their own and at times even diverge from the question originally posed to the team. Work-based learning projects, then, require an organizational culture of risk taking and openness, which permits occasional surfacing of ineffectual or insensitive rules and practices.[82]

Compassionate Leadership

Compassionate leadership uplifts an organization, since it represents a process that dignifies the human spirit, allowing it to grow and achieve. Compassionate communities are characterized by the endorsement of a diversity of views, even those that do not conform to existing mental models and practices. In this way, compassion entails an appreciation of other cultures and sensitivity toward views that are less privileged than those in the dominant culture.

As a grassroots form of learning, work-based learning emphasizes such critical democratic values as humility and sustainability. Participants appreciate any social transformation because they participate in it.[83] By bridging their inner and outer worlds, they can speak with integrity in any effort taken to heal the ecological, economic, and social systems in which they live.[84]

For a work-based learning program to be successful as a vehicle to help transform an institutional culture to a leaderful organization, it is confirmatory when public figures model integrity in their own behavior and discourse. Consider the practice of William Peace, a former executive with Westinghouse and United Technologies, who, as a newly minted executive and against the advice of his closest colleagues, chose to meet alone with fifteen people who had just found out that they were given pink slips. The encounter was an emotionally battering experience for Peace, as he had to listen to former employees' pouring out their grief, anger, and bewilderment. When he got a chance, he tried his best to explain to these employees that the survival of the business required their release, even though there was absolutely nothing wrong with their performance. In the end, the business was sold but the remaining entity flourished sufficiently so that Peace was able to offer the chance for half of the dismissed employees to return. Without exception, every person offered the chance to return accepted, even those who had already found other jobs. In retrospect, here's how Peace later depicted his soft management approach:

> Unlike the classic leaders of business legend with their towering self-confidence, their unflinching tenacity, their hard, lonely lives at the top, I try to be vulnerable to criticism. I do my best to be tentative, and I cherish my own fair share of human frailty.[85]

Critical Work-Based Learning

In the last section of this chapter, I take up both an evolving and a controversial tradition in work-based learning: its potential critical nature. Although not yet pervasively incorporated into practice, *critical action learning* has been seriously broached by a number of academics. This tradition derives from a criticism of conventional work-based learning in its presumed acceptance of current managerial orthodoxies that conceive of organizational actions and changes as largely depoliticized and accepting of current power relationships. In this way, it may give learners a false sense of their participation in a social structure that feigns involvement while sustaining performance coercion.[86] Critical theorists would have work-based learning focus more upon employer-employee relationships as a lived experience that is capable of challenging conventional wisdom.[87]

Criticism in work-based learning can take two forms: it can focus on critical pedagogical content, which tends to politicize the curriculum, or it can focus on critical reflection, which embraces dialogic and emancipatory approaches to teaching and learning.[88] In the former instance, critical pedagogy has as its intent the freeing of people from unnecessarily restrictive traditions and power relations that inhibit opportunity for need fulfillment. As such, it often requires a resistance to established power structures, which may even unwittingly prevent the release of human aspiration.[89] Emancipatory discourse, meanwhile, has a compatible but more social-psychological agenda of freeing people from internal forces that may limit their personal control and autonomy.[90] It is a reflective process that rejects any form of fixed knowledge residing only in those who presume to construct it for others.

Critical work-based learning thus encompasses a reflective, denaturalizing experience, which can encourage participants to find their distinctive voice in tones separate from those of their teachers.[91] They learn to reconstruct their taken-for-granted assumptions even in the moment so as to address the sociocultural conditions that may constrain their self-insight.[92] Participants in such a venue can search for individual and collective meaning that may arise from a discourse among competing interests, one that goes after the tough questions, not the easy answers.[93]

Unfortunately, the evidence as regards the personal value and professional effectiveness of action learning participants questioning the historical, cultural, and political conditions within their own organization is mixed.[94] Gutierrez, in an experimental graduate course in critical analysis of both the corporate organization and the classroom, found it difficult to alter the traditional professor-student dependent relationship.[95] In particular, emancipatory change required students to engage in deep self-analysis at the individual level, to exhibit sensitivity and relinquishment of control at the interpersonal level, and to appreciate the constraints of deeply acculturated social processes at the organizational level. Students who have achieved a level of critical awareness have at the same time reported both discomfort and dissonance when their newfound social awareness and political acuity were contraposed against the utter reality of their powerlessness to effect consistent and substantive change in their work environment.[96]

Nevertheless, Caron and Fisher, in their report of an internship program in business administration that emphasized critical reflection, found that enhanced self-awareness and political consciousness were important achievements that could lead to behavioral change.[97] Rigg and Trehan, in their ethnographic case study of several postgraduate programs in management development, also found that critical action learning could lead to perspective and personal transformation because it gives participants a language to frame how their long-held assumptions can be challenged when mapped against their professed values.[98] Thus, action learning projects can focus as much on the meaning of their accomplishments as on the accomplishments themselves. The ensuing dialogue can raise such critical questions as these: How are we relating to one another as humans? Who has been excluded from our deliberations that ought to be included? Why have we and our managers organized in the way we have? Are there alternative ways to manage our work processes? What cultural or historical processes have led to our current state of being?[99]

4

A Theory of Work-Based Learning

The only person who behaves sensibly is my tailor.
He takes new measurements every time he sees me.
All the rest go on with their old measurements.
—George Bernard Shaw

It may well be that some readers, as I suggested at the outset, will choose to skip this chapter, which focuses on the theory of work-based learning. However, if as a reader you are willing to entertain some academic thought, you might find, as Lewin once opined, that the theory of work-based learning is actually quite practical! One problem with omitting reference to theory is to leave an impression that work-based learning is "vocational," which unfortunately has come to mean suitable for those who don't like to learn in the classroom. But work-based learning is not antagonistic to theory; it respects and uses theory. Therefore, it should make sense that it has its own theoretical tradition. This chapter is an attempt to portray this significant tradition in epistemology.

Theory versus Practice Modes of Learning

Those of us concerned with management development live in two worlds. We speak two different languages. We occasionally come together and exchange views. Although we talk to one another, we are hardly aware that we are not sharing our conceptions of reality. We tend to part company thinking that we had a mutual exchange, but we go back to our respective worlds, for the most part unaffected by the exchange.

We come from the two worlds of theory and practice, and with but few exceptions, we have not figured out how to merge them, how to speak in a language that not only informs each other but also advances our mutual preferences. Theory is depicted as the world of thought, and practice refers to the world of action. Other depictions are less dispassionate. Theory is often construed by practitioners as impractical or as "academic" or "ivory-towerish." Meanwhile, practice is viewed by academics as banal and atheoretical. In normal science, the dominant approach to inquiry is represented by a strategic separation of theory and practice. Theoreticians develop hypotheses, empiricists do theory-testing, and practitioners apply the results.

We are only now beginning to understand the epistemological tradition of work-based learning. By *epistemology*, I refer to the very foundation of what makes up knowledge itself. For years, educators were imbued with a tradition that split knowledge from activities in the world. We now are more accepting of the view that knowledge (and especially its more dynamic agent, learning) is always occurring. It is part of our everyday life. As Wenger suggests, if we believe that knowledge is something that is stored, be it in a library or in a brain, then it makes sense to package it and present it without distraction in a succinct and articulate way to receptive students.[1] However, if knowledge is viewed as arising as much from active participation in the very apparatus of our everyday life and work, then we have to expand our conventional format of the classroom and indeed interpret the home and the workplace as suitable loci of learning.

Work-based learning is much more than the familiar *experiential* learning, which consists of adding a layer of simulated experience to conceptual knowledge. In work-based learning, theory may be acquired in concert with practice. Theory-building, for instance, may be viewed as a practice because those in practice are fully capable of producing theory. The informal activities and patterns of practice can themselves be formalized and disseminated to others in the field.[2] The theory produced by the practitioner may be more a practical, commonsense theory, but a theory nonetheless. According to Schön, practitioners build theory as they consciously reflect on challenges of their practice; reiteratively engage in problem posing, data gathering, action, evaluation, and reflection; and then share the knowledge produced with others in practice.[3]

Consider, in my own field of higher education, how department chairs perform their job. Except for academics coming out of schools of education, there is a dearth of formal preparation in learning how to manage academic professionals and departments. Yet managing in a professional bureaucracy is an enormous challenge because faculty members often behave as individual entrepreneurs rather than as members of a team. In spite of the lack of academic training, some professors become very effective chairpersons. Others often make very good mentors to junior faculty or even to incoming chairs. How do they develop their expertise? How do they know how to work through sticky problems?

Oftentimes, they can be found improvising new theories on the spot, theories without the backing of a sustained literature, but theories nonetheless. If an incoming chair were to face resistance to a department initiative from a senior faculty member, for example, she might be advised to recruit support from another senior professor who could in turn persuade the recalcitrant. What would be the rationale for this approach? The mentor might be using an implicit theory that suggests that peer encouragement based on a professional relationship works better than administrative exhortation. Although such a theory might find support in the literature, in this instance, it most likely was formulated through years of practice and reflection as an actionable knowledge base to be shared with others.

Although there is now a rich source of knowledge to help us understand how work-based learning occurs and may be facilitated, we need a model that integrates the many traditions underlying its construction. In developing such a model, we need to incorporate two dimensions fundamental to the process of work-based learning: (1) theory and practice modes of learning and (2) explicit and tacit forms of knowledge. Let's take up the theory-practice dimension first.

Since theory can be viewed as a frame in which to challenge the assumptions of practice, it makes most sense as a mode of learning when combined with action. Indeed, the connection between the teacher's intentions and the students' understanding is best achieved through action. Practice, meanwhile, is the process by which individuals acquire and practice artistry.[4]

Unfortunately, as noted earlier, a disjunction occurred between theory and practice. Its derivation has very much to do with a view of knowledge espoused by the modernist tradition in epistemology.[5] Although modernism has itself branched into multiple forms, its essence is that, through the use of reason, the course of civilization can be tamed and progress through the regulation of innovation and change controlled.[6] It also holds that human beings, through the commonsense of ordinary discourse, can reach consensus on a reality that exists outside human thought.[7] In probing reality, modernists need to separate themselves from their viewpoints so that they can "know" an objective world.

Among the many branches of modernism, *positivism* (or *logical empiricism*, as it is commonly known) is the one most associated with the view that facts or reality are based on the "positive" data of experience. Moreover, reality can be described and explained through the manipulation of theoretical propositions using the rules of formal logic.[8] As new theories are introduced and current ones are subjected to greater scrutiny and revision, scientists are able to map and predict reality more accurately and thus sustain progress in human endeavors.[9]

Positivists believed that knowledge revealed through science was superior to that produced from values, feelings, or untested experience because of its adherence to scrupulously objective and unbiased methods. Consequently, theory, which affords testable propositions, was deemed best separated from practice. Occupying the domain of thought, which establishes connections or causal relationships among phenomena, theory was thought to be an advance over primitive myths and beliefs.[10] Yet, its detractors, among other things, have seen it evolve as a framework that has distanced us even more from practice than its progenitors.[11]

In concert with the theory-practice divide, teaching was also separated from learning, as it became seen as the process of transferring information from teacher to student. Learning would occur when that information was received, stored, and recapitulated. Faculty were encouraged to develop their research at the expense of more time-consuming teaching strategies, which would require greater intersection with the practice world. The scholarship chosen by faculty would rarely examine their own practice; rather, it would be dedicated to the content of their discipline.[12] Thus, the faculty role became theory-based without necessarily taking context into consideration. It's the students, once in practice, who would have to make the link between the previously learned theory and their current workplace problems. On their own, they might also discover the reasoning behind their practice.

But we now know that knowledge undergoes construction and transformation, that it is as much a dynamic as a static concept, as much a collective activity as individual thought.[13] Abstract knowledge cannot help but be affected by circumstances, and frames of situations are at best inconclusive until verified by their effectiveness in action. Work-based learning, then, must blend theory and action. Theory makes sense only through practice, and practice makes sense only through reflection as enhanced by theory.

Explicit versus Tacit Forms of Knowledge

So far, I have contended that work-based learning requires a new epistemology of practice that seeks to explore not just the explicit instructions and guidelines available in the workplace but also the tacit processes invoked personally by practitioners as they work through the problems of daily management. Let's explore in more depth what I mean by the terms *explicit* and *tacit knowledge*. Explicit knowledge is the familiar codified form that is transmittable in formal, systematic language. Tacit knowledge is the component of knowledge that is not typically reportable since it is deeply rooted in action and involvement in a specific context.[14] In other words, although individuals may be knowledgeable in what they do, they may not have the facility to say what it is they know.[15] Ryle made the distinction between *knowing how* and *knowing that*.[16] Knowing how represents the tacit dimension that often eludes our capacity to know that—or abstractly frame our action.

Another useful distinction proposed by Anderson is between *declarative knowledge* and *procedural knowledge*.[17] Declarative (explicit) knowledge represents our conceptual understanding of phenomena, whereas procedural (tacit) knowledge represents our skill in doing something, be it mentally or physically.

Even though tacit knowledge may not be expressed or codified, it may be teachable. For example, a competent trainer might provide an observable model of tacit skill for the trainee to follow and imitate. The tacit skill would thus be apprehensible and observable in use, even though not articulated or put into words.[18]

Conventional learning methodologies tend to be theory-based classroom experiences, relying on explicit knowledge. Unfortunately, they suffer the risk of leaving inexperienced students with the impression that eventual field problems can be nestled into neat technical packages. But, as Robert Reilly asks, can these students once in practice think independently, function without sufficient data or extrapolate beyond given data, change their approach in midstream, negotiate, and continually reflect and inquire?[19] In a compelling example, he depicts the shock of a fresh MBA-trained manager who finds out that a product line divestment decision has less to do with marginal cost analysis than with personal affinity to the line on the part of the CEO, who began his career with the brand.

Work-based learning is interested in both explicit and tacit knowledge. Heretofore it was thought, especially by classroom epistemologists, that tacit knowledge couldn't be taught; it had to be "picked up" by trial and error at work. However, knowledge creation has been depicted by Nonaka as transforming what is implicit into something that is explicit, especially through spirals of ongoing interaction between individuals, work teams, and organizations.[20]

The neglect of tacit knowledge arose because it is not necessarily mediated by declarative knowledge. However, it serves as the base for many of our conscious operations. It is perhaps at its most accessible point when we think of our actions as intuitive.[21] This is when we have a sense of the correct action or response but are often incapable of explaining why we behaved the way we did.[22] Yet we seem able to quickly and effectively use this knowledge to handle ill-structured tasks, especially when we have contextualized knowledge.[23] Further, our information processing in this case may be social, as we and others in our environment mutually build a knowledge base from the sharing of prior and current episodes or simply from our unique human awareness of our social and collective environment.[24]

In using tacit knowledge, it is often preferable to leave one's performance unanalyzed. This may occur when we attempt to demonstrate but not state our practice or when we are in the middle of a performance.[25] For example, we wouldn't expect musicians in concert to call attention to their fingers because it might disrupt their playing. It is after the experience that one might attempt to bring the inherent tacit knowledge to the surface. In so doing, we might not only improve but even permanently alter our understanding of the situation and as a result our actual performance.[26] The critical issue for an epistemology of practice seems to be not whether but *when* to introduce explicit instructions and reflection into the field to yield optimal performance.[27] The construction of theory in this setting might be more apt during or after rather than before the experience. Hence, theory is not preordained but constituted as a living construction to capture the useful ingredients of the performance.

The Conceptual Model

Using the two aforementioned dimensions of modes of learning and forms of knowledge, we can construct a conceptual model of work-based learning, provided we also consider a third dimension: level of activity. One learns through work at an individual level since the intersection between the learning modes and knowledge forms challenges personal frames of action. However, learning in the workplace requires an extension of learning to the collective level defined as one's co-workers—be they within or even outside the present work unit. My emphasis in this book is clearly on the collective level of activity, but I will digress here briefly to describe the learning styles afforded by the model at the individual level.

Work-Based Learning as an Individual Property

In Table 4.1, the four individual learning types, resulting from a matrix of the two learning modes and two knowledge forms, are depicted. Astute readers will immediately see a similarity between the labels used here and those depicted in David Kolb's well-known *learning style inventory*.[28] In fact, the processes operating in the work-based learning model and Kolb's learning from experience are compatible. However, since Kolb first produced his inventory, much more research has been done on tacit knowledge, especially by the discipline of cognitive science, leading to a deeper understanding of learning processes while working. Furthermore, Kolb's framework was also designed as a way of gaining insight into one's style of learning, which in turn could provide an indication of career interest.[29] The learning types produced in the first matrix of the model of work-based learning do not so much characterize career-oriented styles as processes that individuals may deploy to learn effectively, efficiently, and critically within work. Although like Kolb, I contend that individuals are predisposed to a learning type, all four should be used to engender the most learning in the shortest amount of time. Hence, effectiveness of work-based learning results from the comprehensiveness of facets to which the learner is exposed. It is not

Table 4.1. A Model of Work-Based Learning—Individual Level

| Modes of Learning | Forms of Knowledge | |
	Explicit	*Tacit*
Theory	Conceptualization	Experimentation
Practice	Reflection	Experience

sufficient to learn only through theoretical exposition, nor is it sufficient to engage in tacit practices without making one's mental models accessible. Meanwhile, efficiency of work-based learning results from selective attention to each of the four learning types. For example, as we shall see, experience solidifies the learning made tacit in experimentation but may lead to mastery more quickly when subjected to reflection. As we move from reflection back into conceptualization, we hope to achieve criticalness, defined as the ability and dedication to question our underlying assumptions within the learning process. The four sections that follow demonstrate how each of the four learning types contributes to a solid foundation for work-based learning on the part of individuals.

Conceptualization. Basic theory has contributed a great deal to management practice. Not only does theory challenge the assumptions underlying practice, but as a way of illuminating and describing action, it provides practitioners with a common language and wide powers of analysis.[30] They learn to perceive even standard problems in a new light. Furthermore, by introducing practitioners to new principles, conceptualization gives them a means to tackle new and different problems in different contexts. A consultant who has successfully used the theory of the experience curve in one setting might find it to be equally applicable in a second.

Theory might also reveal problems heretofore undiscovered or left fallow for lack of recognizable solutions. It allows practitioners to explicitly reflect upon and actively experiment with their practice interventions. Consequently, it has become a veritable necessity in work-based learning, if learners are to adopt the capacity to deal with change and with the future—indeed, if they are to imagine.

Conceptualization is often criticized as not being sufficiently real world, meaning not capable of being translated into practice. As Maclagan has shown, however, it is possible that individuals use theories to help them with their reasoning but purposely keep them implicit in communicating with others.[31] In fact, since theoretical language may not be accepted in some cultural settings (consider the tolerance toward using ethical jargon), individuals may choose to translate otherwise obscure concepts into everyday language. It is also possible that theorizing is used by practitioners to help them with their decision making but is kept hidden from consciousness. As noted, conceptualization can also provide a basis for subsequent reflection on and reappraisal of actions.

Experimentation. In his day, Dewey warned educators that mere *doing* or activity was not enough to produce learning; rather, doing should become a trying, an experiment with the world to find out what it is like.[32] At the same time, students need the opportunity to try out their conceptual knowledge so that it becomes contextual or grounded—in a word, that it becomes *do-able*. Reliance on conceptualization alone may limit our problem solving because most new or real problems are not yet sufficiently coherent to be organized into theory.[33]

Once they enter the field, students normally encounter a dissonance between their theory and practice. Argyris and Schön refer to this inconsistency as a difference between one's *espoused theory* and one's *theory-in-use*."[34] The espoused theory is the theory with which one enters a situation; hence it might well be the conceptual knowledge that a student brings to bear on the situation. Once in action, however, we tend to modify or vary our espoused theories usually unconsciously as we employ our theories-in-use. It is important that students have the opportunity to engage in experiments to bring these two theories into alignment. This would be the purpose of experimentation, which often takes the form of case studies, role-plays, in-basket exercises, simulations, and the like.

Consider the plight of a nursing student who enters her clinical experience with visions of attending to the needs of the whole person, only to find that the pressing demands of the unit combined with her sheer exhaustion allow her to attend merely to the urgent, physical needs of her patients. A case study or simulation revealing the demands on an emergency ward nurse might help ground the student's conceptual foundations. Experiments such as these serve to make our espoused theories tacit, thus applicable to the situation at hand and more natural.

Experience. Learning often occurs through experience. Learners first need to undergo a particular experience, and then, as they reflect upon that experience, learn from it.[35] Learning from experience is important to new practitioners, because once they enter the world of practice, no matter how hard they try to apply theoretical criteria, use advanced analytical techniques, or recall a case study, they confront a host of unexpected contingencies associated with organizational life.

Experience reinforces the tacit knowledge acquired in experimentation. It can also be thought of as nonconscious intellectual activity. Practitioners who rely on acquisition of information through such nonconscious intellectual activity can often not only process more quickly than their more "thoughtful" counterparts but can also handle more sophisticated data, such as multidimensional and interactive relations between variables.[36] We all know of athletes who always seem to be at the right place on the field, rink, or court, who are amazingly intelligent in practice but almost totally hamstrung when it comes to articulating their performance. This kind of knowledge is not necessarily mediated by conscious knowledge. There is no abstract theory guiding performance in these cases. We act because we are familiar. Subsequently, we can form an impression, a theory perhaps, of our expert activity.

Learning acquired through experience is often referred to by cognitive psychologists as implicit learning, meaning the acquisition of complex knowledge that takes place without the learners' awareness that they are learning.[37] Implicit learning is thought to be the foundation for tacit knowledge and can be used to solve problems as well as to make reasonable decisions about novel stimulus circumstances. Knowledge acquired during implicit learning is not amenable to verbal report, whereas explicit learning, which proceeds with the subject's awareness of what is being learned, is verbally reportable. It is conceivable that implicit learning serves as the base for conscious operations. It is perhaps at its most responsive point when we think of our actions as intuitive.[38] This is when we have a feeling for the right or correct action but are incapable of explaining why we behaved the way we did. At times, in the "heat" of practice and through the process of sharing with others, we improvise to maintain the flow of activity and in so doing refine and improve our practice.[39] The subsequent step of reflection allows us to bring our intuitive actions to the surface.

Reflection. Reflection constitutes the ability to uncover and make explicit to oneself what one has planned, observed, or achieved in practice. It is concerned with the reconstruction of meaning. In particular, it privileges the process of inquiry, leading to an understanding of experiences that may have been overlooked in practice. Thus, reflection, as pointed out earlier, especially public reflection, is fundamental to all work-based learning practices. Introduced here as a discrete individual learning type, it becomes all the more critical at the collective level.

Unfortunately, most practitioners are unable to develop a cohesive theory and explanation of their work, though they may be very skilled.[40] As a result, they often have difficulty explaining their workplace moves to themselves or to others. Reflective practitioners, on the other hand, become sensitive to why they performed in a certain way, the values that were being manifested, the discrepancies that existed between what was said and what was done, and the way in which forces below the surface may have shaped actions and outcomes. Rather than follow prescribed methods, they question whether new approaches could have led to better solutions. Reflective practitioners are critical thinkers who have the intellectual discipline to avoid confusing viewpoint and reality. They probe whether a socially approved decision is ethically justified and whether a suggested action is ultimately consistent with the very values that they espouse.[41]

Reflection is thought by cognitive psychologists to contribute as much to learning as experience itself to the extent that learners are active observers. In fact, people often learn behavior from observing others before performing the behavior themselves.[42] According to social learning theory (SLT), individuals tend to anticipate actions and their associated consequences. Hence, before trying out new or altered behaviors, they first pay attention to others and develop mental models or cognitive maps to guide their trials.[43] Perhaps you may have noticed that when you are introduced to a new skill involving some dexterity, such as making a wrist shot in hockey, you prefer seeing someone else demonstrate the activity first. That way you can develop a mental picture of what the skill entails before trying it yourself.

Patricia King and Karen Kitchener developed a reflective judgment model that is developmentally sequenced based upon increasingly complex ways of understanding and resolving ill-structured problems.[44] Individuals progress through the stages of the model on the basis of a number of epistemic assumptions: the extent to which they investigate the facts of a situation, the strategies they use to obtain information, their degree of acceptance of divergent interpretations, and the degree of uncertainty they feel about whether a problem has been solved. By the last stage, reflective judgment entails acknowledging that one's understanding of the world is not a given but must be actively constructed and interpreted. Knowledge is understood in relationship to the context in which it was generated.

Mezirow distinguished three forms of reflection.[45] *Content reflection* is based upon what we perceive, think, feel, or act upon. Initially grounded in Dewey's notion of critical inquiry, reflection on content involves a review of the way we have consciously applied ideas in strategizing and implementing each phase of solving a problem. *Process reflection*, on the other hand, is an examination of how we go about problem solving, with a view toward the procedures and assumptions in use. *Premise reflection* goes to a final step of questioning the very presuppositions attending to the problem to begin with. In premise reflection, we question the very questions we have been asking in order to challenge our fundamental beliefs.

Consider a light example of these three reflection forms. Let's say I wish to consider Jim for a job, but I am concerned about his age. I can't ask him directly how old he is because of fair hiring policies, so

I need to invoke my content reflection—how can I get a handle on his age? I might ask him when he graduated from college or I might take a closer look at the lines on his face. Yet these data can be deceptive. My process reflection, considering the assumptions in use, might lead me to posit that Jim may have gone to school later in life or that he might look older than he is. Finally, my premise reflection may be invoked when I consider the more provocative question challenging the presuppositions of my query: What if age doesn't matter in the first place regarding Jim's qualifications for the job?

According to developmental psychologists, such as Broughton, premise reflection or theoretical self-consciousness is only available to adults.[46] It is only in adulthood that one becomes capable of recognizing paradigmatic assumptions in our thinking. However, adults need to engage and to invoke their reflective consciousness to learn at this level. Mezirow calls this learning *transformative*—that is, learning that takes us into new meanings.[47] Transformative learning can help us review and alter any misconstrued meanings arising out of uncritical half-truths found in conventional wisdom or in power relationships. Because higher-level reflection may not occur naturally, learning opportunities need to be provided within the workplace to provoke critical reflection on current meaning perspectives.

Work-Based Learning as a Collective Property

Having explored work-based learning at the individual level, we can now turn to the processes of learning within work in the company of others. In Table 4.2, four different learning types are displayed at the collective level, resulting from a matrix of the now familiar dimensions of learning modes and knowledge forms. As we shall see, each type tends to be derived from a distinct epistemological tradition. Yet these four types should also be integrated, as in the case of the individual level of activity, in order to produce effective, efficient, and critical learning. In the next section of this chapter, I review the contribution of the first collective type, applied science, to the model. Because the remaining three types— action learning, community of practice, and action science—offer

Table 4.2. A Model of Work-Based Learning—Collective Level

Modes of Learning	Forms of Knowledge	
	Explicit	*Tacit*
Theory	Applied Science	Action Learning
Practice	Action Science	Community of Practice

robust practical implications for developing actual programs in work-based learning, they will be expanded upon in the subsequent chapter. Although an essential building block, applied science does not receive much attention here only because it constitutes the classic and familiar approach to learning used in most of the world. For purposes of this book, we are most concerned with its contribution to the emerging tradition of work-based learning.

Applied Science. Although experiments under the carefully controlled conditions of the scientific method can proceed in the domain of learning and work, most academics in professional fields tend to dedicate their research to instrumental or applied problems rather than to pure science. However, as good scientists, they tend not to waver in their commitment to sound empirical methods. Using the guidelines proffered by logical positivism, as introduced earlier in the chapter, they contend that they can gain insight into an objective knowledge or reality that exists outside human thought.[48]

In an attempt to find areas of objective knowledge still left undiscovered, applied researchers further explicitly detach themselves from the situations that might reveal elements of this knowledge, they selectively test out preordained patterns of conceptual relationships, and then they draw conclusions that might generalize to other similar situations. The knowledge subject to this intensity of inquiry has these features: (1) it becomes truer or more valid as it undergoes the rigorous methods of theory testing; (2) it becomes expressed as a series of logical relationships often defined using mathematical language; and (3) it invites reformulation as its precepts and procedures are subjected to further scrutiny.[49] By explaining their methods and elaborating on their data in detail, the researchers are willing to have other investigators assess the results of their experiments for themselves. Others may also offer alternative explanations and propose tests of competing theories. Through this empirical debate, a form of detached community of inquiry is formed that seeks to distinguish valid from invalid claims to our knowledge base.[50]

Although scientific knowledge has led to a bifurcation between theory and practice and has resulted in disciplinary isolation, applied science—in particular, applied social science—can contribute a great deal to collective knowing.[51] Active theory can inform spontaneous inquiry. What can be most helpful to practitioners is not a pure scientific method, which attempts to objectify all organizational phenomena, but an applied science, which takes into consideration the cultural, political, and moral dilemmas within our social systems.[52] We need to correct and qualify what we learn in one discipline by what we learn not only in other disciplines but from everyday life as well.[53]

Applied science can make an important contribution to practice by offering theories of action that are systematically tested using the rigorous conditions of the scientific method, described above. At the same time, practitioners have to be allowed to contribute to theory and comment on gaps between formal research and processes in the field. In this way, theory can be united with the practice world consistent with the philosophy of praxis—the deeply reflective and interactive process of learning from our actions.[54] The history of science and human thought clearly makes room for the contribution of human activity. Conversely, praxis benefits from theory construction and verification that attempt to assess and generalize from our experience.[55] Our work-based learning methods, for example, as I shall detail especially in Chapter Ten, require measurement and evaluation to ensure they are delivering minimally the service they attest to deliver. Work-based learning is thus enhanced from an applied science that deliberately introduces its methods into the practice field and that solicits the contributions of practitioners.

A *Comprehensive Model.*   Although I have yet to detail three of the collective learning types—action learning, community of practice, and action science—I would like to sketch what the conceptual model of work-based learning might look like as a whole, incorporating both the individual and collective levels of activity, but depicted more dynamically than in a 2 × 4 matrix.[56] As exhibited in Figure 4.1, the now comprehensive model of work-based learning illustrates the interplay between the types of knowledge and the modes of learning at both levels. But as learners in practice do not step into a discrete space to perform experience or reflection, the model cannot rigidly classify these behaviors. Rather, the model of work-based learning must represent the integration of these styles. For example, conceptualized knowledge ultimately requires the test of tacit experimentation. Pure tacit experience, representing beliefs-in-action, requires the test of reflection.

Figure 4.1. A Comprehensive Model of Work-Based Learning

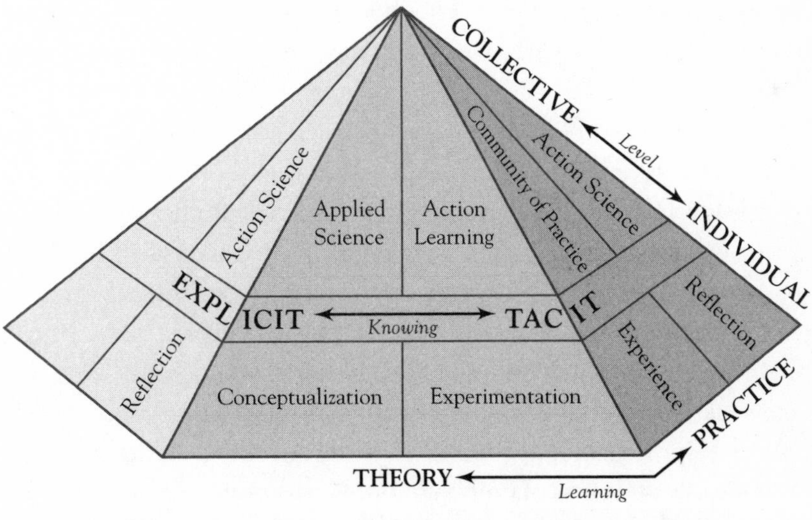

Source: Reprinted by permission from J. A. Raelin, "A Model of Work-Based Learning," *Organization Science*, Volume 8, Number 6, November–December 1997, Copyright ©1997, The Institute of Operations Research and the Management Sciences (INFORMS).

This approach recognizes that practitioners, in order to be proficient, need to bridge the gap between explicit and tacit knowledge and between theory and practice. Work-based learning subscribes to a form of knowing that is context-dependent. Practitioners use theories to frame their understanding of the context and simultaneously incorporate an awareness of the social processes in which contextual activity is embedded.

Each of the eight types of learning needs to be brought into consideration if learners are to achieve proficiency and criticalness of their learning. Although there is a logic to the choice of neighbors among the types, there is no precise rotation that is recommended. For example, experiments of theory are often tentative or successive, requiring frequent reversion to theory, especially during early stages of development. There are also links represented across the levels. For example, reflections lead to theory testing, which can contribute to science. Furthermore, isolated reflection tends ultimately to incorporate the surrounding social context and to invite the reflection of other signifiers. Individual learning can proceed independently for a while, but it may be illusory to think of oneself as autonomous.[57] Most of us work with others, so we need to inquire as to how they see us in action and how they interpret workplace phenomena.

Readers should be able to envision the workings of the model at the collective level even though elaboration of the principal collective learning types awaits coverage in the next chapter. In brief, action learning, one of the most popular of work-based learning methods, places theory into tacit use by having managers learn from their peers while they are all engaged in the solution of real-time problems. Community of practice, an emerging domain of work-based learning, recognizes and encourages the development of tacit collective practices of individuals as they develop a common enterprise and shared ways of doing things. Action science seeks ways to illuminate our practices, especially our untested thoughts and assumptions, so that we can make better choices and enhance our capabilities for effective action.

The collective level is not meant to describe merely group-level phenomena. Although reflections from practice may be shared with an intimate community, the very process of sharing may ultimately spiral out to other communities. Communities of practice, for example, often need to consult with allied subject experts to expand their understanding of tacit behaviors. Hence, although the model has a modest focus on learning through work, it can contribute to the more encompassing domain of organizational learning.

Each of the work-based styles of Figure 4.1 performs an important function, but various intersections are required to achieve comprehensive learning. A perfectly tacit community of practice may exist in a given work setting seemingly requiring minimal intervention. In fact, efforts to intervene may not only be rejected but may actually interrupt the work flow. However, communities of this nature cannot function as closed systems. In the next chapter, we will examine how new processes and technology might accelerate their learning and performance.

Work-based learning as a framework serves to bring together a number of otherwise disparate learning processes, each of which has its own justification as a basis for learning within work. By integrating these processes, we gather insight into the dynamic interplay of forces that can impede or facilitate learning in the workplace.

5

Three Collective Work-Based Learning Types

A problem is an opportunity in work clothes.

—Henry J. Kaiser

For those readers who braved the conceptual account of work-based learning in the last chapter, you are now ready to examine the three principal collective learning types: *action learning, community of practice,* and *action science*. If you're just joining us now in midstream, this chapter details some of the action strategies that integrate the learning processes inherent in work-based learning.

Action Learning

Action learning describes an educational strategy, used in a group setting, that seeks to generate learning from human interaction arising from engagement in the solution of real-time (not simulated) work problems. It can take place either in a formal program offered through a university or as part of a corporate management development effort.[1] It emphasizes learning by doing. The application of real experience cannot be overstated in action learning. Its exponents sincerely believe that the real world needs to be considered the most auspicious location for learning. Inasmuch as practitioners are stakeholders in the problems that they attempt to solve, real problems should become the focus of study.[2]

Active or experiential learning devices, which attempt to introduce a spirit of tacit knowledge into traditional lectures—whether through case analyses, action research using consultancy, field research and observation—though useful, are not sufficient to help students convert theory into tacit knowledge or to learn how to challenge and reflect on their own theoretical assumptions. Students need to take real positions, make moral judgments, and defend them under pressure. Dealing exclusively with simulated events risks defusing or abstracting live conflicts. Cooperation typically is obtained where it otherwise may be impossible, and emotionally laden, complex problems get neatly analyzed into solutions. As Brown and Duguid have aptly put it, a critical issue in action learning is becoming a practitioner, not learning about practice.[3]

It is not unusual to find that practitioners confuse action learning with experiential learning because the word *action* might point to any curricular adaptation that allows trainees to become active rather than passive consumers of dispensed information. However, *action* learning differs from *active* learning. In *active* learning, trainees "actively" try applying course ideas or theories, typically by engaging in experiential or simulated exercises. In *action* learning, learners learn with others by working on and then reflecting on actual "actions" occurring in their real work setting.[4]

Practitioners thus need the opportunity to merge theoretical principles with an understanding of the social construction of the organizations in which they work. Most principles about organizations, for example, cannot anticipate the particular circumstances unique to each organization. In action learning, principles become most useful when they help learners become more effective in action. Furthermore, practitioners often learn best by sharing their theories and experiences with each other. Another way to put this is that organizational members need to enter each other's area of operation in order to provide new perspectives and stimulate inquiry regarding practice experiences.[5]

In action learning, real-time experience, especially problems occurring within one's own work setting, constitutes a good part of the subject matter of the lesson. Opportunities are also provided for substantial debriefing of the real-time experience so that the participant may inquire how others reacted to his or her handling of the situation. Any actions taken are also subject to inquiry about the effectiveness of these actions, including a review of how one's theories were applied into practice. Action learning therefore relies on feedback, which by focusing on the participant's values and behavior ensures that any actions are seen not as neutral stances but as positions with points of view and anticipated consequences. Most action learning advocates believe, however, that the "action" in action learning is there as the pathway to *learning*. Solving the problem is fine, but it isn't as critical that there be problem resolution as much as that there be learning from the experience. Another way to state this is that it is preferable to fail at finding a solution to a problem yet obtain learning than to fail to learn while obtaining a solution to the problem.

Bob Garratt expresses the epistemology of action learning in this way: "Adults learn best from live projects; from the support and constructive criticism of colleagues; from rigourous self-reflection leading to serious reinterpretation of their previous experiences; and from a willingness to test their hypotheses in action."[6]

In action learning's original conceptualization proposed by Revans, learning results from the independent contributions of programmed instruction (designated P) and spontaneous questioning (designated Q).[7] P constitutes information and skill derived from material already formulated and is presented typically through coursework. Q is knowledge and skill gained by apposite questioning, investigation, and experimentation. For Revans, Q was the component that produced most behavioral change and learning because it results from interpretations of experience and knowledge immediately accessible to the learner. These interpretations are bolstered by feedback from mutual learners who participate in a debriefing of the learner's workplace experiences. Actions taken are thus subject to inquiry about the effectiveness of these actions, including a review of how one's theories were applied into practice.

In this way, action learning addresses the pitfalls of conventional training and even of experiential learning, which often overlook the need to engage in mutual reflection as a means to surface the tacit knowledge embedded in live experience. By having peers serve as a sounding board to one another regarding the operating assumptions underlying their project interventions, participants become more equipped to produce the outcomes they desire.[8] They learn from each other how to overcome the blockages that they themselves and others erect to deter project accomplishment.[9] They challenge each other by subjecting their real critical issues to scrutiny from alternative perspectives, giving members a chance to question their underlying perceptions and assumptions.[10] Their learning is tied to knowledge collectively and concurrently co-constructed in service of action.[11]

Because of both the variety and inconsistency in action learning delivery (Revans himself eschewed any single definition), it is challenging to depict a typical action learning program.[12] Nevertheless, here is a characterization of a modal delivery platform. Initially, a series of presentations constituting what Revans referred to as programmed instructions might be given on a designated theory or on several theoretical topics. Concurrent or subsequent to these presentations, participants might be asked to apply the theories to a real live project that is sanctioned by organizational sponsors and that has potential value not only to the participant but also to the organizational unit to which the project is attached. Participants might work on projects individually or in groups. Either way, other organizational members and stakeholders not directly affiliated with the action learning program may be drawn into the project. Projects span any number of critical problems arising in the organization, such as a strategic decision to enter a new market or a new application connected to one of the company's functional areas. Projects have recognized clients—the departments and respective executive managers from which they originate. Clients take a genuine interest in the assignments and are expected to apply normal business pressures to ensure a high-quality outcome within a particular period of time.

As might be expected, not all organizational problems are solved or are even meant to be solved in action learning. Moreover, proposed solutions may be deemed by management to be too costly in time or money. It is even possible that participants may realize that no quick solution is available. Thus, the experience tends to confront participants with the constraints of organizational realities, leading oftentimes to their discovery of alternative and creative means to accomplish their objectives.[13] Projects almost always require some kind of output that can be evaluated. Often, a lengthy written statement detailing project aims, performance, and recommendations is prepared. This report is not merely meant to describe the "results" but also to detail the learnings and competencies addressed in the experience as well as the real constraints that may have blocked proposed interventions.

The advantages of working on such real problems become obvious. Participants are forced to find real, workable answers, not easy, hypothetical ones; leadership and teamwork skills are developed along with the more technical skills; the organization benefits immediately from the participants' contribution to the project; and the lessons learned from the experience tend to stay with the participants longer than if they had learned them from a book or lecture. Moreover, solving problems per se is not necessarily as much the focus in action learning as *dissolving* them. Consistent with Ackoff's notion of *messes*, organizational problems are rarely stand-alone events but rather messy, dynamic, interdependent entanglements.[14] Action learning participants might just as readily change the nature of the system or the environment in which the problem resides as directly "solve" the problem.

In this way, the impact of the action learning project as well as the infusion of organizational members "trained" under this approach can be pervasive. From many accounts in the domain of executive development, it appears that action learning has been deployed effectively in organizations of varying sizes across a wide range of business applications such as: early career programs, new manager assimilation, skill development, high-potential development, team effectiveness, continuous improvement, knowledge management, and organizational transition.[15]

The Leadership for Change program at Boston College's Carroll Graduate School of Management, now in its fourteenth year, features six-month projects that procedurally observe action learning principles and substantively invoke leadership efforts attempting to achieve social as well as economic corporate goals. Participants develop their own projects in conjunction with in-company sponsors. Leadership for Change catalyzes change at many levels of performance. The managers emerge as leaders of change efforts, and the organization obtains a project that tends to produce residual humanizing effects on its culture. To give readers a sense of some of these projects, four of them are described here in the participants' own words (though the names of the sponsoring companies are disguised):

Project A:
Community Jobs Partnership:
Creating Social Capital

Project Description: A community jobs partnership program in conjunction with several community-based organizations was designed and offered as a jobs training program for the position as teller in a bank. Many of the clients were welfare recipients. After completing the four-week training program, most were subsequently hired for full- or part-time positions. The community jobs partnership program leveraged the bank's reputation as a community leader that solved a pressing business problem while finding enthusiastic sales and service people to fill entry-level opportunities in the bank's retail branches.

Project B:
Implementing a Flexible
Work Arrangement

Project Description: This project constituted a policy analysis to assess the current Flexible Work Arrangements policy in place throughout the organization and an implementation of a pilot program within the participant's department. The project was important to the company because recent climate surveys had revealed a need for improved focus on work/life balance. By offering employees various working arrangements, the company would be able to reap many benefits for both organization and employee. The participant's role was to interview the principals, review a working strategy with the management team, and implement a compressed work week plan to all units within the respective department.

Project C:
The Search for a Simpler Way:
Cultural Emergence

Project Description: This project intervention addressed the issue of how to engage employees in the development of a communications plan for disseminating the results of the Job Review process, a critical part of a reorganization which took place after the merger of "Beta" and "Delphi" Companies. The long-term goal of the intervention was to create a culture that supports open communication by sharing information, building relationships, developing a mutual identity, and nurturing the creation of a culture that values employee empowerment. The most immediate purpose was to improve communication within the division by communicating the Job Review process at both the group and individual levels such that employees would have a sense of ownership of the instrument as well as the process of job review.

Project D:
Creating a Balanced Scorecard
for "Well-Being Hospital"

Project Description: The project created a simple set of financial and non-financial performance measures and developed a process to share the information on a regular basis, called the Period Performance Report. Through surveys and in conjunction with a team of staff, the project identified seven factors to be measured and developed measures for five of them. It also drafted an employee survey to aid in the measurement process.

In terms of our comprehensive model of work-based learning, detailed in the last chapter, action learning occupies that cell where conscious theory is placed into tacit practice. So in action learning, theory becomes contextualized. Context becomes important, however, not only as a basis to evaluate theory but also to evaluate plans and actions. An activity that might be seen as harmless in one context can be viewed as antagonistic in another. For instance, it might be acceptable to confront an action learning team member about her overuse of questioning behavior, but that same confronting style might be viewed itself as hostile in one's work team. Hall suggests that in analyzing contexts, we not only consider the subject of an event but the situation in which it is occurring.[16] Further, he suggests that we come to understand the roles of those involved, our past experiences in the situation, and finally the way the situation is defined by the broader culture within which it is occurring.

If we're interested in attempting to export a technology used in our unit to another organizational unit, we need to know how that technology might be deployed in the new situation, who might help us champion its conversion and what that person's role might be, how well our units have cooperated in the past, and what this transference means in terms of the larger culture of our organization. Hall's guidelines can be useful as action learning participants think through the implications of project interventions.

The primary vehicle for providing collective reflection in action learning is the learning team or set, a group of five to seven participants who support each other in their workplace project activity. I will devote an entire section in Chapter Seven to discuss the reflective modality of learning teams, but an introduction is in order here. Learning teams are constituted of participants who, along with a facilitator or coach, help each other make sense of their action learning project experiences in light of relevant theory. Set members become skilled in the art of questioning in order to challenge the assumptions underlying planned interventions in members' projects. Subsequent actions taken tend to be clearer, better informed, and more defensible as a result of the set dialogue.[17] Johnson, reporting a conversation in a set in which he participated, recalled a quip from one participant: "Your advice at the beginning was useless, your anecdotes were boring, but your questions really helped me."[18]

Participants in action learning, then, learn as they work, by taking time to reflect with peers who offer insights into each other's workplace problems. In recent years, there seems to also be a revival in interest in the overlooked *P* (programmed instruction) in Revans's formulation. Programmed instruction and theory can inform spontaneous inquiry and offer alternative frames of problems.[19] Conceptual frameworks, for example, can help set members work through problems in their project work. Moreover, creative devices, such as synectics and counterinduction, can be introduced to stimulate group and individual problem exploration. Many standard group process techniques are also available to advance the development of learning teams, resulting in improved functional efficiency and effectiveness.[20]

Most action learning teams use the time available to focus on the workplace dilemmas of their members. People are given time to fully elaborate on troubling issues facing their unit or themselves personally, and they use each other as sounding boards to prepare for subsequent engagements or interventions. In some instances, no precise action may result from the team process, but the member may have acquired a new understanding or interpretation of past interactions, leading to a reframing of one's perception of the phenomena in question. Most learning team members in assessing their participation tend to report the inherent value of having created a psychologically safe environment in which to share and resolve complex problems.[21]

In one action learning team formed among service workers in a youth services agency, the facilitator, or adviser, as she called herself, reported on the frustrations experienced by one of the members and how, through the active involvement of her learning team peers, she managed to overcome what initially appeared to be an intractable problem:

> Her role within the youth offending team had been curtailed to only a half day a week, after having been told: "We can't afford it." She was tearful and distressed, knowing that she could not do the job she loved. "I feel like I'm deserting the young people," she protested. [One of her first actions was] to tell people clearly what she could and could not do in this role. She was also encouraged by her team

to present them with a "damn good boast" about her work and herself. She did this even though she was very self-conscious. What emerged was her conveying to management her values and her passion for work with young offenders. She reported: "coming to the action learning set made me realize how much control I can have, no matter what other people do." This strengthened her resolve to continue with this work, no matter how small her role. Subsequently, she used the opportunity of new funding to become a full-time member of the team, working as a family support worker.[22]

Community of Practice

Through action learning, we know that learning teams can become a principal vehicle to introduce work-based learning into the work environment. However, we need to consider whether learning teams can also become work teams or vice versa. Among the most referenced of authorities on work teams are Katzenbach and Smith, who, in their *The Wisdom of Teams*, define a team as "a small number of people with complementary skills who are committed to a common purpose, a set of performance goals, and an approach for which they hold themselves mutually accountable."[23] In short, when it comes to work teams, such as task forces, there is a focus on the achievement of performance goals. Learning is equivalent to deriving better methods to become more efficient or more effective in working together and in producing useful outcomes.

There is, however, another type of team, one that is potentially interested in workplace problems, but at least initially is even more interested in learning. We've called this team a *learning team*. Not only are learning teams used in action learning, but as we shall see, they are also relied upon in action science interventions. While individual members may be working on problems in their own work settings, the reason for their coming together is not only to work on these problems but also to use the learning team itself to help them examine and possibly revise their reasoning and behavior in their back-home groups. The focus is more on the development of individual and team capability than on explicit problem solving.

Now, what gets interesting is the question of what happens when one merges these two types of teams. A work team may come together to perform a discrete assignment and eventually disband after completion; however, during the entire process of completing the task, the group may never have congealed as a community of practice. They may never have created meaning together; they may never have focused their attention on their mutual learning or *collective* capability. It could be that only after the task was completed did some of the original members of the task group decide to stay together in a form of learning community that we might call a community of practice.

Communities of practice (CoPs) evolve as people united in a common enterprise develop a shared history as well as particular values, beliefs, ways of talking, and ways of doing things.[24] They come together not so much on the basis of formal memberships or job descriptions, but rather for the purpose of being involved with one another in the process of doing a job. Hence, they don't have an agenda as much as an enterprise. Although their reasoning and behavior become shared, there is considerable variation from standard practices. In time, their efforts as a community become natural. Problem solving becomes more of a social activity than an analytically detached process. Although the knowledge produced is often tacit, community members are capable of surfacing it when needed through dialogue.[25] In other words, their practices become interpersonally instinctive and natural. Meanings are negotiated and the result of such negotiations typically is learning itself. Practices in communities of practice may take such forms as subtle cues, recognized hunches, intense verbal and physical give-and-take, rules of thumb, stories, or shared worldviews.

Wenger cites three dimensions that together create the conditions for the emergence of communities of practice. First, there must be *mutual engagement*.[26] Membership is not just a matter of social category, role, or title. A community comes into existence because people are engaged in actions whose meanings they negotiate with one another. Members are included in what matters. Beyond engagement, they also consider themselves to be part of a *joint enterprise*.

They find a way to work together, to be accountable to one another, to live with their differences, and they coordinate their individual aspirations to become part of a community. Finally, they develop a *shared repertoire*, including routines, words, tools, ways of doing things, stories, gestures, concepts, and the like that symbolize their shared practice.

A colleague once told me about his work on a special operations project team that was charged with building new factories for his company. Initially, team members just saw themselves as performing a job, but over the course of time, the unit jelled in a special way. They took on a unique identity, or a "face," to the outside world. They became enmeshed with each other in practice. Over the course of time, they developed particular ways of doing things and continually added to their knowledge base. Members of the team also created a database of problem resolutions so that newcomers would not have to reinvent the wheel every time they came up against a new problem. Newcomers were not automatically accepted as part of the team, but they gradually learned, and even added to, the symbolic routines that defined how the team operated. The team was self-replicating in that before members would leave the team, they would bring in newcomers who could replicate their work performance. The team would also meet off-site once a month to debrief and discover how they could improve their processes. They would also conduct a two-week debriefing after they completed a project.

Communities of practice tend to evolve informally and are often on the periphery of standard practices, where innovation lies. Groups may form around a common substantive interest or a technology. "Members" may see themselves as current experts who choose to communicate with one another and who may make it their business to become unofficial gatekeepers of any new practices. Within the public sector, there is ample opportunity to share new ways to provide vital services under shrinking budgets. Through foundation sponsorship, a group called CEOs for Cities—consisting of big-city mayors, university presidents, and nonprofit and business

CEOs from fifteen cities—has been organized. The purpose of this CoP is to spur economic development through applied research in such areas as workforce skills, infrastructure development, and housing.[27]

Communities of practice may also arise out of necessity among formally constituted groups. What makes them a community of practice is both their function and their absolute need to commit to one another in order to "perform" their function. Such teams truly represent a collective mind to the extent that it is virtually impossible to detect individual virtuosity. On the other hand, each member of the team possesses partial knowledge of the job to be done. What is critical is how they contribute their partial knowledge to the team so that the collective entity has the full body of knowledge. Moreover, the members of a community of practice have learned how to work with each other as part of their mutual tacit understanding of what needs to be done.[28] They learn together as they work together, in deep trust and with an open spirit.[29]

Consider three examples supplied by Kenneth Labich.[30] The first example is the team represented by the U.S. Navy SEALs (Sea Air Land). Even though SEAL recruits arrive for training as tough physical specimens to begin with, only about three of every ten recruits make it. The one surefire way to wash out is to try to get by without the help of your fellow recruits. SEALs never operate on their own; their commitment to each other is and has to be total. Indeed, no dead SEAL has ever been left behind on a battlefield. This same dedication to one another can be found among members of the world renowned Tokyo String Quartet. No member ever even thinks about showing off his or her individual talent or technique, even though each is skilled enough to be a virtuoso soloist. They realize that they must project as one and maintain the quartet's personality. As a team, they blend their skill by instinctively knowing each other's moods, talents, and preferences.

A third example of a formally constituted community of practice is the pit crew at the Winston Cup races, where, given that races are often settled by fractions of a second, the facility of the crew can determine the outcome. A top crew made up of between fifteen to seventeen people—seven over the wall working on the car itself, the others on the other side handing them things—can change all four tires, power-pump twenty-one gallons of fuel, clean the windshield, and give the driver a drink all in less than twenty-one seconds.

Reaching the state of a community of practice can be achieved without a pronounced leader or a facilitator, but facilitation might potentially accelerate the process. Using some of the techniques described in action learning or action science (as will be discussed in the next section), the facilitator might assist members of the team to reveal more of their hidden assumptions about themselves and about others. Members might learn more about how the group as a whole is functioning and how to improve its process. Facilitation might reveal that the leadership role can be shared and that every member has the opportunity at various times and under certain conditions to perform a leadership function. Facilitators may also create a bridge between the CoP and any formal organization to which it may be attached.

Although there is seemingly little agreement about when and whether the facilitator of a learning team ought to make explicit interventions, clearly for a learning team to function well, the task of managing the learning has to permeate the entire team. Hence, in a community of practice, which operates—as we noted earlier—in part as a learning team, anyone assuming a facilitator role may reach that proverbial point of "working oneself out of a job." Getting to this point may take far longer than the straightforward accomplishment of a task by a work team. Although a work team may share a common goal or accomplish a key assignment or project, it may not require its members to probe to the depth of their underlying assumptions about their values nor about their feelings for each other.

Team members who have never experienced a community of practice may question why one has to reveal assumptions and even inferences if the job is to accomplish a task. Indeed, for mere task accomplishment, such "deeper" processes may not be required. If learning and creating become as important as doing, however, then group members will realize the value of exploring the deeper dimensions of their behavior. As Janov puts it, it is not enough just to understand oneself.[31] To make meaning together in a community of practice, one needs to understand oneself in relationship to the team. In fact, meaning-making becomes the primary basis for holding a community together. Members of such a community realize that it is not as critical that they report on what happened but rather that they commit themselves to interpret what an event that occurred *means*. They realize that each one of them may interpret events differently and that learning in their community can only occur once they share how they see things in a joint manner. Discovering what happened is less important than constructing their own reality together as a community. Furthermore, it is not so much a question of their arriving at the right answer as much as their arriving at a mutual understanding.[32] Once a team reaches this level of mutuality, not only does the role of facilitator fade away, but so does the role of explicit leader. In fact, leadership becomes everyone's responsibility in the sense of reminding group members of their meaning together, be it in accomplishing traditional responsibilities or in facing new work.

An apt example of community of practice development was reported in an account of a group of teachers who became interested in reflecting together and improving their teaching practice.[33] They each took turns describing their actions and mutually drawing each other out to explain the assumptions behind their choices of teaching strategies. Despite a conscious effort to maintain the focus on the presenter, at times the questions posed by the other group members would trigger reflective statements about their own practices. At some point in the process of the group, it appears that with the permission of the presenter, a presumed digression was allowed as an episode in what one member later characterized as the "group thinking together." The thinking in this case was not something that resided in each member's head but represented an open space in the middle of the group. In time, the dialogue took the form of a shared cognitive space. In the course of posing a critical question to the presenter, it became permissible to turn the question on oneself. This process allowed the members to focus both on themselves and on their practices as a collaborative venture for change.

Are there any formal mechanisms for executives and managers involved in potential communities of practice to facilitate their formation and development? The emerging literature on the subject is mixed on this account, with some writers believing that external intervention can actually risk destroying what might evolve naturally. Clearly, careful intervention is called for, akin to "fertilizing the soil."[34] Etienne Wenger presented a case in which a large insurance company in Canada intervened to formally establish a community of practice among its sales agents. Given that these agents are independent and are geographically distributed all over the country but do similar work, there was much they could learn from each other, personally, professionally, and technically.[35] Yet, past efforts had failed, so the company knew it had to enable the emergence of this CoP through specific strategies and resources. In particular, it selected some of its agents to take a community of practice course so that they would have direct experience with the concept. Besides enlisting the support of a number of high-level managers, it also resourced three specific positions on behalf of CoP formation and maintenance: a project manager, a knowledge architect, and a facilitator. The project manager was responsible for setting up the infrastructure to launch the program, the knowledge architect brought experience to bear from prior internal efforts to mobilize corporate knowledge, and the facilitator provided external expertise in mobilizing and documenting online dialogues. The project also assembled a steering group to lay the groundwork for the now new CoPs. This group designed a project plan with an accompanying budget, assembled technical resources, selected a web-based system, prepared and customized the online space for the dialogues, and provided supporting materials, including a guide to the activities supported by the site.

Largely through careful and ongoing planning, the community of practice movement took off at the company. A lively set of CoPs began to operate connecting agents across Canada. They each developed their own rhythm, but a consistent theme was their strong performance focus and need to "talk shop." One of the challenges has been to synthesize and secure the enormous amount of useful information into a searchable database. Over time, however, they have created a model for community development that has become a source of continuous learning.

So, whether through deliberate human or computer programming, collective learning can be accelerated. Compared with nonconscious performance, programmed collective learning can expand the consideration of new conditions and perspectives. It introduces practitioners to a language that is capable of uncovering personal conventions of practice that without programming would not otherwise add to collective memory. Programmed learning in a community of practice bridges to the next learning type—action science—when implicit behavior is made explicit using cognitive and artificial intelligence technologies. Strategies for mobilizing collective learning of this nature can be both formal and informal. A method known as *cognitive task analysis*, for example, analyzes the knowledge and performance requirements for jobs that involve complex cognitive skills.[36] It can help novices accelerate the acquisition of automatic job skills that tend to be associated with the unconscious actions of experts.[37]

There are informal means to cohere communities of practice, which can be just as effective as formal methods. Wenger, McDermott, and Snyder reported on the evolution of a CoP among a company's machine operators and engineers.[38] It started with no fanfare as a small group meeting for lunch once a month to discuss screening issues. In this unobtrusive way, the community built enough trust for the operators to become more comfortable discussing problems and even disagreeing publicly with the engineers. The group eventually developed its own rhythm, and once it began to demonstrate its value, its presence became visible to the organization.

Another well-known case in informal collective learning was depicted by Orr in his account of photocopier technicians who, as most of us working around offices have seen, need to skirt around training manuals as they confront idiosyncratic workplace problems.[39] Designers obviously cannot predict the social context in which the machines are used, so they must rely upon the technicians to understand the user environment. In many instances, problems arise because of operator use or misuse not predicted by the designers. So, the knowledge that is acquired here is social, as if the repairmen are participants in a group mind. Nelson and Winter point out that operator communities build up routines that transcend the sum of individual actions and capabilities.[40] Problem solving becomes more of a social activity than an analytically detached process. It also becomes a natural exercise. Scribner described workers in a commercial dairy, showing how the packers were able to configure mixed orders using calculations based upon changing base numbers depending on the item and its pack size.[41] Their calculations, which were error-free, seemed effortless.

The social and tacit infrastructure of workers is not always productive or even collective. Remedying ineffective team behavior, where differences become polarized, for example, requires team members to learn to observe and experiment with their own collective tacit processes in action. Bohm suggests that breakdowns in team effectiveness be handled through a dialogic process in which participants learn or relearn to reason and act together.[42] In dialogue, members of a team begin to act in an aligned way, rather than segmenting thought into categories with each member presenting a particular position. The dialogue process initially calls for a suspension of judgment of extreme points of view followed by a gradual commitment to inquire together as new insights and meanings unfold.

The expertness of the community of practice as a learning community should not be overlooked. As an element of work-based learning, it often supersedes the formal scientific documentation that can be found in training manuals or designs that are "down-skilled" to operating levels. Learning becomes *enacted*; that is, constructed on the spot as new information comes online.[43] Documenters often assume that the problems their manuals are designed to debug are relatively predictable. Unfortunately, tools such as manuals are mere abstractions, which often fall short in comprehending the complexity of actual field practices.[44] Typically, it is necessary for field workers, through their informal interactions or war stories that represent repositories of accumulated wisdom, to bring coherence to an otherwise random set of conditions.

So the notion of community of practice places knowledge into its context. As a model of work-based learning, it suggests that learning is built out of the materials of the local situation and that it is often collective. Hence, learners cannot be segregated from the communities in which they are to work. Apprenticeships, for example, cannot be complete if training is conducted only in simulated work conditions. Apprentices must have the opportunity to observe and even participate in collective practices. Their job is to learn when, how, and what is to be done according to particular intrinsic practices. They also need to be able to give a reasonable account of why it is done and what kind of person one must become in order to be accepted as a competent member of the community.[45] The knowledge used in a context is often practical as opposed to theoretical, and it is often elegant in its simplicity.

The situated learning literature proposes a progressive learning model in which newcomers move from peripheral to full forms of participation in their respective communities of practice.[46] They learn from a number of different sources and through a variety of methods, most of which are tacit. For example, they may learn from observing others who are more senior or through experimenting on their own from which they may obtain informal or even formal feedback. However, since their communities often overlap, they tend to participate in a number of them at different times and at varying levels.[47]

In a study centered at a consulting firm, junior associates were seen as learning their craft not through a smooth trajectory from peripheral to full participation but through multiple forms. In particular, in one project with a major client, they were limited to observing senior colleagues handling high-level client transactions. In this instance, their learning was thought to be at best vicarious. In another project with a less prestigious smaller client, they were thrown "into the fire" by having to manage client meetings and organize client deliverables. Their learning was direct and unrestrained to the point of shaping their professional identity.[48]

Virtual Team Learning

A critical question in the domain of work-based learning is whether distance learning methods, especially those using electronic communication, can be successfully applied to create collaboration and reflection. There may be occasions when teams might need to coordinate tasks or reflect on past or current practices but are too geographically distant to hold meetings. In particular, communities of practice, evolving as they often do around function, may by design be constituted of members who cross organizational boundaries. What keeps them together might initially be their substantive interest or expertise, not their proximity. They may also wish to discuss real-time work issues in an effort to learn from one another.

In addition to the value of overcoming geographical distance, virtual team meetings by definition can occur when there is a need, rather than having to waste days or even weeks organizing the necessary travel to meet face-to-face. Another critical advantage is the veritable archive made available in real time from the online discussion among the members. Electronic communication has also been found to be actually more effective than face-to-face communication in promoting the widespread sharing of information and for handling divergent-thinking tasks.[49] It can also reduce such barriers as domination by high-status members or inequality of participation. This is because it can remove the distractions of irrelevant stimuli or of invalid stereotypes.[50]

Accordingly, communities of practice may find it convenient to make use of electronic means of communication, becoming what is increasingly being referred to as *virtual communities of practice*, or VCoPs.[51] Using e-mail or more-sophisticated technologies, such as web conferencing or desktop videoconferencing systems, members can keep up-to-date with one another regardless of space or time. On the other hand, without some initial and then quite frequent face-to-face meetings, members may not be able to sufficiently warm up to each other. As Peter Hillen of the semiconductor firm Open Solution once put it, "No one yet has invented a technology that replaces a pitcher of beer."[52]

Although virtual communities allow plenty of opportunity for private reflection, there is a concern that they may not represent a conducive environment for public reflection on members' practices and assumptions. In particular, dialogue is often impeded by a lack of nonverbal cues and by a reduction in the exchange of social-emotional information. As a result, although virtual teams may handle task-oriented exchanges well, they tend to be slow in developing relational links among members based on trust, cohesion, and group identity.[53] Further, though they may work well for task teams as they work through their functional or operational concerns, can they be useful for managers to help them work through fundamental questions of culture and change? Rob Edwards, in reporting on an initial experiment in using online action learning sets to enhance support for students undertaking a master's thesis at the Wolverhampton Business School in the United Kingdom, found that students were far more inclined to take advantage of the face-to-face learning team opportunity than the online exchange.[54]

Perhaps, as Coutu reports, it comes down to a need to build trust, especially when people cannot interact directly with one another.[55] Substituting for the luxury of face-to-face encounter, virtual teams need to begin their interactions with a series of social messages, such as doing full introductions before setting on the task at hand. Virtual team members also need to assume designated roles, helping them to establish their identity and commitment, and to make explicit some of their norms and expectations, especially in regard to goals, tasks, and results.

When it comes to preparing members to participate effectively in virtual endeavors, the very competencies addressed in work-based learning are the ones that need development. It is often not terribly difficult to instruct people in the use of computer-based technologies, but it is challenging to develop skills in interpersonal relations, team contribution, and intercultural communication. For example, team members need to be, at least initially, more sensitive to how their messages might be received because they do not have the benefit of nonverbal expression. Because team membership also tends to be fluid, effective teams require members who can quickly assimilate into a virtual social structure. They also need members who can comfortably communicate with people from diverse cultures.[56] Having experience in project and learning teams that systematically deploy skills to accelerate learning can be critical when it comes to participating in virtual communities.

Although there is not a vast amount of evidence available on the use of virtual or web-based instruction as applied to work-based learning, there are sufficient parallel studies in the general distance learning fields to know the cautions to overcome. Learners tend to become discouraged over time due to competing interests, lack of accountability, an obstructive environment or lack of support by a sponsoring organization, poorly designed courseware, and problems with technology.[57] For example, the distribution of information can become uneven because of variability in the capacity of members' internet service provider (ISP) platforms. Another barrier might be the presence of firewalls, which might inadvertently prevent the delivery of important attachments.[58]

To overcome some of these limitations, besides some of the strategies already discussed, it is important to familiarize each participant in any forming network with the program's operations and norms. Facilitation of this kind should also be available during the course of the experience should individual members begin to experience confusion or encounter technological difficulties. Facilitation is thus of two sorts: group development and technological support. In many cases, these roles will be handled by different principals. The group development facilitator's function is to see that members feel comfortable participating in their team, that they have relevant contextual information, and that barriers preventing full and healthy dialogue are kept to a minimum. For example, at the outset, the facilitator should ensure that members share in the overall aim of the team and have complementary objectives. In addition, members should be encouraged to provide timely, predictable, and detailed contributions about which they should also expect thorough feedback.[59] The technical facilitator ensures that technological problems are kept to a minimum and provides Web-based collaboration tools, such as portals or video conferencing, to enhance learning, whether they be for *asynchronous* (sequential messages) or for *synchronous* (concurrent dialogue) communications.[60]

Experiments are under way to consider the extent to which work-based learning can be delivered online as a virtual community experience. Champlain College offers a project-based learning experience through its MBA program. The program is available entirely online so that the workplace becomes the students' learning lab. An effort is made by the program administrators to tie the curriculum to work in such a way that the learning has a demonstrable, immediate, and profound impact on students' professional lives and on their organizations. Although online academic programs have multiplied in recent years, what makes the Champlain program so unique is its emphasis on work-based reflective practice through a series of virtual teams. Indeed, every course in the program is built around work-based projects that culminate in a major online reflective activity. Founder and former director, Don Haggerty, explained how he structured one of his course assignments along these lines.[61] Students were assembled into small teams of four to produce a deliverable and a team reflection on a work-based change project. Initially, the team prepared its assignment using its own private discussion area. Then, each team posted its results to the full-class discussion area, soliciting feedback from its peers. Here's how Professor Haggerty further described the learning dynamic:

> My thought was to get the class interacting from a perspective of already having reflected on each other's work at the team level but now needing to reflect in a more public forum. The end results were highly received by students because the focus was on the process of applying concepts and learning together at both levels (team and class) and much less on either learning "content" in isolation or posting to a discussion board just for the sake of posting. In effect, I was mimicking "breakout" sessions and bringing the full group together. The "leap of faith" that I took was making this such a big part of the learning process and grading.

Electronic technologies can be used in a variety of ways to support communities both in their processes and in their task endeavors. For example, the computer-based application known as group support systems (GSS) can be used to facilitate group development through its use of team-building procedures, tools, and heuristics.[62] GSS can also be used for electronic brainstorming or for idea organization. In the latter, group members may work in parallel to converge on key issues raised during a brainstorming session. GSS also features electronic voting, group outlining, group writing, shared drawing and diagramming, and structured alternative evaluation. One of the advantages offered by GSS in building a community of practice is that it allows everyone to "talk at once," overcoming the natural effect of losing the train of thought, be it of one's own ideas or those of others. Strong or loud personalities don't have an opportunity to dominate as they would in a totally open forum. All participants have an equal opportunity to contribute, and ideas are considered on their own merits rather than on their sources.[63]

There are many applications of electronic communication as a knowledge management resource. In particular, communities of practice can find the data storage and retrieval facets of knowledge management systems (KMS) to be critical to their work. Consider how collective experience can be captured for online examination using DaimlerChrysler's EBOK system. Short for the Engineering Book of Knowledge, EBOK provides best practice information on car design and building processes, ranging from door panels to tail lamps to engine parts.[64] At DaimlerChrysler, tech clubs form to share knowledge across car platforms, and in turn the knowledge captured through the clubs is consolidated through the EBOK system. Similarly, Xerox maintains an electronic relational database called Eureka, which organizes and categorizes tips generated from the field by its tech reps.[65] The social capital provided by communities of practice is important to activate these knowledge management systems, which otherwise would fail due to lack of motivation or commitment on the part of members to contribute to the repositories.[66] The data contributed need to be stored and accessed with ease and must also be sufficiently detailed to be of practical value to its users, and, of course, must be secure.

Communities of Practice as Organizations

A new variant of communities of practice is the controversial notion of producing a community of practice in an entire organization. Many observers might suggest that this is at best an idyllic, illusory vision that can only be strived for, never to be achieved. There are too many barriers in human systems, especially considerations of power when mass collections of people occur, to create a community where everyone constructs meaning together. Nevertheless, there have been successful experiments in building at least temporary communities by placing the "whole system in the room." Such experiments represent processes that bring up to three hundred organizational members and their stakeholders together for several days to work through critical organizational issues.

There are a few tenets that these large-group interventions have in common. Most critical is that all stakeholders concerned about the problem be present and actively participate in their remediation. Second, it is important that the gathering be structured in advance so that both productive conversation and reflection can ensue in order to generate new ideas and perspectives and to allow people to dream and feel purposeful.[67] Consistent with work-based learning approaches, these approaches recognize the value of private and public reflection to absorb the enormous amount of information exchanged during the meetings. Marvin Weisbord, co-originator of the Future Search technology, talks about the need for "soak time," to give participants a chance to process the network activities both privately and publicly.[68] It is also important that the experience be structured to see how all the parts of a community interact to produce what happened, to help people recognize multiple perspectives, and to give them an opportunity to work together to manage a better future. What large-group interventions attempt is to allow multiple voices to engage in dialogue and thus learn to create meaning together.

Nancy Dixon gives an account of a future search conference held for a group of seventy people from a grocery chain, including store managers, employees, customers, and suppliers.[69] The chain had been struggling with the question of whether to continue its expansion strategy. The store managers voiced the concern that such a strategy would adversely affect quality and other issues. However, through organized discussions held throughout the three days of the conference, they realized that the long-term viability of the chain required continued growth. This realization occurred to them collectively, as all conference members expressed their expectations for the future viability of the business. Other outcomes were likewise produced, such as the need to hire a national purchasing director to centralize buying, all from having everyone in the room learning how to reason together, not necessarily to find a right answer.

There has been a burst of innovation in creating designs for large-system interventions, including the following: Appreciative Inquiry,[70] the Conference Model,[71] Open Space Technology,[72] Participative Design,[73] Public Conversations Project Dialogue,[74] The Search Conference,[75] Wisdom Circles,[76] and the World Café.[77] Perhaps among the most flexible is Open Space Technology, whereby participants are given the opportunity to champion a discourse around an area of concern of their choosing. As long as at least two people are interested, they can continue to meet. Reports to the large community are built into the process. The World Café has become arguably the most popular of these methods. As described by its founders, Juanita Brown and David Isaacs, it is an intentional way to create a living network of conversations around questions that matter, whether in business, government, health, education, or community-based organizations.[78] The construct of *the conversation* is key because it represents how people tend to share knowledge, imagine their future, and create communities of practice. Many critical changes in history can be traced to people conversing informally in their living rooms, church halls, and cafés.

World Café methodology is quite simple. Tables are set with paper tablecloths, flowers, colored pens, and refreshments. A series of conversational rounds lasting from twenty to forty-five minutes are held regarding one or more meaningful questions. Participants are encouraged to write, doodle, or draw key ideas and themes on their tablecloths. At the end of each round, one person remains at the table as the host, while each of the others travels to new tables. The hosts welcome the newcomers and share the essence of that table's conversation so far. The newcomers in turn relate any conversational threads that they are carrying and then the conversation continues. After the last round, participants return to their original table to integrate all the new information. Then the whole community shares and explores emerging themes, insights, and learning, capturing the collective intelligence of the whole.

Thousands of people from around the world have experienced the World Café for a myriad of noble purposes. Chaiwat Thirapantu reported on his use of this large-group methodology at the national level in facilitating a People Assembly for the Democrat (opposition) Party in Thailand.[79] The café imagery works well in a Thai context because of its own tradition of the coffee shop assembly, referred to as Sapa Ga fae. With nearly three thousand people in attendance, Thirapantu and his staff facilitated several cafés to elicit the most challenging goals and issues to which the party should dedicate itself. Not only was the café a success among its participants, but it also galvanized interest in political dialogue throughout the country. Ultimately, seven issues were identified for subsequent deliberation: educational reform, corruption, economic development, ethics, political reform, people empowerment, and provincial violence.

Art Kleiner and George Roth invented the *learning history* to operationalize the collective memory of an organization.[80] In their terms, "A learning history is a written narrative of a company's recent set of critical episodes: a corporate change event, a new initiative, a widespread innovation, a successful product launch, or even a traumatic event such as a major reduction in the workforce." Through interviews, a consultant team prepares up to a one hundred-page document detailing the episode through direct quotes placed on the right-hand side of the document. On the left-hand side, the consultant team, along with some knowledgeable insiders, known as *learning historians*, draw out the recurrent themes, assumptions, implications, and even "undiscussables" from the narrative. The learning history is then used as a basis for group discussions. Kleiner and Roth's technique draws on the ancient practice of community storytelling, wherein individuals would offer their recollection of events and a shaman might comment on the narrative to draw out its significance. Re-experiencing the event together, the group learns collectively. In today's corporate world, the learning history can spark conversations and share knowledge across divisions. It can also generate trust and permit more open conversations about difficult issues. Most critically, it represents a unique way to have organizational members make meaning together.

By studying these large-system methodologies, we might learn what the ingredients need to be to experiment with communities of practice for whole organizations. Dixon has already identified six elements: (1) reliance on discussion not speeches, (2) egalitarian participation, (3) encouragement of multiple perspectives, (4) non-expert–based dialogue, (5) use of a participant-generated database (primary data that are shared by all members present, not as reports from others), and (6) creation of a shared experience.[81]

Action Science

Action science is a work-based intervention strategy for helping learners increase their effectiveness in social situations through heightened awareness of their action and interaction assumptions. Although initially aimed at the individual level of experience, action science is ultimately concerned with improving the level of public discourse both in groups and in organizations. The mental models of people—the images, assumptions, and stories carried inside our minds about ourselves and about others—are often untested and unexamined and consequently often erroneous. In action science, these mental models are brought into consciousness in such a way that new models are formed that may serve us better.[82]

Action science thus calls for the deliberate questioning of existing perspectives and interpretations, referred to by Argyris and Schön as *double-loop learning* (see Chapter Two).[83] When a mismatch occurs between our values and actions, most people attempt to narrow the gap by trial-and-error learning. They also prefer to maintain a sense of control over the situation, over themselves, and over others. In double-loop learning, we subject even our governing values to critical reflection, resulting in free and informed choice, valid information, and high internal commitment to any new behavior attempted.

Robert Putnam sees the goal of action science as improving social discourse in at least two important ways.[84] First, it can improve discourse in the moment so that the people involved can engage with each other in a more productive way. They may be able to do this among themselves, but typically they will require the assistance of a facilitator. Second, action science can invoke the deeper causal factors that lead people to interact as they do. In order to bring about fundamental and lasting improvement in the quality of discourse, people need to reflect upon and alter the assumptions embedded in their behavior and reasoning patterns. Although some of this can occur in the midst of practical conversation, Putnam believes that it more likely requires planned learning sessions.

Donald Schön preferred the term *reflection-in-action* to characterize the rethinking process of action science, which attempts to discover how what one did contributed to an unexpected or expected outcome.[85] In order to engage in reflection-in-action, a practitioner might start by offering a frame of the situation at hand. Then, if in a group situation, he or she might inquire as to how others see it. After receiving feedback, the individual and subsequently the whole group might collectively reflect upon these frames and begin to surface and test their underlying assumptions and respective reasoning processes. The ultimate aim is to narrow inconsistencies between one's *espoused theories* and *theories-in-use*. Espoused theories are those characterizing what we say we will do. Theories-in-use describe how we *actually* behave, although their revision of our espoused values is usually tacit. The goal of action science is to uncover these theories-in-use, in particular to distinguish between those that inhibit and those that promote learning.

Framing and subsequent communication in action science correspond to Habermas's views of knowledge and human interest, which in turn shape human discourse.[86] Technical knowledge involves predictions about observable events, physical or social. This type of knowledge may result in empirical or theoretical discourse, in which claims to truth may be validated by empirical tests. Empirical discourse relies on the scientific method, elaborated on in our previous discussion of applied science.

The second type of knowledge is what Habermas refers to as *practical*, which entails social norms, ideals, values, and moral decisions. Practical or rational discourse, in the absence of empirical tests, may call upon tradition and authority but preferably uses consensus based upon a dialogue over contested meanings. Learning through metaphors—understanding one kind of thing in terms of another—may be a useful method to help resolve contradictions or inconsistencies between concepts and contexts or to allow expression of particularly indeterminate practices.[87] Ultimately, practical discourse will search for meaning rather than attempt to delineate causality.[88]

Habermas's third type of knowledge, *emancipatory*, is gained through critical self-reflection of our taken-for-granted assumptions and feelings. Reflective discourse is used in this instance to determine whether the premises for our interpretation or understanding are themselves valid. The concept of third-order learning, described in Chapter Two, represents this level of discourse. There is some dispute whether reflective discourse should or should not also incorporate such critical dimensions as questioning wider social, political, and cultural practices, including the issues of power, vested interests, and control. Nor is there much talk of ideology in the work of Argyris and Schön. They do not tend to concentrate on questions about the means of production in modern industrial organizations, nor do they tend to directly attack such organizations because they may be exploitative, racist, sexist, or ecologically destructive.

The focus of action science is rather to sustain a methodology that attacks mindless acceptance of organizational routines that can lead to power maintenance regardless of political point of view.[89] Indeed, most action scientists see capitalist and noncapitalist organizations as equally guilty in sustaining particularistic interaction pathologies, such as taking one's own reasoning for granted, asking leading questions, suppressing open inquiry, or keeping thoughts private. Their criticism can even be leveled against critical theorists who at times impose their own interpretations of organizational relationships without being willing to submit these criticisms to alternative inquiries nor to publicly expose the historical processes and social context underlying their own constructions.

An important difference between practical and reflective discourse, to which Habermas has not devoted much attention, is the distinction between perceiving and feeling experience.[90] The latter refers to the explicit referencing of emotional reactions, which are often denied or dismissed, be they defensive reactions, embarrassment, or general anxiety.[91] Action science essentially creates a real-time learning environment that permits and encourages learners to engage in emancipatory discourse, thus testing their mental models, especially their inferences and assumptions about others and about their own behavior. Coworkers come to understand the embedded cultural myths that underlie their felt needs and wants expressed in their relations with others.

Action scientists also make direct comparisons between individual and organizational learning. Argyris and Schön find that people are socially conditioned to use a cognitive model referred to as "Model I."[92] Mostly concerned with detecting errors in our problem solving, Model I is unfortunately characterized by a need to control, maximize winning, suppress emotions, and be rational. Its consequences tend to be defensive behavior, miscommunication, and in actuality, the escalation rather than the reduction of error.[93] Model II behavior, on the other hand, is based on directly observable data and requires that people support their advocacy of positions with illustration and with inquiry into the views of others. Accordingly, Model II practitioners tend more reliably to produce intended consequences and thus increase learning.

Individuals using Model I will create Model I organizational systems. Unfortunately, such systems, characterized by minimal learning capability, are difficult to change because of self-fulfilling processes and defensive reasoning strategies that individuals become unaware of using. Such systems in turn reinforce individuals to continue to act in ways characterized by Model I. On the other hand, Model II attempts to test and make explicit individuals' assumptions about the dynamics going on within their organization. Action strategies reflecting Model II values will serve to create organizations with Model II attributes: most prominently, the ability to learn at an emancipatory level of knowledge.

There are many techniques, such as projective visualization and Socratic dialogue, that can be used in small group settings to elicit and challenge psychocultural assumptions behind habituated ways of perceiving, thinking, feeling, and behaving.[94] One intriguing method, known as *concept mapping*, helps learners, either individually or in groups, reflect critically on concepts and their interrelationships as well as search for alternative ways of interpreting these same or allied concepts.[95]

Concept maps are visualized representations of problem situations that can help teams make sense out of a predicament.[96] Huff suggests that groups involved in concept mapping need to make three choices: (1) which territory the map should cover (individual or group perceptions), (2) which form of data collection should be used as input (post-hoc analysis or interactive generation of the data), and (3) which purpose the map should serve (direct product or a tool).[97] In action science, teams are typically interested in representing their individual and collective mental models in a here-and-now setting. Hence, concept maps may be used as a tool to facilitate this representation process. There are a variety of methods of concept mapping in use today. Three of them will be described here.

Peter Checkland has developed a learning approach known as *soft systems methodology* (SSM).[98] SSM compares pure models of purposeful action with perceptions of what is going on in a real-world problem situation. Using a seven-stage process, SSM teases out and then calls for testing via debate the complex assumptions underlying our actions, including relevant myths and meanings as well as facts and logic.

Strategic Options Development and Analysis, or SODA, was designed by Colin Eden to help consultants work with clients on messy problems, especially during strategy formulation processes.[99] Using interviews with participants, individual cognitive maps are created and then merged into a collective model. In SODA, it is critical that all members of the group be allowed their personal subjective view of the "real" problem. During the merging stage, a process of negotiation permits the aggregation of data without participants feeling that they have lost any of the richness and detail of their own concept maps.

A third mapping technique, based explicitly on action science design, is known as *data mapping* and was introduced in the graduate program in human resource development at the University of Texas.[100] After going through a series of workshops on action science techniques, learning teams are formed in groups of four to six participants. Once in the teams, participants continue to study action science concepts while building trust with one another. They subsequently bring to the group personal cases from their lives as a means to help them become more effective in their human interactions. The cases are representative of incidents that the presenter would classify as demonstrating interpersonal or strategic ineffectiveness. The process is publicly reflective as team members learn to challenge tacit assumptions, whether they belong to the case presenter or to the observers.

As part of a real-time case experience, data mapping would be introduced to extend the action science problem-solving model of diagnosing a problem, inventing action strategies to solve it, producing action to enact the strategies, and evaluating the results (see Table 5.1).

Table 5.1. An Action Science Data Map

Model Components	Model I Map	Model II Map
Contextual cue or triggering condition	When given a task by my boss to delegate to one of my staff—a task that is inappropriate to delegate	When given a task by my boss to delegate to one of my staff—a task that is inappropriate to delegate
Underlying assumptions	I should do it anyway	I should trust my instincts and tell my boss what it is I am concerned about
Action strategies	So I implement my boss's unreasonable request	So I bring my concern to my boss and share why I think the task shouldn't be delegated and then ask if my boss agrees
Consequences in the behavioral world for learning	Which guarantees not pleasing anyone	Which predisposes us to an outcome that may please both of us

As can be discerned from the table, the data map assumes the format of an If-Then or When-So statement, incorporating the following components:

When-So Statement

When _____ (contextual cue or triggering event) _____ happens, I _____ (make the following assumptions about what I should do) _____, so I implement the following _____ (action strategies) _____, which guarantees that the following _____ (consequences in the behavioral world of learning) _____ will occur.

With the help of the team, case presenters progressively revise their case to determine if they can invent an alternative approach more in line with a Model II action strategy. Using action science methods, the presenters learn to develop strategies that can reduce the inhibiting condition of defensive routines in the workplace and replace them with models that encourage mutual learning.

The action science methods discussed here extend the lesson of action learning that at the level of practical discourse is more concerned with meaning-making: helping participants enhance their sensitivity to the ways others perceive or react to them. Whereas action learning seeks to contextualize learning, action science de-contextualizes practice so that learners can become more critical of their behavior and explore the very premises of their beliefs.

Keen has provided language to help us decontextualize our practice. He proposes a three-step process.[101] First, we engage in *phenomenological reduction*. This means that we must try to let whatever we encounter be what it is, apart from our perception of it. As human beings, we find it virtually impossible not to attempt to impute meaning to a phenomenon. In this first step, however, we must try to open ourselves to the situation while holding our preconceived notions to a minimum. For example, when we start up with a new group, we all have a tendency to want to size up each member's contribution even before anyone speaks. Can we learn to be open to each person's potential so as to allow our perception to evolve with experience?

Keen's second step is known as *imaginative variation*. Here we play with all the contingencies in a situation, combining and re-combining them in conventional and in unconventional ways. Again, human instinct forces us to use familiar categories to organize our perception. Keen is asking us to consider multiple combinations of perceptual organization to release the phenomenon from our habitual modes of control.

The third step is the more familiar *interpretation*, wherein we assess the desirability of various scenarios. Although in interpretation we arrive where we may have started, Keen's process helps us consciously and reflectively work through our perceptions of phenomena and our inferences of others so that our mental models become more understandable and coherent to us.

The assumption-challenging process of action science is akin to lateral thinking placed into a public arena. Now part of our common language, *lateral thinking* was invented by Edward de Bono, in his lifelong quest to inspire us to think about our thinking.[102] His work in this domain is remarkably consistent with the broad view of learning advocated in this book. Acknowledging the value of our brain to create and use patterns in helping us make sense of our world, de Bono nevertheless suggests that at times we need to change and to keep on changing our familiar patterns and routines, be it through accident, mistake, humor, or practice. In the latter instance, we can use a variety of approaches within our work groups to help us suspend judgment and through exploration gather new insight. This form of thinking tends to be more difficult in the West, where we prize the clash of opinions or dialectical methods over mind expansion devices. Yet we can be trained in lateral thinking and may experiment with techniques to help us consider problems and relationships in fresh, previously uncharted ways.

One of de Bono's enlightening techniques is known as Six Thinking Hats.[103] It can help participants apply different modes of thinking, especially in regard to Keen's imaginative variation stage of decontextualizing practice. As a problem or issue is being discussed, participants can metaphorically put on six different hats, which they focus on in turn:

White: Focus on the data, dig down to the hard facts.

Black: Spot what can go wrong, identify the fatal flaws in the plan.

Yellow: Take the optimistic viewpoint, think positively.

Green: Generate innovative solutions, be creative.

Red: Use your intuition and emotion, sense how others will react.

Blue: Coordinate the process, orchestrate the meeting.

Chris Argyris and his associates Robert Putnam, Phil McArthur, and Diana Smith have developed a number of unique techniques to surface mental models, including the now-familiar *ladder of inference*.[104] This technique is often used in an action science group in which the facilitator helps members examine their inferences regarding a project situation or work site problem. It can also be used to help members reframe how they currently are working with one another. The ladder of inference is based on an action model, wherein, given the context of the operating situation we are in and our stock of knowledge, we frame how we view ourselves and others in the situation. Based on our framing, we then take action. Unfortunately, as human beings, we don't typically have the time to be totally informed about every contingency we encounter and cannot redesign every action we take, so we respond using models that we have counted on in many prior situations in our lives. By reusing these tried-and-true models, we are able to act fairly expeditiously and do not have to reason through each and every new situation we encounter. To do otherwise would virtually hamstring our ability to act spontaneously.

Unfortunately, by acting instinctively without occasional reframing, we become disconnected from our reasoning processes and even become unaware that we are unaware of our theories-in-use.[105] Consequently, we may create misunderstandings by not testing our views with one another. Using the ladder of inference, we learn to reframe or alter our spontaneous understanding of a particular situation, which can lead to new ways of seeing ourselves and others and thus can also lead to new actions that might accomplish our goals more effectively. Consider how the ladder of inference might be deployed. As shown in Figure 5.1, our mental models may be invoked whenever we place ourselves in a situation affecting us containing observable data.

Let's say that you recently convened a staff meeting and engaged in an interaction that you subsequently wished to process in your action science team. The exchange was between you and a colleague named Paul, and it occurred during a short break.

Paul began the exchange by saying that the way you handled Rebecca during the meeting was "interesting." Rebecca was going

Figure 5.1. The Ladder of Inference

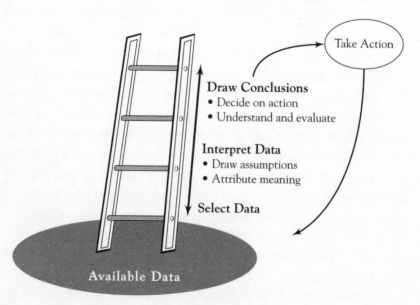

Source: Adapted with permission of Action Design® ©2007.

off on one of her tangents about the team's unwillingness to consider a reengineering of the payroll function, and you had to cut her off by saying, "Thanks, Rebecca. Now let's hear what Paul has to say." (Having attended a process-reengineering seminar, Rebecca was convinced that we could have saved valuable resources by farming out payroll to a reliable contractor, even though you told her repeatedly that you wanted to keep our tradition intact of never firing anyone who was doing a good job because of corporate restructuring.) Paul's comment that your way of handling Rebecca was "interesting" invoked an immediate and tacit response. For you, the word *interesting* is a red-flag word that connotes disapproval. However, if Paul wasn't going to explain what he meant by the word, you weren't going to tolerate his ambiguity. That's why your response was merely to thank him for his approval and move on to other matters.

Now back in your action science team meeting, you want to probe whether you handled the exchange with Paul in an effective manner. You have an uncomfortable feeling that more could have been uncovered from your brief exchange with Paul, but you also believe that little can be done with someone who is so cryptic and unclear all the time.

The action science facilitator can demonstrate, using the ladder of inference, how—from all the available data having to do with your exchanges with Paul and with Rebecca—you moved up the ladder by selecting his one comment about your managing her as having been "interesting." In doing so, you invoked some fundamental assumptions. Primary was the assumption that when an observer says someone has made an "interesting" intervention, that means that the intervenor has made an inappropriate comment. You then further interpreted what Paul said by making an attribution that he was being indirect or offhanded. From this interpretation, you leapt to a higher rung of the ladder when you concluded that when faced with indirectness, your only option is to respond in kind. However, it was the action from this inference that you are now questioning as being potentially ineffective.

Opening up the ladder of inference after the fact, the facilitator can work with you at each rung to show you, first, how you selected just one piece of data (Paul's comment that your intervention was "interesting") from an entire conversation. From there, you made an assumption that Paul disapproved of you, but in turn you attributed a meaning that he often engages in the ineffectual practice of being indirect. Looking at the data, you could have also focused on any number of other interpretations. For example, you could have considered why Rebecca seems to be repeatedly bringing up the subject of reengineering. You could have examined whether there might really be a problem in payroll. As for your attribution of the instant comment from Paul, you could have made a series of alternative interpretations, among which might have been that Paul was afraid of approaching you directly because of past suppressive behavior on your part. Maybe he might have approved in part of how you handled Rebecca, though he was interested in questioning why and when you resort to this approach. Opening up the ladder of inference in this way could have produced not only different conclusions but also alternative actions, which might have led to more effective behavior not only in this one instance but also as a convener of other staff meetings. Essentially, this type of action science intervention can produce a reframing that alters our reasoning and action models to be more consistent with our values and intentions.

Although action science as a pedagogy tends to work on one individual at a time, its practitioners gradually expect to increase the level of public discourse in the organization in order for people to feel free to voice their opinions and shape outcomes according to mutual decision making. An example of this contagion of action science principles occurred in the late 1980s at Knight-Ridder when it undertook a project called 25/43 to increase readership among persons between the ages specified in the label: twenty-five to forty-three. The impetus for the project was that young adult readership of the company's newspapers had dropped. The project sought to change newspaper design to attract readers in the target age group. However, changing the design potentially conflicted with the mental models underlying the chain's journalists, who viewed themselves as first-class writers. Was quality going to be sacrificed to produce more relevance for the desired age group?

In this instance, Knight-Ridder's executives exhibited a high degree of learning and reflection as they worked through the contradictions embedded in the 25/43 project.[106] First, they listened to the journalists and encouraged them to surface their mental models regarding their work preferences and identity. Then they turned their attention to their readers by conducting market research and focus groups with their target audience. In time, the 25/43 process became an institutionalized method of assessing consumer opinion at Knight-Ridder, expanding to other "at-risk" groups beyond baby boomers. Throughout the process, the company kept dialogue alive by trying to uncover underlying assumptions and engage in reflective discourse.

6

Public Reflection as the Basis of Work-Based Learning

> The range of what we think and do is limited by
> what we fail to notice, and because we fail to notice
> that we fail to notice, there is little we can do to
> change, until we notice how failing to notice shapes
> our thoughts and deeds.
>
> —Ronald Laing

I have referred frequently in this book to the process of reflection, initially as an explicit individual learning type and then as a collective property. It is the latter sense that distinguishes work-based learning from standard classroom practices. Through public reflection, we can create a collective identity as a community of inquiry. In this chapter, we examine the process of public reflection, known also as *reflective practice*, in greater detail. In the following chapter, we will look at four explicit reflective practices.

Reflective Practice: What Is It?

Reflection is the practice of stepping back to ponder and express the meaning to self and to others in one's immediate environment of what has, will, or is happening. It illuminates what has been experienced by both self and others, providing a basis for future action. In its public form, it is typically associated with learning dialogues. As noted in Chapter One, these types of discussions, rather than constitute an exchange of statements of points of view, surface in the safe presence of trusting peers the social, political, and emotional data that arise from direct experience with one another. Often these data are precisely those that might be blocking operating effectiveness. Learning dialogues also are concerned with creating mutual caring relationships. However they can reveal—but with permission—a person's solitude and mystery.

Reflective practice tends to probe to a deeper level than trial-and-error experience. It typically is concerned with forms of learning I have already referred to as double-loop and triple-loop, a learning that seeks to inquire about the most fundamental assumptions and premises behind our practices. David Hardy, formerly with the Business Creativity and Employee Involvement group at the Bank of Montreal, would explain it as a *thinking about our thinking*. We noted in the last chapter, for example, that what makes a work team a learning team is its interest in clarifying its thought before and after action. David would point out that our brain, as a sophisticated information-processing organ, can handle some fifty thousand to sixty thousand thoughts per day. Unfortunately, as we encounter problems in our work, we tend to go no further than to consult our *solution database* (as depicted in Figure 6.1) to find an answer.

In thinking about thinking, we are actually able to reflect together about our solution databases and add to them or alter them entirely. The reflection referred to here is more than personal reflection, which is private and introspective. Reflective practice occurs in the midst of practice but is also produced in the presence of others. Taylor goes even further in his insistence that without the medium of relationships, critical reflection can be impotent and hollow, lacking the genuine discourse necessary for thoughtful and in-depth reflection.[1]

Figure 6.1. Our Normal Problem-Solving Pattern

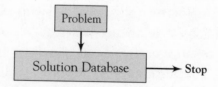

As Plato recounts, Socrates had the idea of relationships in mind when he uttered that famous phrase: "The unexamined life is not worth living." This phrase has often been misinterpreted as a call for additional introspection by people. Although introspection can be useful, the actual meaning is that we need to include others in the examination of experience in our life. Socrates' idea resonated with Aristotle, who recognized that human beings are social animals, whose good is bound up with the good of the polis. Underpinned by these Greek roots, the egalitarian tradition in Western thought has long since recognized that the dignity of human persons is achieved only in community with others.[2] Jürgen Habermas, whom I referenced in the last chapter, sees the reconciliation between individual and society through intersubjective recognition based on mutual understanding and free cognition about disputed claims.[3] It is through communicative action that we are able to realize ourselves within a civic community. We must subject our entire experience to criticism, even our tacit understanding. For Habermas, then, the Enlightenment project of modernity can be saved through open, public dialogue.

Reflective practice with others or public reflectiveness is fundamental to the learning process described in this book. There are a number of reasons why reflection must be brought out in the open:

1. Managers not only need to be aware of their own actions but at times need to move from a position of unawareness to awareness. Oftentimes, we are simply unaware of the consequences of our behavior. To complicate matters, our unawareness occasionally does not allow us to be open to new data or information to help us learn from our actions. We may even be unaware that the questions we ask might be producing defensiveness in others, closing off the possibility of generating new information, even new questions. It is often only through the support of and feedback from others that we can become receptive to alternative ways of reasoning and behaving. For example, an executive may see herself as having an open-door

policy, but she may be unaware that she "kills" nearly every idea brought to her attention by some of her associates.

2. There is an unfortunate gap between what many of us say we will do and what we actually do. Recall how action science refers to this gap: an inconsistency between our *espoused theories* and our *theories-in-use*.[4] We are simply all guilty of deceiving ourselves that we can practice what we preach, though what we preach may be very difficult to accomplish in particular organizational cultures. For example, managers are often pressured to produce reports without sufficient time to get all the facts. Under these circumstances, though one might believe in and espouse the value of participative processes, one might be unaware that he has begun to order subordinates to come up with subsidiary reports. Once the pressure has subsided, the same manager might still fail to notice that his behavior has persisted.

3. Most of us are biased in how we obtain information, which in turn produces "errors" in our perceptions of reality. According to Bright, errors constitute such practices as collecting data superficially, ignoring certain pieces of information, making assumptions about data rather than investigating them, or using self-confirming reasoning.[5] However, if we are interested in improving our professional practices, we have to become aware of these so-called errors. Such an awareness is extremely difficult to awaken without the involvement of peers who can detect the use of untested assumptions and raw biases.

4. Although past practices can give us very cogent clues in deciphering future situations, oftentimes the new situation presents itself in a different context. Prior solutions may not fit, even if the situations appear alike. We tend to look, however, for the similarities between the situations rather than their differences. This type of normal cognitive processing can play tricks on us. Even when we consult a repertoire of available responses (recall the solution database), we may not find one

that fits the new situation. Consider a scenario in which an executive exudes great confidence in making an acquisition, having successfully acquired a firm in a prior year. In a year's time, however, the environment may have changed, be it as a result of economic or political conditions. The target may have little resemblance to the recently acquired firm, perhaps due as much to elusive cultural and personal contingencies as to financial considerations. It is only through reflective practice, exercised in the presence of critical and even disinterested peers, that such an executive can distinguish between the part of his or her reasoning that is measured and critical and the part that is self-fulfilling and self-justificatory.

Reflection and Experience

Although I have been using the notion of experience as representing the identity of practice, it also carries the meaning of preparation for practice. Research by Ferry and Ross-Gordon suggests that experience in the second sense may *not* be sufficient to explain practitioners' use of reflective practices.[6] Rather, it is *how* one uses experience that is critical to understanding why some individuals use reflection to grow in their professional learning. Reflective practitioners *reinvest* in learning by participating in continuing education, by seeking out greater challenges in their work, and by tackling more complex representations of recurrent problems.[7] As a consequence of their learning reinvestment, reflective practitioners engage in problem posing as much as problem solving, continually expand their solution database rather than select the first solution that works, view inconsistencies as opportunities rather than inconveniences, and enjoy reflecting back on their decision making rather than sealing off debate. Of most relevance to work-based learning, reflective practitioners also seek to involve others in their search for new solutions.[8]

When experience is viewed as representing the world of practice, it becomes coterminous with public reflectiveness. Consider that when people in interpersonal transactions sometimes pause for a moment to catch their breath and reflect, the process of reflection does not end once the conversation resumes. Reflection continues on into the engagement as one becomes absorbed in practice. So, consistent with prior formulations about work-based learning, reflection is mixed up with practice. Our experience with others informs us, pulls us, and even transforms us. Our collective framing of events infuses these events with meaning, allowing us to negotiate a shared understanding with other adherents.[9] As Wenger suggests, we create ways of learning in practice in the very process of contributing to making that practice what it is.[10]

In addition, the social and political setting of our experience can contribute significantly to our reflection. We tend to assume that everyone has the psychological and even physical security of reflecting with others, but in fact this may not be the case for marginalized groups in particular settings. Although not well researched, it is likely that cultural background may play an important role in the encouragement or discouragement of reflective practices.[11]

In our everyday work activity, although we may be learning, we may not be subjecting that learning to conscious activity. Such concentration might indeed disturb our performance. We Western positivists tend to think of learning as that time when we stop our performance, assess how we're doing, and then determine how we can improve. We may choose at that point not to change anything. But when we stop and reflect, we at best capture what we had already learned tacitly in the past. Our learning may be continuing beyond that point of capture.

The stopping, however, is important, if not to help us figure out what we had learned, then at least to help others learn what we have done well (or poorly). Work-based learning is concerned with what we can do collectively during this stop-and-reflect period. How might we observe and experiment with our own collective tacit processes in action? One way to think about the reflective process in action is through the metaphor of the self-guided tour bus, the kind that allows you to hop on and off to explore some areas of the city on foot. If you choose never to get off the bus, your experience is broad but perhaps superficial. Stopping gives you the chance to see more deeply what is being experienced. It gives you, in the words of Isabel Rimanóczy of LIM Ltd., an opportunity to "lean over" an event and even to melt inside the situation, becoming part of the scene.[12] Note also that once you've completed the excursion on foot, you normally have the option of reboarding the bus to continue the general tour.

Consider as a more practical example the instance of time-outs or adjournments in meetings used to give us time for private reflection on the transactions that took place, thus helping us prepare for the next meeting. In fact, this version of reality may be oversimplified and even misplaced. Private reflection does occur and may well help us prepare for the meeting, but any subsequent communication during the meeting extends that reflection because meaning derived from that interaction is as much social as it is an internal activity.[13] In other words, we may be just beginning our reflection when we do it in private. Our thoughts are constantly reshaped when converted into language and brought out in the presence of others. Indeed, as we use language to persuade others about our points of view, we may notice that in our very process of argumentation, we begin to reframe our position. Furthermore, most of us find that we change our viewpoints slightly, or even a great deal, as the conversation ensues.

There are other qualities that tie reflective practice to experience and to work-based learning. For example, practitioners are sometimes called upon to improvise on the job. Often, the use of real-time improvisation is enhanced through conscious moments of reflection. Beyond improvisation, however, is the need for managers to question the contradictory forces that often impinge on their decision making.[14] How does one respond, for instance, when asked by one's executive supervisor to "bury" an expense in order to show a positive quarterly result? What if one becomes aware of unsanitary practices in a plant owned by the company? It is one thing to speak about how one would redress these ethical issues; it is another to "practice" taking action in one's work-based learning project and then reflect upon that practice.

Reflection also considers the affect experienced by the practitioner. Often overlooked, emotions can play a significant role in enhancing or in distorting the facts within a situation. Since emotions may not work in concert with rational behavior, public reflection can act as a validity check against decisions made in haste or in the spirit of the moment. Emotions arising from interpersonal relationships can also contribute to or detract from learning experiences. Such subjective elements as trust, friendship, and support tend to enhance learning resulting from interpersonal reflective processes.

The "Practicality" of Reflection

One wonders, nevertheless, whether reflective practice is possible or practical in this age of the busy executive who, as noted in Chapter Two, is virtually socialized to be a person of action, not of reflection. Nor are CEOs, according to some fatalistic observers, prone to inspire reflection in others. They want an answer rather than a question; they are looking for solutions rather than problems. They want to take credit for successes rather than be part of the "team."[15]

Recall the exercise in Chapter Two, where executives were invited to participate in the exercise known as Actors and Reflectors. They were faced with the following questions:

- What is the quality of your work and personal experience?
- What are others at work saying about the intense pace of the workplace?
- What is your desire for personal reflection time?
- Do you desire more genuine conversation in a group or with a colleague?
- What is the community saying it needs from business?

By examining questions such as these, we begin to see the short-sightedness of pure action as a worldview. Lee Bolman and Terrence Deal believe that action without reflection—or without *reframing*, as they call it—can be fatal to corporate success.[16] The decline of Sears in the face of its stronger competitor, Wal-Mart, or the pre-cipitous decline in market share of General Motors can be attrib-uted, in their view, to an inability to use reframing. For example, when Roger Smith assumed the role as CEO of GM, he killed a de-sign for a new small car to compete with the high-quality compact cars from Japan. It was thought that his commitment to rational thinking and financial logic got in the way of his mobilizing his company to undertake the necessary visionary strategy that would have been necessary to compete with the Japanese car manufactur-ers throughout the 1980s. As Bolman and Deal suggest, Smith's in-ability to reframe comprehensively kept him from seeing in a new light the problems confronting his company. In other words, he was unable to question the fundamental assumptions of his business to generate sufficiently creative responses to cope with the treacher-ous environment characterizing his industry.

The authors go on to suggest that managers consider at least four different frames or perspectives as they work through critical business decisions:

- The *structural frame* emphasizes goals, specialized roles, and formal relationships.

- The *human resource frame* sees an organization as an extended family, inhabited by individuals who have needs, feelings, prejudices, skills, and limitations that must be attended to.

- The *political frame* sees organizations as arenas in which differ-ent interests compete for power and scarce resources.

- The *symbolic frame* treats organizations as cultures, propelled more by rituals, ceremonies, and myths than by rules or mana-gerial authority.

In our turbulent global environment, it appears almost definitional that we need executives who can encourage the widespread use of reflection to the extent of generating new ways of coping with change. There is a natural inertia that seems to accompany size and structure in organizations. A reflective culture is one that makes it possible for people to constantly challenge things without fear of retaliation. Hammer and Stanton believe that of all the tasks involved in the reflective process, breaking assumptions is the most critical.[17] In their view, businesses operate on fundamental assumptions, such as the following:

"We are and always will be the low-cost producer."

"Every new product we develop must be unique."

"Our people are the best and brightest in the industry."

"We are known for being the first to bring out new models."

Although these assumptions are important, they must be subject to review and revision as change occurs. Yet this almost natural step is the most difficult to undertake since change requires having people in control lose their grip on the status quo.

An assumption-breaking culture is one that deliberately keeps an organization off-center. Executives also need to determine ways to make reflection and learning contagious within their organization. Perhaps one indicator of whether executives are prepared to accept reflective practices is the extent to which they themselves are receptive to feedback—the extent to which they can allow others to have an effect over them.

In fact, encouraging reflective practice in an organization does not have to be an onerous task for executives. Consider the role of the manager, considered in most cultures to be the person of action. Yet in a hospitable environment, managers are people who like to share their experiences and moreover to help one another. Unfortunately, any formal reflective sharing that is made available to managers typically arises through discussions at training events or on strategic plans already formulated. However, managers are almost always working on challenges and puzzles in their daily work that would benefit from public dialogue. Many come to realize that they do not have a monopoly on good ideas and solutions. They might even crave the opportunity to share their experiences, insights, questions, and even failures with others if given the right climate—a climate receptive to open discourse. Indeed, they might appreciate an opportunity to replay their plans and actions in front of like-minded colleagues, who are not assembled to take advantage politically of their faults but who want to help because they realize that they too need the understanding of others.

In this age of strategic planning, it is also important to note that reflective practice is not equivalent to planning. Planning—be it determining one's strategic advantage, gathering competitive intelligence, or exploiting one's strategic competencies—constitutes reflection at a somewhat superficial level. It takes for granted the goals we are working on in solving our problems. Higher levels of reflection, noted earlier as process and premise reflection, examine not only the assumptions and procedures in use but also the very presuppositions attending to the problem to begin with. Reflection of this order requires an institutionalized capacity to rethink the nature of the business, including its strategic goals.

To truly shape organizational learning, reflective practices should also occur simultaneously with knowledge sharing so that new meaning and methods can be accessed by organizational members and partners. Shared meaning often gives way to new plans as well as to new or renewed action. Whether the action produced from reflection is new or renewed, it tends to be more coordinated than before since it has presumably engaged everyone involved in a publicly reflective process. Action then precipitates more reflection and the process begins again.

Finally, is public reflection a practice that should be reserved for those unpredictable times in corporate life when we have to reason our way out of turbulence? In fact, there isn't much routine in organizational practices among most organizations these days, but if there were to be, it might be the perfect time to engage in reflective behavior in order to reengineer taken-for-granted processes.

Why Reflection Leads to a Better World

Most of us accept the view that we human beings do not behave that well under stress. We can become defensive, mean, combative, sullen. Jensen refers to our behaviors in this mode as our *pain-avoidance model*.[18] It is compatible with a learning style that Chris Argyris has called Model I (in contrast to Model II, discussed in the last chapter). Under pain avoidance, we tend to avoid personal error, remain in control, maximize winning and avoid losing, act as "rational" as possible, cling to our theories of the world and our view of self, and suppress negative feelings. These reactions are more often than not nonproductive for us today, though as automatic responses programmed through our brain, in particular our amygdala, they were helpful to us some four hundred thousand years ago. Now as we have become more populous, have created more of a global society, and have devised organizations as a basis for working and even living in society, we need to adopt a different pattern of response, one characterized by learning. However, this pattern may be invoked only through a process of reflection. It is reflection that will allow us to search for truths even if they are unpleasant to us, to take personal causal responsibility for problems, and to allow us to accept some pain in order to learn how to become a better societal participant.

Recalling our initial thoughts in this chapter, the reflection we are talking about is more public than introspective. Private reflection affords us the chance to cool down and come back with a presumably more rational response. However, walking away to reflect might rob not just us but also those in our immediate—perhaps intimate—environment of a potentially productive, albeit highly charged, moment. In *The Drama of Leadership*, Pitcher cautions us that emotion can impair judgment, but its absence can result in even worse judgment.[19]

So we return to the need for learning dialogues that encourage reflection, even after one of our temporary rages, in the presence of trusting others. That way, we don't have to walk away. We can work with others to help us make productive use of our emotional energy, and we can do so in a way that is sensitive to others, if not always perfectly pleasant. The reflection in this instance may not only be about our statements but also about our thoughts, feelings, and actions. The dialogue might also extend to what was not said or done. Hence, even under the grip of emotion and tension, we can develop the discipline of acknowledging our feelings and inquiring about the feelings of others, at least to the extent that we can understand the frames or meanings afforded by our statements and actions.

Sigmund Freud understood the value of inquiry and dialogue even on his deathbed. There is a story that one of his students approached him, and seeing how much pain Freud was in, due to an afflictive mouth cancer, sheepishly uttered, "I presume your illness is so serious that you won't be interested in talking about the tenets of psychology." Freud immediately retorted, "My illness is fatal but not serious."

Reflective practice addresses two fundamental dilemmas posed by Giddens underlying the very process of reflection.[20] Giddens referred to the "unification versus fragmentation" of ourselves and our being in the world. In unification, one protects one's self-identity from the seductive influences of modern society. In fragmentation, the self yields in conforming to the expectations of these outside influences.

Giddens' dilemma can be addressed by public reflection, especially in view of the two endpoints. Unification may be overcome if people show a willingness to confront themselves and ongoingly create alternative interpretations of their own constructed reality in the company of trusting others. They become receptive to what Alvin Gouldner once referred to as "hostile information," or data that run contrary to their comfortable stance.[21] They submit to the critical gaze of others. As for fragmentation, public reflection encourages people to distinguish themselves from their social contexts. They learn to posit viewpoints that might not be accepted in their community. They become willing to face the utter isolation that may come from ostracism from the group. Most of us have been in situations in which someone has asked for a second look at a proposal.

In so doing, that person faces the stern rebuke from nearly everyone in the room. Do we have to go over this one more time? Yet how often does the second review lead to new critical insights? Are we not better off encouraging voice—or at least having a public debate about it—than suppressing it?

The account of these dilemmas brings up reflection's critical nature. Critical reflection is often associated with praxis, since, derived from the Greek word for action, it connotes not only what one does but also what one thinks about what one and others do. As an interdependent process that links the human mind with the external world through activity with others, it can also take an emancipatory stance if it results in eliciting the contradictions in the current power structure.[22] The critical analyst would thus be interested in knowing who was not included in a particular conversation since some discourses may privilege particular stakeholders at the expense of others.

Yet, critical reflective practice need not take a political or ideological stance other than its insistence on an inquiry that is genuine and that actually seeks out disconfirmation of immanent mind-sets. What may be strange or contradictory can produce zeal in the actions of reflective practitioners because of its potential to disclose new knowledge. Reflective practitioners thus are known to: question why things are done in a certain way; to accredit local and informal knowledge that has been acquired on the subject at hand; to consider the historical and social processes that affect their decision making; to admit nontraditional forms of knowledge, such as emotions, sensory perception, and aesthetics, into the inquiry; to question the questions that they tend to resort to; to look for discrepancies between what they and others say they do and what they actually do; and to try to become aware of how their reasoning may at times become self-referential and self-confirming.[23]

Reflective practice, then, considers data beyond our personal and interpersonal taken-for-granted assumptions. It is just as interested in exploring historical and social processes that go even beyond the individualistic notion of *learning to learn*. As Giroux advocates, reflection can help us understand how knowledge has been constructed and managed and how what is deemed to be relevant or even common sense has been arrived at.[24] Critical theorists, such as Freire, are also concerned with how we consciously or unconsciously use power, privilege, and voice to exert influence and suppress dissent.[25] We need to examine whose interests are served by the forms of knowing in popular use, be they instructional methods, curricula, or classroom technologies. Lectures and case studies provide the means for control to remain securely in the hands of the instructor. Dialogue, on the other hand, encourages learner voice because it attempts to develop critical consciousness by engaging learners in desocializing discovery and linking experience with text. Dialogue ensures that multiple points of view are heard, leading to new ways of thinking and ultimately of acting. Learners enter the conversation knowing that it will produce something totally new to each one of them. Dialogic practice, then, moves from an instructor-identified beginning point through numerous, subsequent rounds of interaction. Questions are raised by both learners and instructor as a given theme is explored.[26]

A publicly reflective approach, then, takes up the challenge posed by critical theorists that current human resource development methods are not only openly or subtly performative but also at best engage learners in a *false consciousness* about their presumed participation in a social structure. Those who are subjugated are given to believe that their mistreatment is natural and inevitable under an erroneous presumption that material goods satisfy their needs and lead to contentment.[27] The picture painted by critical theorists is one of a *Brave New World* à la Huxley, in which, deprived of historical and critical information, citizens become languid by the appearance of a constructed munificence that belies their subjugated state.[28] The term *cultural doping* has even been used to characterize how organizations use socialization techniques to dull the consciousness of workers.[29] Even if workers become aware of their subjugated state, they may despair that their individualized social consciousness has no outlet for expression within the organization.

Under this condition, critical learning remains ensconced at an individual level of change.[30]

But public reflection invites the critical commentary of trusted-other signifiers. Decision makers are encouraged to place their assumptions on the table to reveal their epistemological and political preferences.[31] Further, individual self-knowledge can lead to team and organizational learning—for example, individuals may include in their personal learning goals the elucidation of barriers preventing them from finding their voice or reaching their potential in the world, independent of prescriptive forces, be they corporate or radical. In finding their voice, participants learn to "speak up" in ways not merely sanctioned by privileged social authorities but also because of their self-identified interests and commitment to their community.

Critical consciousness enhanced through public reflection thus recognizes the connection between individual problems and the social context within which they are embedded. Once this connection is made, learners can participate in educational projects that may transform their world by their very participation in them. Consider the case of Mark Twain's Huckleberry Finn, who believed he was committing a moral sin because he was harboring a slave, his friend Jim.[32] Huck eventually gave up on his morality because of his feelings for his friend. Most of us can agree that acting on his feelings was correct. Turning in a slave who also happens to be your friend is immoral to begin with. However, Huck did make one error. He did not question the underlying values behind the morality of the day. In public reflection, one learns to criticize even societal norms and values by surfacing one's own beliefs and—in Huck's case—one's own tacit wisdom. By engaging in civic dialogue, wherein we take others' points of view into consideration but in which we also advocate and illustrate our own viewpoints as well as surface our underlying assumptions, we advance the cause of community. We mobilize to create a genuine community and thus a better world.

7

Reflective Practices

If I continue to believe as I have always believed,
I will continue to act as I have always acted; and
if I continue to act as I have always acted, I will
continue to get what I have always gotten.
                              —Marilyn Ferguson

Having laid out the rationale for public reflection as the critical component of work-based learning, I would like to turn our attention to four explicit reflective practices: learning teams, journaling and portfolios, developmental planning, and developmental relationships. They can be deployed individually or in combination. Each represents a distinct method for integrating public reflection into the workplace as a basis for learning.

Learning Teams

In most work-based learning programs, but especially in action learning, participants work on projects with assistance from other participants, as well as from qualified facilitators or advisers, who help them make sense of their project experiences in light of relevant theory. This feedback feature principally occurs in learning teams or sets.

During the learning team sessions, participants discuss not only the practical dilemmas arising from actions in their work settings but also the application or misapplication of concepts and theories to these actions. The rationale for the learning team structure is simply that people engaged in similar work tend to encounter similar difficulties and hence will be likely to offer practical suggestions to one another and through this process learn how to manage their own problems. J. R. Mercer, who wrote about his experiences in an action learning set, put it this way: "To my surprise I found that they [the other set members] could often look at my problem from an entirely different perspective and yet arrive at the same conclusion."[1]

The typical conversational device in most learning teams is questioning rather than advice giving. Through apposite questioning, the problem solver is led to reflect on a problem from different perspectives. The type of question used in an action learning team matters in that questions are not designed to (1) place the focal person on the defensive or (2) illustrate the cleverness of the questioner. Rather, questions are designed to open up the focal person's own view of the situation. They should keep the focus on the focal person and not on the questioner. Questions tend to be open-ended rather than closed (requiring a yes or no answer); they tend to ask for specifics; and when asked in a "why" format, they are typically applied to future actions rather than past actions. The idea is to create an environment for exploration rather than rationalization.[2] As the process unfolds, the questioners might themselves come to appreciate, through the very process of inquiry, particular nuances that affect their own problems and environments.

Frank suggests a number of conditions that make for what he calls "good questions."[3] A good or nondefensive question has the following criteria:

- It is based on human curiosity or knowledge gathering.
- It does not presume that the questioner already knows the right answer.
- It is received in a constructive way.
- It is not stopped by the fear that in questioning one is ignorant.
- It does not cut off further inquiry.
- It is not based on the assumption that a past answer will be the best answer.

Ultimately, a good question leads to possible changes in action as one is led to challenge the assumptions of practice. In a set for small business consultants, one of the members was asked in a non-judgmental way why she engaged in constant note-taking. Did it not prevent her from active engagement in the set? The set's facilitator summarized what happened next:

> A brief upset from the challenged person was followed by her abandoning pen and paper. However, what was so unexpected was how she then participated and offered some of the most helpful questions and insights. She had always taken notes. Following feedback from the set on how helpful she had been, she admitted that although she felt slightly bereft, she was bemused at how she had successfully changed her behavior. Her note taking, she admitted, had been a smoke-screen to hide behind, in case her comments were silly or of no use.[4]

In an in-service program for teachers, using a community of practice approach, one participant expressed how she experienced her learning team's inquiry process: "I felt my own teaching at that moment, when I started to compare it to this [inquiry-led] system, quite absurd. When I was looking at that system, I started to question myself how could teaching be carried out otherwise."[5]

In addition to asking nondefensive questions, learning team members also need to practice *active listening*, wherein they can demonstrate to the focal person their interest in listening with such undivided attention that they truly understand both the content and feelings of the message. Active listening is a difficult skill to learn. Most of the time, rather than deeply listening, we use our listening time to prepare our next response. To practice active listening, team members might occasionally try paraphrasing, which, rather than asking a question, makes a statement or expression that shows the focal person that you understand the meaning of what has just been said. They might also use *perception-checking*, which makes a statement or expression that shows the focal person that you understand the feelings behind what has just been expressed. When used effectively, active listening conveys a sense of empathy, perhaps the most important attitude to cultivate as a learning team member.[6] Using empathy, listeners try to feel what it might be like to be "that person with that problem."

Consequently, rather than give advice, listeners try to open up cognitive avenues to help the focal person solve the problem. No one is a better expert on a problem than the person with the problem, so advice may not only be naive from the focal person's point of view, it may even be counterproductive to learning. There are countless factors, both known and unknown, in the focal person's environment that impinge on the problem, and it is the focal person's prerogative to choose what to share. Focal members of the team have autonomy to choose how to use the other members as mutual helpers in the design of solutions to their problems. For example, they might choose to focus on events that recently occurred in their project or they might prefer to focus on plans for future actions.

Empathy also has implications for feedback in the learning team. Feedback should report on specific, observable actions without placing value judgments on them as good or bad, right or wrong. But team members are hard-pressed to comment on actions that the focal person chooses not to disclose or chooses to avoid or keep hidden. This consideration is depicted vividly in the well-known Jo-Hari Window (see Figure 7.1), developed by Joe Luft and Harry Ingram.[7]

Figure 7.1. The Jo-Hari Window

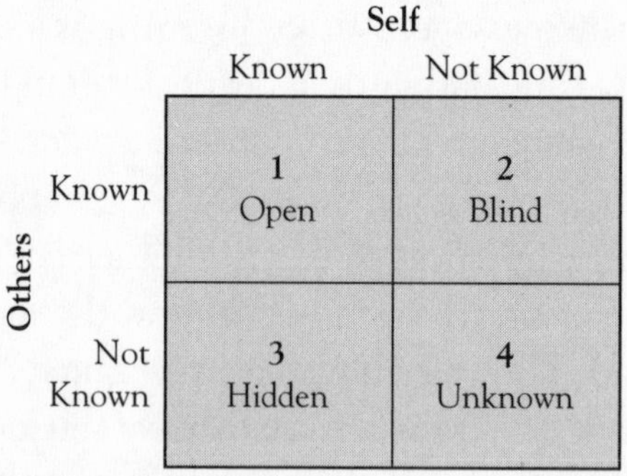

	Self	
	Known	Not Known
Others Known	1 Open	2 Blind
Others Not Known	3 Hidden	4 Unknown

Source: Joseph Luft, Group Processes: An Introduction to Group Dynamics, Third Edition, Copyright © 1984, 1970, 1963 by Joseph Luft. Reprinted with permission of The McGraw-Hill Companies.

According to the model, four quadrants are displayed, representing different aspects of a team member's experience in the group. Some behaviors and feelings, which he or she may choose or not choose to disclose, are known only to the individual. Other feelings and reactions to the focal person are known to the team members, which they may choose or not choose to reveal.

Quadrant 1 is the open area, known to self and to others. Everyone in the team can notice such things as other people's height or eye color, but teams are unlikely to operate well unless more critical behaviors and feelings are revealed.

Quadrant 2 is the "blind spot," representing mannerisms and other personality characteristics observed by others but not revealed to the focal person. For example, someone might believe himself to be calm, unaware that he gets easily perturbed.

Quadrant 3 is the hidden quadrant, also known as the facade, which represents things about ourselves that we prefer to keep to ourselves. Perhaps, for example, we don't wish to reveal prior negative reactions that we have had toward other members.

Quadrant 4 is the unknown domain, representing behaviors and feelings that lie below the surface and thus are hidden from our conscious awareness and also not known to others.

When it comes to interactions between members in the learning team as well as to the group's overall development, it is advisable to enlarge the open area of Quadrant 1 in the Jo-Hari Window, though not completely for fear of overexposing the self. The way to enlarge the open quadrant is to move the line dividing the 'others' axis down and the line dividing the 'self' axis to the right. This would mean having the focal person disclose more of himself or herself and having the other team members provide more feedback. However, members of the learning team typically take cues from the focal person regarding whether, when, and how to provide critical feedback. Initially, it might be important for whoever volunteers to be the first focal person to *ask* for feedback. That individual also has the opportunity to ask for information of a certain type to keep the focus on his or her issues. Not every comment from the team can be absorbed by the focal person—nor is it necessary to debate every point.

On the other hand, it is equally important to disclose more and more of oneself to show a receptiveness to open feedback. Beaty, Bourner, and Frost talk about learning how to receive feedback as follows:

> It is important to really hear the questions that are asked and the comments that are made. It is easy to keep the blinkers on our own ideas and sometimes hard to accept that there may be other ways of doing things. If you decide to reject the ideas you hear, then your own ideas will have been strengthened by having considered alternatives.[8]

In order to encourage feedback from others, it is helpful to let down one's guard a little. It is not exhibiting weakness to demonstrate a need for support and encouragement. In this way, empathy works both sides of the street. An appreciation of empathy from others breeds more empathy from them and perhaps later by you to them. As is demonstrated in the Jo-Hari Window model, one has to learn to both give and receive interpersonal attention if the learning team is to function at its optimal level.

The support generated among members in a learning team establishes close bonds, which subsequently may account for dramatic expressions of teamwork and encouragement, one member to another. In a learning set organized through the Britvic Soft Drinks Developing to Lead action learning program, the following anonymous quote was recorded by the company's training manager:

> I was seriously considering defaulting. I sent Jane an e-mail, just saying the word "help." She responded immediately: "We cannot complete without you, we all do it together or not at all. Don't give up now, we are so close. Where can I help you most?"[9]

In observing a typical action learning team, members will be seen listening, posing questions, and offering suggestions to another team member whose project is under scrutiny. Occasionally, the focal individual might listen as the other set members brainstorm ideas regarding his or her issue or project. Participants often decide to experiment with new approaches in light of the group discussion, leading to new theories or ideas to be tested in action during the intervening periods between set meetings. The results are then brought up at subsequent set meetings.

Since the pattern of the meeting tends to be sequential, moving from one member to the next, sufficient time is required to give each member a chance to develop his or her project situation. Hence, meetings require a minimum of two hours and in some cases even up to a full day to give every member a chance to present. If meeting times are relatively short, they should be scheduled at frequent intervals, perhaps every two weeks, so that members who have not had a turn get a chance to air their project or team concerns. In any event, learning teams should meet as often as monthly in order to sustain momentum and to give members a chance to bring up issues before they become stale or are forgotten.

The matter of where and when to meet is not a trivial issue. Many a learning team has become stuck when it is time to take out one's calendar and schedule meetings. It is usually advisable to have learning teams meet away from the workplaces of the participants to reduce the likelihood of members' being called away for on-site emergencies.[10] As for meeting times, it is typically useful to schedule a full slate of meetings at the very first session. That way, dates can become fixed for nearly all members, aside from prior commitments or unexpected emergencies.

An important programmatic issue for learning teams is whether to staff them with in-company or mixed-company members. It should not be assumed that the familiarity of in-company membership makes the process easier. One still has to deal with the admixture of expertise, background, role, and level in the same-company format. In fact, in-company teams can occasionally produce political repercussions, leading some work-based learning exponents to advise programs not to constitute a team with direct supervisors present. On the other hand, staffing teams with diagonal hierarchical levels provides a unique opportunity to see how the other levels "think," giving participants a chance to dislodge their assumptions and biases. Staffing teams with in-company members who represent diverse functions also gives participants a unique networking opportunity. Such teams also tend to create a sense of community as participants discover how things are done in other parts of the organization. It is not unusual for the team experience to lead to contacts that can last for years. Finally, when the number of in-company teams reaches a critical mass, they can become infectious as a learning vehicle or approach that can extend throughout the entire organization.

Mixed-company learning teams offer their own distinct set of advantages. They expose members to ways that other organizations use to cope with comparable problems. For example, there are advantages to seeing how participants from other industries and sectors or from organizations of very different sizes address particular issues. Members also tend to report feeling freer to disclose sensitive matters, especially as they enter the team with others' having fewer preconceived notions about their position and responsibilities. They might feel that they can start their participation with a cleaner slate, giving them a chance to try out new roles and behaviors. Finally, mixed-company teams constitute the only work-based learning method for lone senior executives to interact with their peers.

Perhaps the most critical concern regarding learning team membership is to provide for some diversity of background and ways of knowing so as to avoid having the team begin with an entrenched mental model that inhibits divergent thinking. It is thus advisable that members display variety in their learning and cognitive styles. In that way, members can enjoy the opportunity to work with others who have different ways of learning and thinking in order to improve the quality of sharing within the team.

Beyond the contribution of learning teams to project operations, some teams provide feedback to members to help them assess their effectiveness in a group setting. As we shall see, participants may also develop personal agendas or development plans for individual and managerial change and share these with the rest of the group. Team members then discuss each other's plans, identify potential pitfalls, and suggest improvements. Occasionally, participants may even be called back together six to eight months later to report on the successes and frustrations in implementing their personal development plans.

Learning teams thus provide many opportunities for members to develop their interpersonal and professional skills. Learning tends to be enhanced because, compared with other teams, the learning team explicitly focuses on member development. Among the lessons available to members are such managerial practices as providing and accepting positive and negative feedback, negotiating with others, dealing with internal and external politics, testing publicly one's espoused values and beliefs, fielding a new strategy, and managing change. The experience is designed to encourage participants to challenge their own actions and consider novel views and processes. At the same time, participants are encouraged to be critical of academic theories placed into their use. Finally, the experience leaves ample room for making mistakes, provided that participants learn from them.

Weinstein and Mumford have identified a number of other skill opportunities available to members:[11]

- Time and space for reflection
- Support in setting goals and timescales
- Insights and inquiries from others
- Different perspectives
- Knowledge, expertise, and experience of others
- Sharing of ideas, confusion, and successes
- Support from others, especially to try out new behaviors and actions
- Challenge by others
- Confidence from hearing oneself be helpful
- Opportunity to hear oneself think—and respond

- Learning how to manage oneself in a group and to manage the overall group process and group learning
- Space to experiment with new ways of behaving in order to become more effective in interpersonal situations
- Opportunity to be "out of role"

Learning teams also develop a social culture in their own right, which presents participants with lessons regarding group dynamics. They are not unlike other groups that must confront the inevitable processes of their own development.[12] As learning teams, however, there tends to be explicit focus, in this case on group learning. Hence, learning teams, as a special form of team, might reflect a different set of norms compared with performance or task teams. Although each learning team is unique, the following norms would not be unusual:

- We should strive to become more and more open and honest with each other.
- We try to be supportive of one another; we are concerned about each other.
- We actively listen to one another.
- We are interested in giving and receiving constructive feedback from one another.
- As our main purpose is learning, we are committed to reviewing our individual and group learning processes.
- We commit to distribute our workload equally.
- We arrive fully prepared for our meetings.
- We are as committed to each other's and the group's agendas as our own.
- We act in complete confidence and never reveal our deliberations outside the group unless we receive permission to do so from respective members.

- We are committed to learn how to develop deep trust in one another; that is, we don't have to "stand on ceremony" or be an authority. We can at times be tentative and even vulnerable.
- We agree to accommodate our team schedule and make all meetings unless there is an emergency that we must attend to.
- We try to have fun.

It goes without saying that in order for development of the learning team to proceed, it is critical that it not change its membership on any regular basis. The team is designed for team members and team members alone. However, visitors may certainly be invited from time to time, especially if they can offer some expertise unavailable from any of the members. Clients may also be invited to the team to provide some perspective on a troublesome issue within a project.

As a method of reflective practice, learning teams allow participants to engage in critical reflection of the assumptions underlying actions in their own organizations. Some organizations, though sponsors of work-based learning interventions, are not always hospitable to the probing that characterizes the dynamics of this form of learning. Hence, participants appreciate the opportunity to try out their ideas and examine their values and assumptions in the learning team. With the help and encouragement of their team members, especially their facilitator, they can also try out some new interpersonal skills or professional competencies based on reframed assumptions derived from public reflection within the team.[13]

In an evaluation of the Leadership for Change graduate program at Boston College, referred to earlier, one of the members in commenting on the contribution of her learning team, pointed to the growth in her reflective orientation:

> In terms of personal growth, I think I have become much more aware of the world outside of my immediate circle of influence. I have come to realize that I spend much of my time focused on my

day-to-day responsibilities without giving much thought to how I might engage others or further engage myself. I have learned to be more reflective and thoughtful in my approaches to work and relationships. I have also learned that having the confidence to reveal your vulnerabilities as a leader may be viewed as a strength.

The Journal and Portfolio

This section describes two valuable tools for reflective learning practice: journals and portfolios. The journal helps participants distill lessons from everyday experience to help them track their learning. Although similar, the portfolio tends to be more inclusive and is often a more public document compared to the journal.

Journal

It may seem contradictory to think of journal writing as a *publicly* reflective learning practice. After all, the journal is completed in private and is not necessarily shared with other persons. It is viewed most often as a powerful technique to enhance our self-reflection. Often used as an introspective tool for personal growth, it can also serve as an aid to bring together the inner and outer parts of our lives. It offers a lens to view experience—before, during, or after the event under scrutiny—and it even allows further reflection on the journal entries themselves.

Given that most people bring their journal insights into public dialogue, however, it has a direct bearing on the work-based learning principles discussed in this book. It is a potent vehicle for reflecting with others on experience, for clarifying our assumptions and behavior, for improving our powers of observation, and for promoting consistency between our beliefs and our practices.[14] Journal writing also requires support from a variety of sources, such as from peers, mentors, or supervisors, to provide feedback and encouragement to continue the writer's self-development through reflection.[15]

One of the most influential writers in the domain of journal writing was Ira Progoff, whose approach, referred to as the intensive journal process, was designed to bring people back to critical events in their lives and give them a chance to relive them and make decisions based upon them.[16] Within this overall approach, Progoff formulated three fundamental methods:

1. *Dialogues*. Conversations with people from the past or present, from literature or history, or even from within oneself are held in order to confront events, ideas, images, assumptions, and even unconscious motivations.

2. *Depth dimension*. Creative forces are used to explore hidden meanings, as when journal writers free-associate, using dreams, metaphors, unsent letters, and images.

3. *Life study*. The writer becomes a *trustee* for another person's life, by writing a journal as that person, looking at the world through that person, thus intensively empathizing with that person.

In work-based learning settings, journals can be useful in helping participants reflect on experiences, be they in their learning team, in their projects, or just in everyday life. The journal can serve as a vehicle to integrate information and experiences that run counter to preexisting viewpoints. It can also help participants more deeply understand their current reasoning and associated behavior, or it can spur their consideration of new methods or skills introduced in the program. A participant in a professional self-development program produced the following journal entry regarding the workshop skills that he was hoping to incorporate into his work practice:[17]

I notice that I automatically started to use the small range of lateral thinking techniques that I found interesting over the last six months. I consciously realized when I was "black-hatting" [see the reference to de Bono in Chapter Five]. These techniques definitely helped as the bank of normal personal ideas ran out. I must spend time reviewing, reflecting on, and practicing these techniques, as they appear to work.

Newcomers to journal writing might wish to begin with some express questions to help them work through interpretations of their experience:[18]

1. How have you processed the particular experience? Note your thoughts, reactions, and judgments (though try not to prejudge your own behavior or the behavior of others). Be aware of the context surrounding the experience and try to recall the sequence of events.

2. What were your feelings attending to the experience? Try to understand their range and depth—emerging both at the time of the experience and the time subsequent to it. Be aware of feelings that may hinder your learning or that may distort your recollection of what happened. Include positive as well as negative feelings. Recall incidents when you felt similarly. Be prepared to check with others about your affective reactions.

3. How do you now evaluate the experience? What new insights or information have been revealed? Perhaps you might relate the incident to other experiences or compare it with your personal beliefs and attitudes. After this process of association, be prepared to integrate the data to see if they form any coherent whole. Once you have a sense of the new knowledge that has been generated, subject it to tests of validity by asking whether the integrated information squares with reality as you know it. Check whether the new knowledge has internal consistency— that it remains consistent with other experiences as well as values in your life. Try also to visualize how the new knowledge would apply to new experiences that might arise. Be prepared to actualize the new knowledge into current and future practices and thereupon reflect again on its utility.

The aforementioned characterization can be said to follow a *row* or sequential approach to journaling, as depicted in Figure 7.2, in comparison with a *column* approach. In the row approach, one begins by anticipating an event or encounter and then explaining how one plans to engage with another or with others. During the engagement, the journal writer may be able to make some mental notes on how things are going. As soon as possible after the event, the journal writer prepares a full description of how things went, to be followed by an assessment of differences between the actual engagement and one's prior expectations. The last row is saved for any insights that may have arisen from the reflective journaling process so far. Perhaps the individual may have generated a fresh or enlightened understanding of the problem, which may lead to new solutions.[19]

The column approach may proceed using the "left-hand" column method, initially designed by Chris Argyris.[20] Accordingly, the journal writer will divide a page into a right and left column and start on the right by transcribing either a prospective dialogue she might have with someone regarding an irksome but important problem or an actual dialogue about such a problem that had occurred recently. On the left side, upon completing a page or two of the dialogue, the journal writer would annotate the dialogue by inserting any thoughts or feelings that for whatever reason she could *not* bring up. Then, often with the assistance of learning team members, the individual might reflect on what prevented her from offering some of these thoughts and feelings and whether and how some of them—if stated—may have led to a more productive discourse.

Figure 7.2. Journaling—Two Sample Approaches

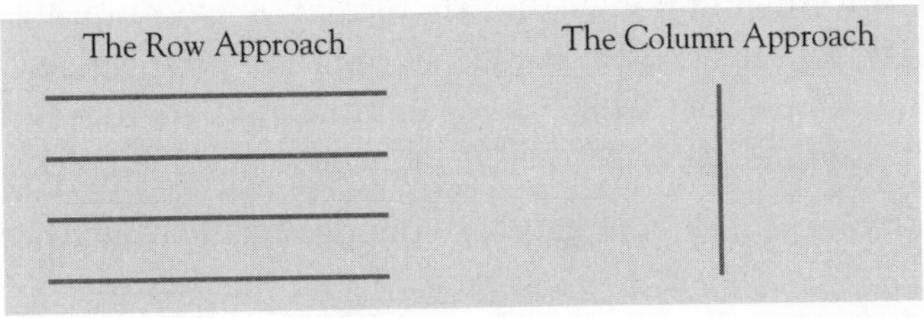

The Row Approach   The Column Approach

During this analysis, the individual might come to appreciate some of the inferences she had drawn about the other person that may have been inaccurate and likewise review the other person's assumptions and inferences.

Many academic programs use the journaling process as a strategy to spur metacognitive thinking from a reflective learning perspective. Metacognitive thinking constitutes a thinking about self, others, context, and even about our own thinking in action. It asks learners to be more self-conscious about their assumptions and their ways of being, acting, and relating.[21] Within the academic setting, journaling can enhance learning in a number of ways. Consider five here:[22]

1. It can promote learner autonomy to work on areas of personal and professional interest.
2. It can enhance associated experiential learning activities.
3. It can encourage critical reflection to challenge personal and organizational practices.
4. It can enable holistic learning involving all the senses.
5. It can promote self-development and self-understanding through real-world experience.

In undertaking a journal assignment, there are bound to be constraints that students will face, such as beginning the discipline of writing on a regular basis. McKernan suggests that if participants make the commitment to use a journal but do not attend to it on a regular basis, they will likely forget key events or observations, even if left for completion later on.[23] Further, it is through practice that participants might progress to higher levels of reasoning and reflection that begin to analyze data from multiple perspectives. Persistency in journal writing (along with skilled support from the work-based learning program) can help participants overcome the frustration of acquiring unfamiliar skills, especially when these skills reflect back on the self. Cunliffe also cautions against letting journals get out of hand in their scope and size.[24] They are not life histories that can go on forever. Although excerpts of one's life can be incorporated into one's journal, the focus is more on one's thinking, interpretations, and assumptions about self and others in action. Furthermore, although journals allow for focus on the self, the aim is to learn more about oneself and one's reasoning about phenomena rather than to merely describe what one does. Recalling our prior discussions about praxis, students should be encouraged to critically question their past actions and future possibilities as a way to become reflective about their being in the world.

It is sometimes scary for students to confront themselves, in some cases for the first time. The reflective journal process may dredge up some past or current events that are unpleasant to face. Eventually, students may find that journaling, rather than merely rehashing objectionable memories, often allows them to consider events in a new light, leading to new alternatives, fresh insights, and ultimately behavioral choice. Here's how one student expressed this *opening-up* process, as captured by Christine Hogan in a class in human resource development:

> The use of the journal initially presented a major blockage. It had the potential to unlock some inner secrets, such as my original perceptions of early childhood, the agony of personal and professional self-doubts . . . all the little "checkpoint Charlies" I had designed to prevent breaching. Out of this bubbling cauldron of negativity came an acceptance of the journal. It became a friend, a secret closet one could open at any time and into which frustrations could be unloaded, and then close the door.[25]

Once participants develop some comfort with the journal-writing process, they will likely develop their own style. In addition, it may be useful to consult some of the following learning formats that have been discussed in the literature:[26]

Logs or reports represent factual accounts of specific experiences.

Lists represent clusters of ideas on a topic; for example, my ten pet peeves, a "table of contents" of the person I am at this moment.

Portraits are descriptions of people who are admired or disliked. They help one learn more about oneself as portraits of others are developed.

Memoirs are personal accounts of oneself that are written to be objective, perhaps as might be told to others, and that include the landscape of events swirling around the writer.

Catalogue of feelings lists what the writer likes or does not like about particular experiences, ideas, or people.

Intimate accounts set down personal notes and logs rich in personal sentiments, even confessions. These represent the most personal of the journal types.

Dialogues entail the writing of both sides of a conversation to obtain insight into multiple points of view and perspective.

Conceptual understanding represents an attempt to write about a new or existing theory in which one may not have had much exposure or prior appreciation.

Applications take relevant concepts and attempt to apply them into practice, normally with commentary as to their potential or worthwhileness.

Social histories record consensual and conflicting ideas between various individuals and groups.

Maps of consciousness are drawings that capture the writer's feelings or state of mind at a given moment.

Guided imagery constitutes a meditated frame of reference that could include the recording of daydreams or the development of dream images into the waking state (as in "imagine yourself in a forest" or "imagine yourself taking the last shot in a tied game").

Stepping-stones characterize the milestones that have enabled the writer to reach a present moment.

Mandalas or *domain maps* plot segments of one's life or illustrate one's evolving social network.

Altered point of view has one writing about oneself in the third person or about someone else in the first person in order to gain empathy, to experience something painful, or just to imagine oneself in a different place or in a different time.

Contradictions and dilemmas compare aspirations and reality or reveal decisions around competing values.

Inconsistencies pick up on differences between what one or others espouse and actual behavior.

Surprises note differences between what one expected to occur and what ultimately did occur or between the expected behavior of people and how they actually behaved.

Unsent letters express to someone what one couldn't say in real life, perhaps to a loved one or to a deceased person.

Portfolios

The portfolio, now often produced in electronic format, can be thought to be inclusive of the journal, though it is often prepared as a more public document. Portfolios tend to contain collections of self-generated artifacts and reflections that demonstrate the author's knowledge, skills, dispositions, and growth over time.[27] They allow learners to illustrate their work in a self-directed and comprehensive fashion, well beyond the presentation of mere résumés or curriculum vitae. Portfolios are also constructivist in their approach, meaning that learners are expected to take responsibility for selecting their own artifacts, connecting them to the overriding purpose of the portfolio, and drawing implications from them on behalf of their own learning.[28]

Portfolios have a number of purposes beyond their use as a reflective tool in work-based learning. They are often employed to showcase the knowledge and skills of the writer for job-seeking or promotion purposes. They are also designed to meet the needs of programs to satisfy institutional standards.[29] Some academic programs require them as part of their course of study. Students obtain such benefits as the chance to share their work with advisers, faculty members, and employers; to master valuable information technology skills; and to demonstrate knowledge and skills gained beyond the classroom. At Penn State University, every student is allocated up to 1 GB of online storage space to create a personal e-portfolio.[30]

Within the realm of work-based learning, portfolios are inherently developmental, helping the learner focus not only on current accomplishments but also on future needs. When using portfolios, learners become engaged as they record, interpret, and evaluate their own learning.[31] When reviewing one's portfolio with advisers and mentors, one can extract the skills already possessed and those in need of development. In addition, the comprehensive account in the portfolio can provide the adviser (or even a peer mentor) with a basis for providing useful feedback to the learner.

At a university that relied heavily on the use of portfolios for professional development, one teacher described the value of the portfolio for reflection purposes:

> Our final reflection is structured for them to go back through the entire portfolio, look at what they had completed over the semester, and reflect on what it meant in terms of their development. The idea is to get them to really state where they are right now. How far have you come? How did you get there? And then to take the next step and say, "What is this going to mean for your first couple of years [in your field]? What are you going to have to focus on? What do you think your professional development's going to need to look like? What are your strengths and weaknesses?"[32]

In recent years, the portfolio has been transitioning to electronic formats. There are many advantages to electronic portfolios:[33]

1. Many artifacts—reports, presentations, web sites—are already in electronic format, so it is much easier and less cumbersome to report them out digitally.

2. Since they are portable, electronic portfolios can be easily reproduced and distributed.

3. They capture the dynamics of knowledge work by employing and combining a variety of media, such as text, graphics, audio, and video.

4. The structure of electronic portfolios can be hierarchical rather than linear by showing the relationships among major headings, thereby reflecting the complex interactions that exist in most professional practices.

Developmental Planning

Developmental planning is often carried out in conjunction with professional and executive education and thus represents a practical form of reflective practice. Its principal rationale is to allow participants to anticipate their learning needs prior to or concurrent with any development program, under the assumption that the self-generation of personal and professional objectives will provide a substantial incentive for learning.

The responsibility for developmental planning devolves to two principal constituents: the organization and the individual. The organization has the responsibility for providing opportunities and resources to the individual in order that he or she may plan developmental goals and meet personal and professional needs in concert with the organization's strategy. The individual needs to take responsibility for his or her own growth and development. The ongoing principles underlying developmental planning include the valuing of feedback, in particular encouraging employees to solicit feedback from as many sources as possible; the interpretation of any job assignment as a potential opportunity for development; and the search for work and relationship experiences that might provide opportunities for stretching and learning.

As for the nature of planning, there are many approaches to choose from, but a popular one to precipitate the process through objective-setting and that is also easy to remember asks five principal questions: Who, will do what, when, under what conditions, and to what extent? Let's consider each of these five questions in turn. First, the participant identifies himself or herself (for example, by role) and then develops some challenging and specific objectives, which, though difficult, are nonetheless attainable. Through objective-setting, the participant is able to more objectively and precisely track progress toward predetermined development goals. As the goals are revisited throughout the feedback process, they can be changed since they are not rigid quotas to be met.

The *what* question needs to be prepared in as specific a language as possible in order that progress be measured. Objectives can be qualitative as well as quantitative. For example, a participant may desire to improve her working rapport with another member of the staff with whom she has had a rocky relationship in the past. Perhaps this person reminds her of people with whom she has had difficulty. Objectives should also tie in, to the extent practical, with both organization and unit goals. Although some objectives may be of a personal or professional nature, and thus specific to individual development perhaps within one's field, it also makes sense to tie some objectives to work tasks and resultant needs within one's department or within the organization as a whole. Objectives should also be set in conjunction with one's program sponsor, mentor, buddy, or perhaps work supervisor. Developmental programs may vary in regard to who serves as the adviser to the participant. Although the development plan is a personal document, its learning potential is enhanced as it is made public both within a learning team and with a personal confidant who can reflect on the participant's plans and progress.

The next question, the *when*, is determined by specifying a timetable with milestones to assist in establishing some temporal parameters for accomplishing the objectives. Although the time horizon should be kept flexible, it seems best to plan for shorter rather than longer cycles to enhance the feedback process. If the objective is considerable in terms of time to accomplishment, it may be useful to break down the objective into subgoals that might be accomplished within shorter time frames.

The conditions establish the legitimate constraints that need to be overcome or actions to be undertaken in order to succeed. The participant might specify how particular resources or experiences in the company might be necessary in order to develop the necessary competencies to accomplish particular objectives. Other conditions might include particular people to interview, textual resources to consult, educational opportunities to take advantage of, feedback from certain individuals to solicit, senior staff to consider as mentors.

Finally, developmental objectives need to incorporate measures to assess accomplishment—that is, criteria that would indicate how the participant as well as the sponsors would know that the goals have been achieved. Participants can learn to become quite creative in establishing useful performance criteria. They might develop so-called unobtrusive measures that are less obvious indicators of performance but nevertheless are quite useful. For example, if a participant wants to develop his listening ability, he might practice certain techniques, such as perception-checking, which could be assessed by using a standard fill-in-the-blank test or by receiving direct feedback from learning team members. However, a more interesting, unobtrusive, measure might be to have him tally how many times during the course of a week associates have sought him out to share their personal or work concerns. Increased listening acuity often begets more trust and contact from subordinates or associates.

Once the plan is written, it should be reviewed on a periodic basis. It is also useful to recurrently assess results from the ongoing developmental activities to be sure that the participant is learning what he or she planned to achieve. Perhaps a given activity has not been sufficient or needs to be replaced with another method to exemplify the competency under consideration.

Mentors and sponsors play a number of critical roles in the development process. Mentors can assist participants in diagnosing their learning needs, in preparing their objectives, and in assessing progress toward the achievement of the objectives. Here are some other responsibilities for mentors and sponsors:

- Clarifying how the learner plans to learn
- Assisting learners in setting realistic target dates for completion
- Helping devise creative measurement techniques
- Monitoring the learner's progress toward completion of goals and objectives
- Serving as a resource or even as a role model
- Evaluating and renegotiating the development plan as needed.[34]

Plan Unfolding

Developmental planning may be triggered by the process of reviewing already-established objectives. During a consultation with one's sponsor (or supervisor), the participant becomes aware of those areas of performance that are strong and those that require improvement. Although development planning recognizes and builds on areas of strength, it tends to concentrate on performance deficiencies, in particular on the gaps between expected and actual performance. The essence of the development action plan is to identify the types of learning activities that can be undertaken to fill these gaps. Remember that the process is a joint undertaking between participant and sponsor. Often there is considerable discussion and negotiation regarding the appropriate action.

There are a number of activities that can be undertaken to fill gaps in one's knowledge base. These may include the following:

- On-the-job training
- Personal reading and videotape viewing
- Planned task rotation

- Formal training courses
- Coaching
- Shadowing
- Volunteering
- Special assignments
- Task force membership
- Community service

Most proponents of developmental planning believe it should be separated from the performance appraisal process, which tends to focus on the evaluation of employees for purposes of merit increases and promotion and layoff decisions. Feedback from development is designed to help individuals grow in ways of their choosing, not necessarily for pecuniary benefit. It should also be psychologically safe and used for the recipient's benefit, not the organization's.[35] If used for administrative purposes, not only does it lose its integrity, but it also can become subject to manipulation by both parties. For example, the feedback recipient might resort to what is called *strategic self-presentation* to manipulate how one is perceived rather than to seek sincere behavioral change.[36]

General Mills, according to chief learning officer, Kevin Wilde, separates appraisal and development discussions, which may explain in part why 80 percent of General Mills employees participate in a personal development process. Another reason for its success may be due to the sensitivity of the process to respond to the life-cycle needs of its employees. For example, discussions with senior audiences vary significantly from those held with people who are early in their careers. Among the former, there tends to be more of a focus on such topics as leaving a legacy, mentoring, achieving world-class expertise, and easing into retirement.[37]

Development plans can also take the form of personal learning goals, goals that are designed purely to benefit the personal life of participants and that may only indirectly improve their work performance. However, in most work-based learning programs, participants are inclined to derive goals that are professional in character or that affect their communication and leadership competencies. Some of the goals that I have monitored through my own coaching include the following: improving listening skills so that others are not cut off when speaking, asserting oneself within one's work team, knowing when to stop talking to give others a chance to speak, allowing subordinates to complete a delegated assignment without premature interference, learning to speak more effectively and with more confidence in public, attempting to diversify one's leadership style with different staff, and aligning one's body language with one's verbal communication.

It is one thing to construct a goal; it is another to nurture it throughout the course of a program and commit to it even after the program's conclusion. Goal construction and evolution are taken most seriously when the program devotes time to the goal development process. Participants need to be given a chance to publicly state their goals and say how they plan to achieve them. The program also needs to provide time for review of each participant's progress toward goal accomplishment. For example, a specific time on the agenda might be allocated for the participants to receive feedback from each member of their learning team regarding how other members see their progress.

In a personal journal prepared by a graduate student in a skill- and work-based MBA program at Northeastern University in Boston, the writer demonstrates how the personal development process intersects with the feedback function provided through one's learning team:

> The greatest area that I need to continue to improve on is my creative problem solving. I focused on this during the fall semester and feel that I have improved immensely. However, it does not surprise me that my learning team continues to score me low in this area as a couple of them are quite strong in this domain. I am much stronger in analytical problem solving than the creative side. Since my undergrad degree is in chemistry, I never would have been able to succeed

in this field without impeccable analytical and technical knowledge. It is important for me to continue to work on and improve my creative and "soft" skills as these will be important when managing people.

Whatever their form, personal development plans need to be viewed as flexible, living agreements. All parties need to acknowledge that unanticipated events create changes in how one looks at particular phenomena. Participants change their views as they learn. They encounter different experiences and people as their projects evolve. They may change career plans after going through a soul-searching personal development process. Caren Ulrich Stacy, director of professional development and recruiting at the law firm Arnold & Porter reports that it's not unusual at her firm to see an associate transition from one of the firm's divisions to another, such as IP (intellectual property) to Environment. She further explains that a personal development plan is "not like a mission statement; it can't be static. It is a very dynamic piece of paper. Anything going on in your life can change it, so there's a constant revisiting of your needs."[38]

The personal nature of development plans is bolstered by evidence from the field that most individuals, when explaining the sources of major influences on their development, do not tend to mention the books that they've read, seminars attended, or training received.[39] Instead they talk about assignments they have completed and relationships they have formed. Often they talk about a significant boss who has influenced them or someone they have observed carefully or even modeled themselves after. They may also focus on their failures or on particularly stressful experiences they have overcome. But their images of success or overcoming are typically based on real experiences with a real person. In their account of experiential learning, Lombardo and Eichinger sustain this personalized view by contending that people learn most of the skills they need on the job through four kinds of experiences that teach the most: (1) critical jobs, (2) important other people, (3) personal hardships, and (4) training.[40]

Lex Dilworth has posed a number of questions to help participants develop their personal learning plan once it is initially formulated.[41] He believes that by giving people space for personal self-examination, the surface layers of the original goal can be peeled back to reveal a more fundamental goal of potentially greater importance. He asks participants to consider such questions as:

- What motivates this goal? Do I really care about it?
- What specific incidents in my life have led me to it?
- Will the goal help me avoid mistakes that I often make in my life?
- How will I benefit if I make the change specified?
- How will I know whether I am successful?

The espoused goal, when peeled back, as Dilworth suggests, might also reveal some deeper psychological processes that might benefit from surfacing. For example, a manager might initially project a goal of learning to delegate more. Beyond learning the conventional techniques of delegation, however, the development plan, with the assistance of a good coach, might delve into such challenging issues as the manager's perfectionism or conceit that only he or she can reliably get the job done.

The goal-setting and development processes are comparable to journal writing in that they promote a personal reflective experience, which the participant can choose to bring into public view as desired. Personal developmental planning arises from a philosophy that sees personal growth as emanating from personal reflection on both achievements and mistakes. As people engage in personal dialogue or *self-talk*, they may establish a personal vision of where they want to go and how they can make it a reality.

On the other hand, developmental planning need not take place in a vacuum. Most work-based learning programs provide opportunities for the sharing of personal learning goals. Teammates in learning teams are available to provide feedback on one another's accomplishments or even on one another's lack of progress. Participants may also seek out mentors or coaches to assist in the developmental process, as the next section on developmental relationships will expand upon.

Participants often find that the process of developmental planning can be even more rewarding than the achievement of the goals themselves. For many individuals, personal development planning may represent the first explicit opportunity for reflection afforded them within their work environment. Work is often construed as a place for doing, not for reflecting, especially with others. The simple idea of stepping back in order to move forward is so often overlooked in cultures of action and progress.

Multisource Feedback

A popular tool that by some estimates is deployed by some 29 percent of U.S. firms is multisource feedback, also known as 360-degree assessment. Under this format, participants or focal persons compare their perceptions of their own knowledge, skills, and abilities (KSAs) against feedback from their supervisors, subordinates, peers, and customers, each of whom can provide a unique perspective on their performance and potential. There are a myriad of assessment instruments that can be developed or purchased "off-the-shelf" from training suppliers. For example, some assessments reflect KSAs based on one's job, on a set of competencies associated with categories of performance, or on strategic plans.[42] Some organizations offer online access to 360-degree tools and include self-directed workbooks to guide participants through a personal development planning process. Online delivery has been found to promote anonymity, which in turn increases the amount of trust among users.[43]

The effectiveness of multisource feedback appears to rest on particular attributes and behaviors of two principal parties, the ratee and the coach. Not everyone is predisposed to receive negative feedback in particular. Ratees with an internal locus of control, with high self-efficacy, and with a learning goal orientation tend to benefit the most from 360-degree feedback because they view their ability as modifiable and because they believe themselves to be capable of improving on their KSA levels.[44]

Meanwhile, the competence of coaches, be they mentors or supervisors, to help explain the feedback from the assessment instrument and plan both strategic and personal activities to overcome any noted deficiencies becomes paramount.[45] Ratees who had the benefit of coaching have been found to be predisposed to development on a number of dimensions: they set more specific goals for themselves, they analyze gaps more intensively between their current and anticipated performance, and they solicit more ideas for improvement from others.[46] Furthermore, when ratees see that not only their coaches but also their coworkers support development-related activities, they report a more positive attitude toward multisource feedback and become more involved in such activities after receiving their feedback.[47]

For developmental planning purposes, it is preferable to build assessments mutually with participants who normally have a good sense of the KSAs needed to develop their own effectiveness and potential. Hence, participants might very well participate in the construction of any instrument and in the selection of relevant appraisers. Assessments should also be given more than once, perhaps semiannually or annually.

After the assessment instrument is administered, feedback can be provided to the focal person using a number of methods. For example, scoring can be presented as a comparison to one's peers, or participants can choose to compare their own scores over time, using the first set of results as a baseline. It is important for coaches, sponsors, and supervisors to participate in interpreting and applying the results of the assessments as a basis for supporting the development plan. Furthermore, as the assessments tend to be sensitive documents, the feedback associated with them needs to be delivered in a constructive manner. For instance, coaching tends to be far more effective when it emphasizes the behavior of the participant under scrutiny as opposed to the individual's personality dimensions. Other skills that coaches might incorporate in working with feedback assessments include: active listening; focused interviewing; dealing with feelings, especially from unexpected negative appraisal; targeting improvement areas; helping shape the development of new behaviors; setting specific goals and action plans; and following up.[48]

There have been encouraging signs that 360-degree feedback can have salutary effects on the employees of those managers who are the recipients of constructive feedback. In particular, such employees have been found to have higher levels of satisfaction and engagement and reduced intentions to leave.[49] Engagement refers to their enthusiasm for work, their emotional connection to others within the workplace, and their cognitive involvement in their role.[50]

Multisource feedback as a development approach can also be incorporated to support an organization's strategy. According to Douglas Shuit, Yum Brands, the world's largest restaurant company, with such brands as KFC, Long John Silver's, Pizza Hut, and Taco Bell, had to alter its strategy when it broke off from parent company PepsiCo in 1997.[51] While PepsiCo emphasizes marketing and sales to major customers such as supermarket chains, Yum's customers are mostly single individuals who care about fresh and hot food. Tim Galbraith, Yum's vice president of people development, explained that being successful at Yum means "delivering our passion, which is to put a yum, or smile, on customers' faces. We want to do that on every transaction."

The 360-degree feedback system had a lot to do with helping the company become more people-friendly, especially by turning managers officially into coaches. First, as a web-based system, its multisource assessment can be completed in a compressed three-week cycle and is efficient enough to involve not just executives; it also drops down to the store-manager level. Although a range of issues are covered, the focus is clearly on employee and customer development. Since the company operates worldwide, with a large presence in China, the tool has been translated into the language of each focal person's local region. The assessment is not tied to compensation, which is considered a separate process. As a long-time supporter of development and to emphasize his commitment to it, CEO David Novak himself asked for feedback on the job he was doing. Over one hundred employees responded, providing him with a report that ran sixty-five pages!

Developmental Relationships

Another option in work-based learning programs using reflective practice is the formal or informal organization of developmental relationships. Typically, this option is referred to under the familiar labels of coaching or mentorship programs. The labels, however, become confusing as the terms become intertwined. For example, some authors refer to coaching as outside advisement and mentoring as internal advisement. On the other hand, professional mentorships sometimes evolve by taking advantage of people from outside organizations.

Using work-based learning precepts, we avoid stumbling on these unnecessary distinctions by merely suggesting that one's learning at work can be facilitated through the advisement of one or more significant individuals with whom to engage in a reflective process about one's thoughts and behaviors. This clarification does not require that the adviser be a peer, a senior member of staff, or an outside practitioner; that the purpose be remedial or enriching; that the content be substantive or therapeutic; nor does it insist that the adviser give advice or merely actively listen. Developmental relationships evolve under various memberships and using a variety of styles and can occur frequently without formal organization. In fact, group mentorships can be a viable option, wherein a senior colleague would meet simultaneously with several junior protégés.[52] What makes each relationship unique as a work-based learning approach is the interest of the parties in mutual reflection and learning.[53] Recall that in the last chapter, I suggested that developmental relationships entail dialogue, meaning that the parties are committed to surfacing those social, political, and even emotional reactions that might be blocking their own operating effectiveness.

The parties consciously reflect on experience and even upon their own problem-solving processes and communication patterns. Otherwise confidential issues, be they working relationships with other managers, strategic business issues, or the participant's own growth and development, are given a forum for open consideration. Individuals get a rare opportunity to think out loud and receive constructive feedback on critical and even undiscussable problems.[54] In fact, the coaching discussion might even discern ways to make what has been heretofore undiscussable discussable.

Developmental relationships often tie to the developmental planning process described previously. Many action learning programs, for example, feature coaches working with participants to create agendas and action plans. As a role distinct from that of the supervisor, sponsor, or learning team facilitator, the coach provides individual feedback to the participant on progress in accomplishing developmental goals. The coach, however, offers the benefit of not exerting or representing formal line authority, most likely making it easier for the participant to share confidences. The firm MDA, in a successful engagement with a high-end clothing retailer, sponsored a six-month action learning intervention, featuring the convening of a Breakthrough Learning Team. The team was composed of senior leaders responsible for reducing costs at the company's primary distribution facility. Besides several days of skill-building and interim meetings to help the team develop a viable change process, members received one-on-one executive coaching tied specifically to their role in the change effort but also dedicated to each individual's growth and development.[55]

The intent of the developmental relationship is for both parties to learn and to further their own self-development. Hence, they need not be one-way. There is as much for the coach to learn as the participant. Developing others can be considered a critical managerial competency, especially in an age when team structures and two-way communication have become commonplace. Coaches and mentors might also find that the unique perspective of a protégé can provide them with new insights about different segments of their own organization and about other careers.[56] They might even obtain organizational recognition from the success of their protégé.[57] Aside from its career implications, development can also be a source of great personal accomplishment. Mentors report an exhilaration from the fresh energy provided by protégés.[58]

There is a built-in check on the effectiveness of these relationships. In reflective practice, the parties *check in* with each other as a matter of course to assess their ongoing value to one another. Developmental relationships also entail situated learning, in the sense that the parties do not rely on pre-existing knowledge but instead develop their learning as they go and as they adjust to the challenges of their own practice. Furthermore, they are not didactic in the form of master instructing apprentice but rather allow for the progressive accumulation of values and skills as they are applied to real problems. Participants in a coaching relationship are encouraged to consult with a variety of knowledge resources in order to develop an appreciation of how expertise and insight are distributed within an organization.[59] Such exposure helps them understand that work tasks can be confronted in multiple ways and that no one individual embodies all the necessary expertise. Learners need to be encouraged to view all their associates as mutual learners who can offer insight into their personal and organizational performance. In this way, they begin to appreciate learning as a progressive process. Coaches, however, can help them establish benchmarks to measure their own progress.

Some of the mentoring literature suggests that this form of developmental relationship may have performance effects on protégés as well as direct bottom-line effects on the organization. A meta-analysis found that protégés tend to be paid more, promoted more often, and more satisfied with their career compared with those who have not been mentored.[60] Considering the organization as a whole, the evidence is more anecdotal. A report from First Direct, an online English bank, publicized a nearly £1 million savings in recruitment costs, directly attributable to its mentoring program, which is conducted concurrently with the bank's five-week training program for new call center workers.[61] The program entails new recruits meeting with a senior manager for a half hour each week to discuss any issues that might come up. One recruit, for instance, needed to know whether and how to ask for a change of shift due to child care demands. The cost savings from the program resulted from attrition levels falling from 30 percent to 17 percent.

Evidence from the Field

There are lessons from research on mentoring and coaching that can guide the creation and operation of successful development relationships. A program called LeaderLab, conducted by the Center for Creative Leadership throughout the 1990s, featured three developmental roles: a process adviser (PA), represented by a staff professional; an in-course change partner, represented by a peer in the program; and a back-home change partner, represented by a peer back at the work site.[62] A subsequent evaluation of LeaderLab found the PA role to be the most critical feature of the program.[63] The PA represented an ongoing link between the program and the individual, tailoring the activities of LeaderLab to the participant's needs. The evaluation found that participants valued their PAs more for their process concern than for their substantive expertise. It was not the PA's intimate knowledge of the participant's job or industry that was valuable. Rather it was the encouragement that the PA provided, which in turn was based upon knowledge of change and developmental processes, as well as the PA's closeness to the individual. Two typical comments made in this regard by participants were:

> My PA acted as a mirror for myself so I could see patterns, maintain consistency.

> The PA challenged me to explore my feelings and develop different strategies.

PAs were also found to be especially useful in ameliorating some of the stress that most participants were experiencing in their back-home environment. It was thought, for example, that PAs provided a positive influence on participants' self-efficacy by expressing confidence in the participant's ability to overcome hardship.

With regard to the change partner roles in LeaderLab, especially the back-home partner, the results of the evaluation were mixed. There were two critical ingredients to enhancing these roles. First, the participant needed to be open in sharing and accepting feedback from the change partner. Second, the change partner needed to be seen as trustworthy, discreet, committed, and available.

Clearly, for development relationships to work, learners need someone who can be committed to them and who can afford the time for the relationship to evolve. There is no point in having a mentor, for example, in name only. Nor do you want to have a relationship of this caliber with someone who might be competing with you or who might be "looking over your shoulder" in a controlling sense. Accordingly, some supervisors make for good coaches; others do not. Not all bosses are inherently good at developing others, nor unfortunately is development always rewarded in the corporate culture.

In an intensive study of twenty-seven mentors by Allen, Poteet, and Burroughs, the most critical organizational factor that facilitated mentoring was organizational support for employee learning and development.[64] This factor, represented by such comments as "It is important to have a learning environment system where people are encouraged to teach and learn from each other" was followed by manager and co-worker support and a team approach to work. Another critical success factor that has been amply reinforced is mentorship training, since the inherent skills are not necessarily natural.[65] It is interesting to note that by far the most inhibiting factor to mentoring was time and work demands, a condition that I have earlier cited as stifling reflective practices. In fact, the study also found time requirements to constitute the overwhelming response to a query regarding the negative consequences of mentoring.

Although most individuals are lucky to have one good mentor during their entire career, there is something to be said for attempting to develop more than one mentor at any given time. Different mentors can serve different needs or provide alternative competencies. One might be helpful in interpreting office politics; another might understand corporate strategy.[66] This perhaps presupposes that mentors are widely available, and in fact there are companies whose mentorship program founders on the lack of participation by potential mentors. In the late 1980s, Motorola University created the Application Consulting Team (ACT), a program staffed by managers with twenty-plus years of experience. Rather than pursue their traditional management responsibilities, ACT managers served as mentors or coaches in the workplace to help transfer knowledge gained from Motorola courses.[67] McDermott, Levenson, and Newton found that such internal coaches were very effective in helping managers overcome instances of derailment, likely due to their ability to leverage organizational resources to help solve the issues that led to derailment in the first instance.[68] In work-based learning programs, a good source of mentors is the recruitment of past participants. Having experienced the benefits and challenges of work-based learning involving reflective practices, past participants are in an expedient position to empathize with current participants.

The deployment of past participants brings up the consideration of *peer mentoring* as a viable developmental relationship. Indeed, the opportunity for mutual learning can be great in this setting and can be propitious, especially in an era of corporate delayering, wherein the number of managers in the hierarchy has been reduced and at a time when horizontal ties between peers are replacing vertical ties as channels of communication. On the other hand, a peer can become resistant to an exchange that may threaten his or her security. The secret is to build a relationship that honors the complementarity between the parties and develops their mutual wisdom. One study found that individuals were more likely to discuss personal feelings and insecurities with their peer mentor than with a hierarchical mentor, although the latter was thought to be more effective in providing insight into organizational politics.[69] A peer might also be particularly sensitive to diversity issues, such as race and gender, and any consequent feelings of exclusion that may arise.

A program known as the International Masters Program in Practicing Management (IMPM), sponsored by McGill University, Hitotsubashi University, the Indian Institute of Management, INSEAD, and Lancaster University, has come up with an interesting peer mentoring approach.[70] After developing participant observation techniques, participants from different cultures and industries pair up and spend a week visiting, observing, and reflecting on each other's daily work. The guest shadows the host for the better part of the week and then prepares a draft report on the experience. The report is shared with the host, who then responds with a brief report. The experience is then repeated in reverse at the guest's home site.

A variant of the peer mentoring approach is the supportive relationship that may evolve between a manager and an external consultant. This may occur when the consultant and manager work collaboratively and incrementally over the course of time to design innovative interventions in the organization, which may not only effect change but may also encourage learning. Robert Schaffer reported one such instance at a manufacturer.[71] Karen Prasch, a customer service manager responsible for processing international orders, worked closely with a consultant who had been hired to improve the company's order processing problems. Not only did the consultant's interventions solve the immediate problem, but the effort grew into a program of continuous improvement, which Prasch extended to her own peers. The learning generated was as much competency-based as functional. In particular, Prasch and her order processing group developed a repertoire of new process redesign and leadership skills and in the meantime doubled their order-processing capacity.

Of all the qualities necessary to develop a relationship that can be constructive and inductive of healthy reflection, it is most critical to find someone who respects the learner as an individual and can work with him or her in a supportive and nonjudgmental way. Second, it is helpful to have a mentor who understands the organizational culture and can interpret how the individual's behavior matches with that culture. It is also important to have a mentor who is willing to reassess the mentoring relationship, after a period of time has elapsed, to ensure its ongoing value. Lynda McDermott, in a survey of senior-level professionals, offers these other qualities to describe an ideal coach:[72]

- Creates a relationship that isn't forced or contrived
- Is comfortable and secure; lets people grow
- Provides honest information
- Takes time to develop the relationship by showing a personal interest in the employee's development
- Displays empathy for personal as well as professional issues
- Provides specific guidance, where possible, on substantive issues
- Leads by example—works at improving his or her own development needs
- Doesn't force his or her own goals or agendas on employees
- Paints the big picture
- Talks with employees, not to them
- Provides informal feedback, not just a checklist
- Works with specific performance criteria
- Helps employees plan for improvement

To keep it short, Bell uses the mnemonic SAGE to help mentors remember the key qualities in the developmental relationship:[73]

Surrendering—mentors are capable of yielding the process to the protégé rather than controlling it, which only results in depriving the parties of the freedom needed to foster discovery.

Accepting—mentors try to rid themselves of bias, preconceived judgments, and human labeling; they embrace rather than evaluate or judge.

Gifting—mentors are committed to bestowing something of value without expecting anything in return, and the gifts they bestow, they give abundantly and unconditionally.

Extending—mentors push the developmental relationship beyond expected boundaries in the interest of seeking alternative ways to foster learning and growth.

Although these items are behaviors, suggesting that mentoring can be learned, they may derive from key personality traits that predispose certain individuals to becoming effective in developmental relationships. In particular, mentors have been characterized as having the attributes of high sociability, high openness, but low dominance.[74] Hence, effective mentors tend to build rapport and lead individuals into dialogue with relative ease. They like to be open and candid about themselves, giving protégés the encouragement to do likewise. Finally, they have no trouble giving up control to others and work hard to listen rather than to talk.

Since developmental relationships are two way, there are also qualities that might characterize the predisposing behavior and attitude of the protégé. In one model, the person being coached is advised to be interested in and able to do the following:[75]

- Change.
- Ask for help.
- Share feedback.
- Learn from shortcomings, not hide them.
- Examine ways to improve.
- Try out new and different approaches.
- Listen openly, not defensively.

Another mentoring study pointed out the qualities that mentors look for in their protégés.[76] Most important was the openness and willingness to learn, followed by the actual competence of the protégé. Mentors also expected protégés to be "willing to work hard," to be self-starters, and to have "the drive to succeed." Mentors also sought individuals who were people-oriented and had high integrity. Finally, it was important that protégés display a willingness to accept constructive feedback.

The Coaching Session

What does a session with a coach look like? There is no prescribed format, but we might be able to provide a sense of some popular practices.[77] Most coaches are willing to provide a familiarization session with the participant to set the parameters for their subsequent work together, including their respective roles, anticipated results, and the amount of time to be invested. A contract may also be worked out for a certain number of sessions over a given period of time. Monthly or twice-monthly sessions for a period of six to eighteen months are common. Coaches also offer "check-up" service between scheduled meetings, often consisting of telephone conversations or an exchange of e-mail.

The first formal session typically involves some kind of assessment of current practice. Many coaches now recommend 360-degree assessments, which, as pointed out earlier, entail survey or interview feedback from the participant's subordinates, bosses, and peers. Self-assessment data are sometimes included as well as input from customers and suppliers. The coach initially reviews the feedback from the assessments with the participant, occasionally even with the rater present. Once these data are understood and integrated, the participant is next encouraged to work on a plan for improving particular behaviors identified in the assessments or cited as a matter of personal or professional preference. Working in a manner consistent with our prior discussion of developmental planning, the coach then encourages the participant to plan workplace interventions to try out these new behaviors. At subsequent sessions, these actions in the workplace would be subject to reflection on their effectiveness, both in terms of consistency with the participant's original plan and intentions and in terms of his or her accomplishment of personal or professional goals in the workplace. For example, the participant might be interested in learning how to build a sense of teamwork in his or her unit, how to increase the level of trust, how to relate better with certain "difficult" members of the staff, and so forth. Problems of this nature would be addressed until both parties feel sufficient progress has been made to allow the participant to proceed without the need for explicit coaching.

Good coaches emphasize the need for ongoing reflection and inquiry. As participants attempt to use new knowledge in practice, which may lead to novel actions or interventions, they will need to reflect on their progress introspectively but also with their peers and with their coach. The coach's role in this case may be to model *reflection-in-action,* in which they help participants frame problems, devise and experiment with solutions, and reframe as "situations talk back."[78] Through this process, the participant may learn to distill important lessons from workplace interactions and become more aware of his or her assumptions. In this way, the coach can engage the learner in deeper forms of reflection in which meaning structures can be examined.[79] As Newman puts it, we learn not only how we see the world and ourselves more clearly, but how we see ourselves see the world.[80] In this more in-depth form of coaching, learners come to see that our meanings are shaped by our frames of reference.

Coaches might also expose participants to learning that involves both explicit and tacit forms of knowledge. For example, one participant might benefit from reading selected literature on team building. He or she might also take advantage of training resources offered through the company or be advised about organizational policies and practices in team development. These explicit sources of knowledge, however, would need to be supplemented by implicit strategies (call them "hints" or "tips") that could be addressed directly in conversation or surmised from observation, experimentation, and subsequently from reflection and dialogue.[81] For example, a coach might suggest that a particular director prefers to read supporting documentation before sitting down to meet with staff. In this instance, the participant might learn the contextual value of anticipating a boss's style.

As for the dynamics of each session, naturally the coaching process will vary, but good coaches will tend to use a lot of probing into delicate issues, be they blind spots, biases, or unfounded assumptions. Hutcheson recommends that coaches pay as much attention to what is not being said as to what they hear.[82] Probing should also be as open-ended as possible in order not to come off as an inquisition. As opposed to a question such as, "Why would you do that?" the coach might lead with "Tell me a little more about your thinking behind that." This type of open-ended query tends to produce more expansive thinking such that both parties feel free to explore new information or test unfounded assumptions. In a similar vein, the coach might guide the participant to his or her own solution rather than offer unsolicited advice. The idea is to facilitate the reflective process, asking about likely consequences attending to a particular alternative rather than condemning the viewpoint as naive or ill-advised. Another critical goal in coaching is to help participants come to realize how others might be reacting to their behavior.

As the relationship evolves, the coach might try to uncover the individual's defenses, especially where they may be blocking useful interpersonal and professional relationships. New skills or new perspectives might also be introduced to help the individual plan and implement workplace changes. In instances where changes in behavior are likely to be difficult to make, the coach and participant might prepare scripts and role-play possible scenarios. Another useful technique is to set microgoals, which represent successive approximations to the ultimate goal.[83] For example, if the learner wishes to become more approachable, successive microgoals might call for asking a staff member how his or her weekend went or soliciting other people's opinion about a matter instead of launching into one's own. Among the issues that appear to really challenge participants is the establishment of useful boundaries between family and work life as well as between personal and professional relationships.

There are abundant variations of the coaching format. Some coaches do not necessarily believe that workplace problems need to become the substantive focus of the relationship. A holistic approach to coaching would focus on the learner's personal history and current personal life as context for his or her work role resulting in an alignment of "head and heart."[84] Former chairman and CEO Roger Enrico of PepsiCo reported that one of his earliest mentorships was hardly conventional, though it was vital to his development.[85] For a couple of hours in the middle of the workday, Enrico would meet informally with then CEO of PepsiCo, Don Kendall. Kendall would close the door and hold all calls. Enrico recalls showing up the first time with a three hundred–page fact book and a flip-book of charts, but Kendall spent the meeting talking about opera.

Subsequently, they moved on to a wide range of other subjects and never viewed Enrico's slides. Instead, Kendall kept the focus on what Enrico would later consider the perspectives of good leadership. The personally reflective meta-skills that coaching may emphasize often are indeed those precisely associated with enhanced leadership competencies.[86]

Robert Krim described an interesting process of mentorship in helping him work through some difficult projects as assistant director of human resources for a large city government.[87] Krim had the benefit of two mentors—one a consultant for the city, the other a university faculty member. He was encouraged to tape-record his reflections of critical incidents in his work, both before and after they occurred. In the recordings taped prior to the incident, he might reflect upon his intentions before attending a meeting. In his tapings after the incident, he would address whether his intentions were actually practiced and what the outcomes were. Krim also used the tapes to record his ongoing personal feelings throughout the process. Finally, his mentors also encouraged him to rehearse publicly with them particular scenarios that might evolve. They would then provide feedback on how they saw his proposed behavior and what likely effects may occur. Through this process, he not only was able to practice new behaviors, but he also developed a greater consciousness of his own performance as well as the impact of that performance on others.[88]

In particular, Krim learned that in the work environment, he came across as manipulative because his style was so self-effacing. His mentors felt that his instincts were on the right track but that he should act on them, not suppress them when under pressure. As a result of this developmental experience, Krim created a set of working rules that helped him through many subsequent crises, including this very important one: learn to state a view clearly and when challenged aggressively by others, to listen, to come to terms with your feelings, and then to respond by challenging back.

8

Facilitation in Work-Based Learning

There is no human problem which could not be
solved if people would simply do as I advise.

—Gore Vidal

In the last chapter, the practice of learning teams was depicted as the principal means of supplying work-based learning program participants with feedback on their planned and unplanned actions or interventions in their work environment. To enhance its value as a learning methodology, learning teams benefit enormously from the skillfulness and artfulness of a trained facilitator. I devote attention in this chapter to the practice of facilitation. Please note that some of the ideas introduced here can be applied to other work-based learning practices, such as project teams and group mentorships.

Facilitation Methods

Although facilitation methods vary, there are some common principles and practices that distinguish facilitation from, say, meeting management or group therapy. A review of some of the classics of group behavior as well as of popular accounts of facilitation, including a plethora of resources available through the International Association of Facilitators (IAF), delimits facilitation as focusing on process rather than on content.[1] The root definition of facilitation is *to make easy*: thus, group facilitators provide assistance, not control, making it easy for the group to do its work.

Most of the literature also calls for the facilitator to take a neutral stance on the content of the discussion in order to help the group free itself from internal obstacles that may be hampering effective decision making. As a servant to the group, the facilitator has one goal—to help the group achieve its purpose by assisting the participants in having a constructive dialogue, as free as possible from internal dynamics that may block productive discourse.

The Organization Development and Change Division of the Academy of Management specifies in its competency guidelines that facilitation of individual and group processes ensures that clients "maintain ownership of the issue, increase their capacity for reflection on the consequences of their behaviors and actions, and develop a sense of increased control and ability."[2] Facilitators thus tend to rely on the group members themselves to offer suggestions to one another rather than solve their problems for them. However, facilitators do provide resource suggestions and advice on learning how to learn. We have referred to this level of learning as *second-order learning*, which is learning that takes the learner out of a context or frame of reference. Instead of teaching about finance (in which the facilitator may not even have expertise), the facilitator offers ways of learning how to learn finance. Participants also learn how to use *third-order learning*, in which case they might challenge existing assumptions and beliefs in order to come up with new theories about financial systems.[3] Facilitators also encourage participants to question their own values and assumptions. Finally, facilitators can provide alternative ways to frame the subjects of inquiry—in other words, ways to look at things differently. They encourage a group to maintain a healthy appraisal of alternatives, thus avoiding the dreaded groupthink, made famous by Janis's account of the Bay of Pigs fiasco.[4]

In practice, some facilitators find it difficult to stay clear of directing the group. In some action learning settings, for example, it has often been found that the more active the facilitator, the better the project outcomes on the part of the participants. Yet there is a paradox in this view of project outcomes. Admittedly, the facilitator's advanced technical knowledge might lead to a better "economic" outcome, but at the same time it may deprive the project team of some less tangible benefits or competencies, such as learning-to-learn, use of judgment, deployment of balance and perspective, and the handling and creation of change. Task achievement may also come at the expense of personal development. Moreover, pre-structuring by a facilitator may also circumvent creative solutions generated by a participative project team. Kevin Wheeler, the president of General Learning Resources, provides the example of a project group assigned to a CFO sponsor who charged them with coming up with a system to help one of his units close its books faster.[5] Unfortunately, in Wheeler's view, the facilitator helped the team prestructure the problem by looking at what was realistic given their prior experience. They might have come up with a better process had they set a seemingly unrealistic goal of twenty-four hours as the time frame for closing the books rather than working toward the more "realistic" one, which they had selected as three days.

Malcolm Knowles, famed adult educator, distinguished between *andragogy*—that is, participant-directed learning, and *pedagogy*—teacher-directed learning.[6] In andragogy, participants are allowed to be more autonomous in their actions, more reliable in their assessment of their own capacities and developmental needs, and more capable of accepting greater levels of responsibility for their own actions and the actions of others. According to andragogical practice, then, facilitators model such behaviors in the group as tolerance of ambiguity, openness and frankness, patience and suspension of judgment, empathy and unconditional positive regard, and commitment to learning. Eventually, group members will begin to adopt some of these same behaviors, thus all the more limiting the proactivity of the facilitator. Some other andragogical facilitator skills discussed in the literature include:

- Listening and attending
- Clarifying goals, agendas, and norms
- Promoting airing of problems from diverse viewpoints

- Openly but sensitively confronting conflict or disagreement
- Looking at the underlying assumptions operating in a situation
- Revealing one's own assumptions and inferences
- Being aware of inconsistencies between one's beliefs and actions
- Giving feedback in a nondefensive way
- Soliciting and receiving feedback from others
- Reflecting on self
- Allowing and encouraging the airing of emotions and feelings
- Taking note of group dynamics to help the group with its own development
- Encouraging group members to take ownership of their own learning
- Reinforcing an open and participative environment

There is a subtle difference between actual intervention in a group, on the part of the facilitator, and the orchestration of actions by others. Reason and Rowan discuss a number of methods that facilitators could adopt to encourage the development of member involvement and team leadership:[7]

1. One or more members could be charged with keeping a diary of events and experiences for later examination.

2. Members could be invited to visit others in their work settings to observe them as they experiment with new behaviors and practices. Later, during a team meeting, feedback could be given to those who were observed.

3. Questionnaires and other assessments could be introduced from time to time to evaluate the group's or particular individuals' styles, experiences, or progress.

4. Members could be encouraged to interview each other and bring results to the entire group.

5. The facilitator could interview members of the group and develop a descriptive model of team behavior to be shared with the entire group once together.

6. Members with a creative flair could be asked to make drawings or other expressive works to tap both conscious and unconscious aspects of experience.

A related issue in work-based learning contexts is whether the project team is better off with a facilitator who is a subject specialist or with one who is strategically ignorant of the project's technical environment. In the latter sense, ignorance implies a need to ask difficult questions that participants might find useful in framing problems. In terms of acquiring team performance competencies, especially those that induce a process of inquiry within the group, the answer to this question is clear. More learning of such *meta-competencies* will likely result if the facilitator is more of an expert in group process than in the technical domains of the project. Accordingly, the facilitator can comment on such process concerns as the distribution of workload responsibilities, group member participation, the management of deviance or isolation of particular members, the expected mood swings in the group from early excitement to subsequent discouragement, and so forth. Nor should project domain ignorance cause the facilitator to refrain from sharing his or her knowledge of the organizational culture that envelops the project. Facilitators are often experienced practitioners and may know a fair amount about the norms of practice in the units affected by the project. For example, they may be able to guide participants to the best people to speak to, or they may have a good hunch of how best to obtain relevant data; be it by survey, interview, or observation. In sum, there are different ways that facilitators can share their expertise other than by providing technical direction.

Even when it comes to group process considerations, the facilitator has to tread a fine line between offering direction and exhibiting forbearance. Especially in the early phases of group development, if the facilitator comes across as too discretionary, group members may ramble from subject to subject or from content to process in a way that may overly frustrate particular members. On the other hand, if the facilitator comes across as being too directive about the content and process of the group, many of its members may become overly dependent on the continued supervision of the facilitator. Part of the craft of facilitation is knowing when to offer counsel to help the group overcome obstacles and when to hold back to allow group members to assume leadership roles critical to the group's internal development.

The facilitator is thus depicted as eclectic in the use of intervention strategies. The art of facilitation is knowing when to use which. Heron offers six types of interventions to choose from:[8]

Prescriptive interventions deliberately offer advice and direction.

Informative interventions offer leads or ideas about how to proceed on a given matter, for example, where to find an appropriate resource to contribute to a project.

Confronting interventions directly challenge members of the team on such issues as the team's current process, evolving relationships within the team, restricted intellectual frameworks.

Cathartic interventions address emotional undercurrents and seek to release tension, for example, by prompting the expression of grief or anger.

Catalytic interventions provide a structure or framework to encourage the development of an idea or to remove a blockage; for example, suggesting that a member stop, reflect, and write down her thoughts or asking someone to role-play an individual with whom a member is reporting to have difficulty.

Supportive interventions display care and attention and offer empathy.

The dexterous facilitator knows when to use each of these styles and activities, including when to use them in sequence or even in combination. For example, cathartic and catalytic interventions might be used concurrently; a confronting intervention might be followed up with a number of supportive gestures. Whatever style is chosen at a given point, the underlying philosophy of most facilitation in a work-based learning setting is to allow the participant ample room for self-discovery and personal learning.

Charles Donaghue describes four sets of interconnected activities, including intervention, which should preoccupy the facilitator.[9] Note that his work expands the domain of facilitation to incorporate some responsibility for brokering relationships between learning teams and the organizations to which members are affiliated.

Understanding—having a good sense of the membership of the learning team, their backgrounds, their jobs, their frames of reference, and the nature of their projects

Intervening—knowing how and when to act to influence the team, given the facilitator's understanding of each member, the member's project, and the group as a whole

Reviewing—providing feedback to the team on its original intentions, commitments, and plans as well as to individual members on their learning plans and personal development

Integrating—establishing a link between the members and their projects to the client system or organization in order to establish sound working relationships

To these four activities of facilitators, Donaghue adds four dimensions, or issues, that need to be managed along predictable, even developmental, lines, suggesting a role for the facilitator as mobilizer of the group from one dimension to the next. The first dimension to be tackled by the group is that of *administration*, which entails such procedures as the frequency and duration of meetings, logistics, and the relationship of the learning and project teams (if they are not one and the same) to the sponsoring organization. After the basic security or hygiene needs of the team are satisfied, groups typically transition into a *content* dimension. During this period, there tends to be a focus on task achievement related to the projects of the members, especially their diagnosis, planning, and operation. During the next phase, the *process* dimension, the group becomes interested in processes underlying their surface content, considering such group and interpersonal issues as communication, leadership and authority, group norms, and group development. The fourth dimension is the *feelings* domain, wherein affect and interpersonal relationships are dealt with openly and honestly as members acknowledge their importance not only to their learning but also to the team's performance.

Weaver and Farrell suggest fairly concrete roles for facilitators, at least during the early phases of group development.[10] At the outset, for example, they recommend that the facilitator work with the group to establish both a charge and a charter. The charge or mission entails the group's overall assignment; hence, it defines the scope of work and the results expected. The charter details the group's goals, roles, and procedures. The goals clarify what must be done to fulfill the mission, such as who will do what, when, and how. Roles characterize the skills, knowledge, and abilities that individual members will offer to the group to help it achieve its purpose. Finally, the procedures or norms establish the ground rules that will be necessary to keep the group on track and may include such items as the nature of group meetings, guidelines for communication, making decisions, experiencing conflict, and introducing new members.

Facilitation and Group Development

Part of the role of the facilitator is to raise awareness of the natural dynamics of groups so that members realize the challenge but also the benefit of developing their team. Some writers have used developmental theory to propose specific styles of intervention to move groups through their natural stages of development. There is not unanimous concurrence that all groups go through the same stages since such variables as purpose of the group, constitution, duration, and organizational context will cause a fair degree of diversity. Yet the classic study of Tuckman, with its rhyming stages, has gained a great deal of credibility among "team-building" aficionados.[11]

In Tuckman's model, there are four stages that groups must contend with in their life cycle. A group will achieve greater effectiveness to the extent it can manage the unique challenges attending to each stage. In the *forming* stage, members begin to determine what is acceptable behavior within the group and how to approach their task at hand. As they orient to the task, they begin to establish some group rules, yet they tend to become dependent on the designated leader or authority figure (if there is one). They also begin to test their individual styles and personality to see if they will be accepted by others.

During the *storming* stage, as the group redefines its task and members try to agree on objectives and strategy, conflict inevitably results. Members find that their styles do not coincide. They may differ in the amount of time they want to commit to a particular task, the priority they may assign to it, or even the means they might use to accomplish it. As a result, this tends to be a time of high emotionality and tension. Members may compete to establish their preferences for the group and to achieve their desired personal position or status.

It is during the third stage, *norming*, that members begin to come together as a coordinated unit. The jockeying behaviors of the storming stage now give way to a precarious balancing of forces. Members begin to resolve their differences by exchanging their interpretations and opinions about group operations and as a result act more cohesively. Team norms and roles also become accepted at this juncture, as members display an increased willingness to listen and to contribute to the team. However, for some members, holding the group together may take precedence over successfully working on the group's tasks.

By the fourth stage of group development, the *performing* stage, the integration begun in the norming stage is completed. Members not only dedicate themselves to the tasks of the group, but they also do so as they simultaneously support one another. There is also energy for developing ways for the group to continuously improve and renew itself. The group structure becomes stable yet fluid, disagreements are handled in creative ways, and members become motivated by group goals. Further, members understand their individual and collective responsibilities to other units in the wider organizational environment.

If the role of the facilitator (or facilitating supervisor) is to help a learning team move through its natural stages, then some behaviors may be specified for each of the four stages indicated here. Among the models of group leadership, the situational leadership model developed by Hersey and Blanchard, although initially created for one-on-one manager-subordinate interaction, can be instructive when applied to group development.[12] Revising the original situational leadership model, Carew, Parisi-Carew, and Blanchard designed a group development model that can link facilitator intervention style with stages of group development.[13] Accordingly, facilitators might deploy different degrees of two principal behaviors in their work in groups. Directive behavior, related to task functions, is depicted as being directive about member roles and assignments and about what the group needs to do. Supportive behavior, also referred to as the *maintenance functions,* is concerned with providing support and encouragement to group members, facilitating their interaction, and involving them in decision making.

The situational leadership model is based on the notion that leaders can adapt their style to fit the situation. Hence, a proper combination of directive and supportive behaviors is advised, depending upon the stage of development of the learning team in question. The facilitator can help move a group through the four stages previously described. The four stages may also be depicted in terms of the amount of work expected from each stage as well as the morale or socioemotional tone of the group. The amount of work accomplished steadily increases through the stages. On the other hand, morale starts out high during the forming stage but then takes a dip during the storming stage as the expectations of the members confront the stern reality of trying to reach a high level of task performance without having worked through the requisite maintenance functions. As members discuss and begin to define norms in this and the subsequent norming stage, morale begins to pick up until it reaches a high level in the performing stage.

Table 8.1 depicts the four stages, the relative degree of directive and supportive behavior advised for each stage, and the resulting intervention style recommended for the facilitator.

"Telling" is most appropriate at the forming stage of group development as the learning team struggles to clarify its task and to set realistic and attainable goals. Although supportive behavior is low at this stage, it has to be sufficient to establish a climate for member acceptance of one another and to initially introduce the process goals of open communication and shared leadership.

By the storming stage, the facilitator is seen as having to increase the level of supportive behavior to balance task provision. Essentially, a "coaching" style is called for as the facilitator trains learning team members in the skills and knowledge associated with task and group process while engaging in more active listening, acknowledging difficulties, and focusing on building supportive member relationships and group cohesion. The goal at this stage is to work toward less dependency on the facilitator and more self-sufficiency within the group.

"Supporting" aligns with the norming stage as the facilitator diminishes emphasis on task and goal clarification. The facilitator at this stage can be seen as encouraging group members to assume more and more of task and maintenance functions that were once his or her province. As this stage evolves, the facilitator can even begin to lessen his or her supportive behavior because group members will be seen as assuming more of the process work. However, the facilitator needs to be alert to an inclination on the part of some members to avoid conflict and disagreement for fear of losing their

Table 8.1. Group Development and Facilitator Style

Stage	Directive Behavior	Supportive Behavior	Style
Forming	High	Low	Telling
Storming	High	High	Coaching
Norming	Low	Moderate	Supporting
Performing	Low	Low	Delegating

newfound cohesion. The facilitator needs to encourage continued free expression and valuing of differences among members.

In the last performing stage, the facilitator uses "delegating" as the group itself can begin to take responsibility for task and maintenance functions. Although the facilitator continues to monitor the goals and performance of the group, he or she can become more of a resource for individuals and the group as a whole—for example, in providing technical support for members' projects. The facilitator also has to be aware of the need, as the occasion arises, to bring back supportive and directive behaviors as conditions in the team change—for example, if new members were to enter or if a crisis, such as the loss of a sponsor, were to occur.

Facilitation and Change

Just as there are natural rhythms in group development, there are some relative constancies, oddly enough, in the world of change. Work-based learning is by nature about change, so participants— by subscribing to this form of learning—need to accept change as an inevitable course of events. Certainly the learning team is a vehicle for individual and group change, as was demonstrated earlier in our discussion of group development. However, it is also the case that participants in undertaking an action project (to be discussed in more detail in the next chapter) become themselves agents of change in their organizations. Facilitators of learning teams can play an important role in helping participants understand some of the dynamics of change when the participants come together to reflect on their actions in their sponsoring organizations.

Facilitators might first help participants understand the forces for stability and the forces for change that likely exist in their company.[14] Some of these forces will be very influential, whereas others will have little impact on the course of change. Assessing the strength of each force as well as determining whether the force facilitates or resists the change in question are critical diagnostic points for the change agent. For example, a project might be undertaken in the area of mergers and acquisitions. Particular departments might be very much in favor of an acquisition because of the synergies it might bring. Perhaps the new partner might offer a product that will significantly complement the company's product line. On the other hand, other departments might resist the change for fear of losing staff, resources, or prestige. Perhaps the new company has a comparable staff, which will cause redundancies once the acquisition is completed. Kurt Lewin originally characterized the balance of forces, depicted here as a force-field, and their diagnosis as a force-field analysis.[15] It can be graphically displayed, as in Figure 8.1.

As can be seen from the diagram, each force has a strength or intensity depicted by the length of its vector. In order to move toward a changed or new state, one has a choice of increasing the strength of the facilitating forces or reducing the strength of the resisting forces. Lewin was clear that it is preferable to try the latter since increasing the strength of the facilitating forces can often produce unintended counter-reactions. Focusing on the resisting forces can lead to strategies for change that may ameliorate some of the legitimate resistance. Continuing the previous example, perhaps the manager of the department fearing layoffs from redundancies as a

Figure 8.1. Force-Field Analysis

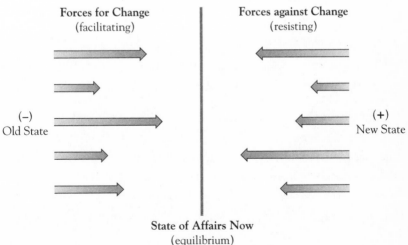

result of the acquisition could have his or her fears allayed by a promise that natural attrition would be used to reduce head count, followed by a commitment to reassign all other redundant staff.

It may also be important to help members of a learning team who are involved in change projects learn the natural effects on people from experiencing transitions brought about by the change process. Change inevitably translates into letting go of the old and embracing the new. However, people and groups respond differently to the transition process, often depending upon their psychological security from experiencing change. The most important lesson is that during change, people need time to adjust. Helping people overcome the losses typically associated with change can serve as an important contribution on the part of change agents. Scott and Jaffe indicate five types of losses that employees might experience when facing a change:[16]

1. *Security*. They may not feel in control or may no longer feel that they know where they stand.

2. *Competence*. They may not know what to do or how to do it, which in turn may cause them considerable embarrassment.

3. *Relationships*. They may fear the loss of old customers, co-workers, or managers, which in turn may affect their sense of belonging to a group or an organization.

4. *Sense of direction*. They may lose a sense of where they are going and why.

5. *Territory*. They may fear losing the area that used to belong to them, such as a work space or job assignments.

Transitions are also characterized as moving through some fairly predictable stages. Each stage may require a different strategy to help people make a positive transition. Again, in learning teams, facilitators can help participants understand these stages so that appropriate interventions can be made in their project work. Reflective discourse in the team can also help participants understand if they've correctly diagnosed where their organization or unit might be in the transition process. In the following section, four stages of change are characterized, with a brief description as well as suggestions for some appropriate change agent interventions.[17]

Phase One: Denial

Denial, which may also be characterized by numbness or confusion, is often a manifestation of an unconscious unwillingness to accept change. Those endorsing the change may miss the intensity of this stage since it is not always behaviorally visible. But by trying to move too fast, they may miss the natural need to mourn and unwittingly push the next phase, resistance, underground.

During denial, change agents should equip all individuals with ample information to help them understand what to expect. They need to give them time to let things sink in and schedule forums to allow them to talk things over.

Phase Two: Resistance

Resistance occurs when people, having gone through the denial stage, begin to focus on how the change affects them. At this time, they may experience self-doubt, anger, depression, or any number of manifestations of anxiety. Some people may engage in nonproductive behavior by converting their energy elsewhere, perhaps by trying to obtain another job. Others may become counterproductive and begin to take out their frustrations on the company, perhaps by reducing their output or by staying out of work.

Change agents, acknowledging the natural resistance stage, need to allow people to express their feelings and share their experience. It is important that concerns about the prospective change be aired in the open so that they can be addressed in a forthright manner. It may also be comforting to discover through a sharing process that others in the organization feel the same way.

Phase Three: Exploration

During exploration, people finally begin to accept the idea of the change and can begin to focus their attention on the future. Things are still unsettled, though, as they attempt to determine what their new responsibilities may be, how they may have to change in relating to one another, and what the form of the new organization may look like.

Since this phase can still be confusing, change agents can assist organizational members by trying to get management to conduct brainstorming, visioning, and planning sessions. The organization needs to set priorities and goals, follow up on current projects, and provide resources to help people make any necessary transitions in their knowledge and skills.

Phase Four: Commitment

By the commitment phase, people become willing to refocus on the new mission and build action plans to make it work. They have re-negotiated their roles and expectations and have re-aligned their values and actions to commit to a new era of productivity.

This is the phase for building teams and aligning the entire organization toward a mission and long-term goals. The change agent can help management design development and reward systems to keep the organization in a learning mode that will also help it cope with future events.

Facilitator Training

The practice of facilitation is not natural for most people. Facilitators often require some form of facilitator training so that they can apply the skills until they become second nature. Through facilitator training, novices not only increase their proficiency in facilitation tools, they also enhance their confidence in handling challenging groups, difficult group members, and outside circumstances. Often, training will also link any facilitation strategy to the stage of development of the group and to the particular needs of given teams.

A critical issue in work-based learning that affects facilitator training is the fallout expected from both participants and facilitators in transforming learning from a planned approach, typical in conventional training, to the emergent or reflective basis characterizing work-based learning. Participants unaccustomed to directing their own learning or who separate learning from work might resist this approach. They might find reflective practices to be "soft" or too emotional and become defensive if forced to face their own practice assumptions or explore their own inferences about self and others. They often attend training programs to get answers, not to create questions. They don't intend to "look bad" or not in control in front of their peers. And even if they find the experience useful, they may find little invitation to use reflective skills when they return to their regular job, especially if some of the learning experience has occurred off-site.

Meanwhile, facilitators, accustomed to positive reactions from participants and content to control the learning process, may find it threatening to hand over the responsibility for learning to the learners. They may unwittingly collude with participants to return to a planned, control approach under the guise of reflective practice. For example, without sufficient practice in inquiry processes, some facilitators might use probing to get participants to arrive at pre-planned responses or solutions.

Facilitator training might well include a segment, therefore, that acknowledges the resistance anticipated on the part of both participant and self. The comfort level of the group and of particular group members with regard to emergent learning and reflective practices will predetermine how fast facilitators can move in turning the learning over to the group itself. Facilitators need to be sure that they will have sufficient time to create a team climate for self-examination and self-development. Relinquishing control too quickly might expose group members to unproductive anxiety. Participants might experience the attendant lack of structure as an abdication of responsibility by the facilitator. Having the courage to face one's full range of behavior, including one's reasoning processes, takes time, patience, and above all, skill. Facilitators need to acquire a practical artistry that can guide them in knowing when they can gradually yield control of the group to the members themselves.

Considering more formally the content of facilitator training programs, a few constants seem to emerge. Typically, there is a didactic component on basic group dynamics, including such topics as group process, group roles and norms, stages of development, and intervention methods. Trainees are then given time to practice facilitation in small groups. Often, videotaping is available to help them see their own actions and the verbal and nonverbal responses of group members. A key to the process is the opportunity for immediate feedback from the other trainees as well as from an instructor regarding the effectiveness of various intervention approaches and styles. Some training programs also form learning teams to help support novices as they try out experiments in facilitation in their back-home settings. In learning teams, trainees can also practice the tools and skills introduced in the classroom segments.

Training approaches might align with the ideology represented by the respective work-based learning approach. Action learning purists would most likely suggest that immersion in learning team experiences is the best device to learn how to become a set adviser. In action learning, the facilitator tends to be most committed to keeping individuals and the team as a whole focused on learning from one another's real-time work experiences. The emphasis in this case is on the rational behavior of the set members. In other work-based learning settings, the learning team may focus on some of the underlying and even unconscious activity going on below the surface. Facilitators interested in this level of discovery, according to Manfred Kets de Vries, require a modicum of clinical training in addition to reasonably sophisticated comprehension of group and organizational dynamics.[18] Like it or not, defensive and irrational dynamics are bound to arise in group settings. Furthermore, project experiences occur in an organizational environment that at times may be dysfunctional. Knowing how to work through a holistic analysis of barriers to learning would be an important complement to the skill set of the trained learning team facilitator.

Facilitator Differences

Beyond the constants of basic facilitator behavior, differences across work-based learning approaches may call for differences in facilitator styles. As examples, let's consider some differences in facilitation between action learning and action science methods.

In classic action learning, the facilitator's role is by most accounts more passive than in action science. Revans conceived of the role as that of a *mirror* to merely illustrate conditions in the set such that participants learn by themselves and from each other.[19] Hence, facilitators need to display a good deal of patience in order to permit member skills in insight and inquiry to unfold. Naturally, some early modeling of active reflection might be required. Facilitators, however, are not to forget a critical precept of action learning: make the learner the center of the experience.

Although action science facilitators would subscribe to the action learning tenet that eventually the group assume the management of the experience, action science skills require more practice and development. It is difficult to learn how to surface inconsistencies between a participant's governing values and action strategies. Besides modeling, the facilitator needs to spend time actually teaching and demonstrating Model II learning skills. In working through individual and interpersonal problems, learners at times may have to reveal their defenses, placing them at given moments in a personally vulnerable position. Facilitators need to be not only adequately trained but also quite active in helping members work through their feelings. Eventually, as the membership of the group gains confidence in using action science skills, learners can serve as co-facilitators and even begin to challenge the facilitator's action strategies. At this point, the facilitator and the membership can transform themselves into a collaborative learning community.

Level of Discourse

One way to view facilitator differences is to consider whether an intervention is to entail a practical or emancipatory level of discourse. The practical level, most associated with action learning, solicits inquiry regarding how others see someone who has been or is currently engaged in action. Action science, by using emancipatory discourse, takes the intervention into another, perhaps sequential, level. It becomes permissible to challenge not only the actor's theories-in-use but also the questioner's perceptions and inferences to the point of questioning the entire system's frame of reference. For many participants, and even for the system under scrutiny, action science intervention can be threatening because it has the potential to cause an entire reframing of the practice world. Even participants in responsible positions may not have sufficient authority or independence of action to challenge their cultures at the level of exposure sanctioned by action science.

Consider how the respective processes might work. Action learning focuses more on problems arising from the handling or *mis*handling of on-the-job project interventions. Although these problems might be recent, they are not necessarily here-and-now issues arising from ongoing interactions among members of the set. Occasionally, interpersonal issues are surfaced, but their elicitation is designed more to increase the communication effectiveness among set members than to probe into the mental models of individual members. When the action learning set is functioning smoothly, feedback to individuals tends to be open, direct, and unburdened by hidden agendas.

Action science process meanwhile may work on workplace problems but is just as likely to focus on here-and-now interactions occurring among members of the learning team. Where workplace problems are chosen, the group process is not necessarily designed to improve the work activity directly. Rather, the selection of the problem is merely a means to help participants learn to appreciate their reasoning processes better. Facilitators are also just as likely to create real-time experiments (perhaps using other members as role players) to help participants focus on their mental models. For example, they might elicit the attributions and evaluations the participants are making about themselves, about others, or about the situation being depicted, or they might have the participants slow down and—using the ladder of inference—reflect upon the inferential steps taken in leaping from data to conclusions.

A Case in Point

Consider the case of a vice president of a retailer of lumber and hardware products, who is concerned about the lack of commitment to the business on the part of the chain's part-time check-out clerks.[20] He has undertaken a project to assess their concerns to see if he can determine why their motivation is lower than their full-time counterparts. In an action learning set, the facilitator might start by having this member, call him Jim, describe his project and anticipated intervention in full detail. In a fairly well-developed set, members may join in by probing into these details and the underlying assumptions of his plans and actions. For example, Jim might determine that the best way to obtain data from the part-time clerks would be to conduct focus groups in groups of three or four corresponding to their work shifts. A group member in the set might challenge the focus group methodology as too intimidating to obtain reliable information, suggesting that Jim would be better off interviewing select clerks individually or even having someone else less senior in the company interview them. Jim would then reflect on his intervention approach and decide whether he might change his plan of action. Other questions might attempt to ascertain why Jim has chosen this project over others. Is this one that the president has a particular interest in, or is it a genuine concern of Jim's?

In some action learning sets, questions and responses of this nature might ensue for the entire duration of the meeting. Notice that the focus tends to be on this one member alone, at least until time is allocated to another member or to the set as a whole. There is a lot of probing going on, but it tends to focus on the member's plans and actions that are typically taking place or about to take place in the work setting. When the focus shifts to the set itself, attention is directed to how to make the group more effective as a learning vehicle for its membership. This might require learning how to engage in active listening and offer feedback more effectively, how to check on one's assumptions about others, how to apply classroom theories in practice, and so on.

An action science group in probing the underlying reasoning processes used by individuals in the group has a different texture. It might start by focusing on Jim's problem with his part-time checkout clerks. But rather than spend time planning and offering suggestions to him regarding useful interventions, the facilitator and group members will focus a lot more on Jim and his organization.

For example, the facilitator might start out by asking Jim why this problem has been standing around looking for a solution. Jim might answer that it's because it hasn't been a high-priority item and that the managers assumed that the "de-motivation" of the part-time staff couldn't be helped. The facilitator might then ask Jim if he feels the same way as "management." Jim might answer that he has always been concerned but didn't feel that the president considered it a priority. At this point, the facilitator might ask whether Jim as a rule disavows those issues with which he believes the president won't agree. Jim explains that not only does he monitor what he says but that others in management do the same. No one, including him, wants to be seen as contradictory. In action science terms, Jim has not only offered an observation but has also provided an inference regarding his perception of the behavior of others.

Although it might be possible to stop here, most action science facilitators would inquire whether Jim would like to pursue the issue further. Assuming he would, the facilitation could proceed using a number of different methods. For example, Jim's inferences could be drawn out more by asking what he assumes drives the president's behavior. The facilitator and group might also ask what makes Jim and his colleagues so reluctant to bring up so-called contradictory issues with the president. Another technique might be to have Jim prepare a case in which he recounts a conversation he might have with the president about a controversial issue. In the margin or on one side of the page adjoining the narrative, he would indicate what he and the president were thinking when they responded in particular ways. A data map might also be drawn wherein Jim compares his action strategies using Model I and Model II learning approaches. Jim might be invited to role-play a conversation with the president, played by another group member, wherein he might practice a Model II action strategy. Further, real-time conversations might be constructed whereby members of the group agree to role-play certain key figures in this scenario to demonstrate Jim's cognitive and behavioral responses. Whatever method is chosen, the ultimate purpose is to surface defensive or inhibiting behaviors that might be blocking Jim and his colleagues from engaging in a productive dialogue, one that permits them to achieve useful and just outcomes.

The case suggests that facilitators may need to clarify ahead of time whether they will be pursuing action learning or action science change. Participants need to know in advance whether anticipated changes will arise from frequent questioning of their action interventions, common in action learning, or from in-depth exploration of their reasoning processes, more typical of action science. Likewise, organizational sponsors need to know whether they'll get a completed project of significance in addition to prospectively more effective interventionists or an organizational culture in which there is far more consistency, even under stressful conditions, between what people say they will do and what in fact they do.

Distress Facilitation

As groups develop in work-based learning, it is likely that facilitators might have to confront the emergence of emotional reactions on the part of team members. Social power relations and emotions associated with differences among people, although not sufficiently addressed in group facilitation accounts, represent facts of life for groups that can either be sidestepped or faced directly.[21] Learning teams clearly evoke more than just rational behavior among members. Although typically left within the unconscious, feelings develop almost immediately among members, and some might come out in the normal course of dialogue. Craig Johnson, a former set member enrolled in the action learning program at the University of Huddersfield in the United Kingdom, noting his reactions from the experience, quipped, "[Such programs] should perhaps come with a health warning on the back of the books. Becoming aware of the depth of one's own ignorance and being reminded of one's own weaknesses is not a particularly palatable process at times."

It is disputable whether deeply held emotions should be brought out in a learning team or whether they should be set aside. Many of our emotions are simply not accessible to us, having been safely placed into our unconscious. They remain there unless solicited or pointed out by others in the group. Since learning teams are by no means therapy groups, it is important to know the role that emotions should play in the deliberations and process of the team. Should the facilitator encourage the release of affective content?

Facilitators have to keep in mind that members of learning teams typically come from organizations that are built on bureaucratic principles, which make little room for the expression of emotions.[22] Emotions are seen as an interference in an organization's functional purposes. Yet most of us in organizations recognize that we respond to phenomena emotionally, oftentimes without conscious awareness. From a work-based learning perspective, facilitators need to consider a number of delicate issues that might have a considerable impact on learning itself:

1. Teams need not focus only on pleasant feelings. There are times when learning requires the surfacing of unpleasant experiences and memories. People arrive at their learning team with their life issues, some uplifting, others unpleasant.

2. There are typically certain emotions that are not only encouraged but even indulged in organizations (for example, pride in being first, bearing up in the face of adversity). On the other hand, there might be emotions otherwise proscribed that might be bottled up in individuals, keeping them from performing their best work (for example, a resentment toward a co-worker who is thought to have stolen one's ideas).

3. Human beings find themselves in difficult emotional states—fear, guilt, depression, rage—in the course of their lives. Although it is not the job of a manager or of one's associates to alleviate these states, they may deserve attention to the extent that they significantly affect on-the-job performance.

4. Personal development is a legitimate topic for learning. For some people, the struggle for self-realization requires the need to uncover and work through the sources of their fears and anxiety. Members of a learning team might also choose to try out new ways of behaving in order to alter ineffectual patterns in their existing behavior.

5. There are instances when employees are manipulated in their work through seduction or coercion. Although "victims" may initially be unaware of such manipulation, they may need encouragement to face the conditions of manipulation, be it by acknowledging the circumstances, changing their environment, or even confronting the perpetrator.

Höpfl and Linstead contend that there are two dimensions of emotions at work that are legitimate for learning teams to address—learning to feel and feeling to learn:[23]

Learning to Feel. How do we recognize the emotional learning that is taking place, to know what we feel, to discuss which of our feelings are problematic, to become sensitive to the feelings of others?

Feeling to Learn. How do we transfer a threatening and
oppressive atmosphere in the workplace to one that is
relaxed and supportive?

Although the treatment of emotions within the workplace and
within learning teams per se is a controversial subject, I believe that
facilitators need to endorse the communication of emotions. Feelings can either expedite or block our learning. Perhaps the most
eloquent spokesperson in behalf of this perspective is Peter Reason,
whose action strategy, known as *cooperative inquiry*, explicitly makes
room for the management of anxiety that arises as participants examine their world and their practice.[24] Cooperative inquiry, however, has other characteristics familiar to the work-based learning
approaches already described in this book. In particular, Reason
views participants in cooperative inquiry as co-researchers and co-
subjects. As co-researchers, participants contribute to generating
ideas, designing and managing projects, and drawing conclusions
from their experiences. As co-subjects, they willingly participate in
the activity that is being researched. As in the case of action learning, participants might choose to work on some kind of action taking place in the outside world; however, cooperative inquiry also
makes room for introspective experiences among members, be they
examinations of the self or of states of consciousness.

What is most particularistic about cooperative inquiry is the
straightforward view that underlying conflicts and distresses among
members be explicitly acknowledged and worked through.[25] Accordingly, Reason suggests that facilitators receive sufficient training
in counseling to minimally facilitate the expression and exploration
of feelings and emotions, be they within their project experiences
or even within the group.

Although I might not wish to go as far as Reason in advocating
the use of counseling as a facilitation tool, the exploration of affect
strikes me as a useful agenda for learning teams, provided that individuals do not become so distraught that they lose minimal control
within the team environment. In these instances, the facilitator

needs to acknowledge that certain members may require additional psychotherapeutic resources to help them work through some of the deeper, troubling sources of their anxiety.

An example might provide some insight into the types of emotional problems that learning teams can safely examine under the watchful eye of a trained facilitator. Vince and Martin present the case of an individual manager in an action learning set working through a concern relating to a member of her staff.[26] One of the members of the set (not the facilitator) points out that this manager seems to be avoiding her strong competitive feelings toward her associate. The manager's immediate impulse is to deny the competition, but something in what her set colleague has said rings true. Vince and Martin go on to describe what happened:

> She feels suddenly on the spot, uncertain, as if she would rather be elsewhere. However, because she felt some truth had been acknowledged, she talks about envying her staff member's ability to be liked by the rest of the team and the competitiveness this envy generated. Through their questioning, set members . . . provide her with the insight that her envy is a block to her effectiveness both with the specific individual and with her team. She resolves to undertake some practical actions which she imagines will overcome this particular problem.

This case demonstrates how providing a forum for examining emotional content can also lead to learning. In some cases, it can even lead to a breakthrough that can produce new practices more in sync with our values, intentions, and desires.

Critical Facilitation

Earlier in this book, I have referred to the philosophy of praxis as that deeply reflective and interactive process of learning from our actions. In some quarters, it has also assumed a critical nature not because it is directly associated with a change in the social order but because its inquisitive orientation can highlight contradictions inherent in the power structure. It often requires self-transformation at the same time that it scrutinizes the world around us. Given this view of praxis, the facilitator may assume a more particularistic process role. Critical facilitation promotes a discourse in which members of the group are encouraged to challenge not only the statements they and others make but also the assumptions they may be relying upon in producing the statements. Habermas referred to this kind of discourse as *argumentation*, an intersubjective exchange that can occur under an ideal speech situation—in which no single individual nor point of view would be privileged or free from challenge.[27] Equal power is extended to all participants, and decisions are based upon mutual consent rather than on tradition, greed, dogma, or coercion.

Once engaged in critical discourse, even the facilitator's statements and interventions are themselves subject to validity testing. In this way, the facilitator's open inquiry can model critical praxis for the group. In addition to modeling, the facilitator can also ask the participants to debrief critical exchanges, using four tests suggested by Habermas: comprehensibility, normative acceptance, sincerity, and interpretation. These four tests have been converted by Wendy Gregory, Norma Romm, and myself into specific questions that may be asked during the debriefing:[28]

1. Do you understand what the speaker has said?

2. Do you agree with the speaker's point?

3. Do you believe the speaker is being sincere?

4. Do you agree with the speaker's interpretation of the facts and how his or her conclusions were arrived at?

By debriefing group discussions using such questions, group members can be encouraged to engage in critical praxis that allows for challenge to expressed views. It is through such validity-checking discourse that groups can build a forum for open exchange and mutual learning.

Advanced Facilitator Skills
in Reflective Practice

Now that we've considered how facilitators can encourage open dialogue and critical reflection in a group, it might be useful to bring some of these ideas together in developing a portfolio of skills for consideration by facilitators. Consistent with my views about group development, these skills may be introduced by facilitators but can gradually be assumed by other facilitating members of the group itself. In the model presented in Figure 8.2, five principal skills are illustrated, which my colleague, Robert Leaver, and I believe represent such a portfolio. The five skills are *being, speaking, disclosing, testing,* and *probing.* The skill of being is central and pervasive, cutting across the other skills, for it represents the facilitator's presence and vulnerability in creating a reflective climate in the group. Recalling the definition of reflection introduced in Chapter Six, reflection is a stepping back to ponder meaning. The first step of reflection is to experience or even more simply to be. In accomplishing being,

Figure 8.2. The Five Skills of Reflective Practice

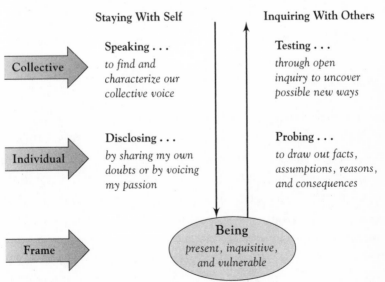

we try to experience and describe situations, even our own involvement in them, without imputing meaning to them or without evaluating them. If facilitators are successful in modeling or helping team members learn *to be*, they can begin to explore differences and diverse experiences together and learn from one another without initial polarization. In this way, they learn to explain together.[29]

The skill of *being* can place us in a vulnerable state in the sense that we do not rely on defending ourselves against experience. The focus is rather on opening up to experience and to the interpersonal environment around us. Bill Isaacs refers to this process as *suspending*, in which one makes the contents of our consciousness available to others.[30] One doesn't have to change anything but rather just notices. This process produces a reflective response, which can be characterized by a number of attributes that are in direct contrast to the defensive posture.[31]

Instead of maintaining unrealistic standards	One sets realistic expectations
Instead of expressing doubt	One displays tolerance
Instead of concentrating on self-expression	One uses listening
Instead of being self absorbed	One conveys humility
Instead of feeling out of depth	One feels open to learn
Instead of feeling out of context	One becomes open to experience

Referring to the dimensions of the model, being itself occupies the dimension we call the *frame mode*. Framing refers to how we think about a situation, more specifically, how we select, name, and organize facts to make a story to ourselves about what is going on and what to do in a particular situation. In the collective mode, we extend our contributions and inquiry to all members of the group, whereas in the individual mode, we listen to our own voice or address one individual at a time. The cross-dimensions are *staying with self* and *inquiring with others*. At times, we make personal contributions to the group or focus attention on ourselves. At other times, we extend and dedicate attention to others.

Returning to the skill of *being,* as a central skill it may entail staying with oneself or taking action toward others. It is most concerned with exploring differences and diverse experiences apart from the preconceived notions of members. The being skill models an inquisitive, nonjudgmental attitude toward group phenomena. It is not about achieving; it is about being present. Some of its components include inviting questions and comments, considering one's own positions as hypotheses to be tested, and acknowledging expressions of vulnerability by others. An example of being might occur in an advertising group about ready to launch a new campaign. Everything seems to be in place, but the group leader (who might also be a facilitator of reflective practices), who has actually pushed a particular design, might ask the group to pause with her in a state of vulnerability. She wonders aloud if something has been overlooked or whether the group might take one more look at the design.

The second reflective skill, *speaking,* is in the upper-left section of the diagram, signifying that it seeks to articulate a collective voice from within ourselves. The purpose of speaking is to use language to help people slow down and understand one another and to help them explore their processes beyond an immediate agenda. It may entail summarizing the true and full words of a group participant, or it may call for reciting a poem to open people's hearts. Facilitators using speaking like to develop images that may characterize the state of a group at different points. For example, one group never lost the image presented at an earlier time by their facilitator, who said the team was operating like "a cargo plane having to make its destination to Istanbul but with one engine knocked out."

In the third skill, *disclosing,* the facilitator stays with oneself but at the same time shares doubts or voices passion. By using disclosing, the facilitator may unveil his or her feelings at a given moment based on what has transpired or may present a story to reveal the depth of one's experience. The idea is to help the group learn more about its own membership. Another cue to promote disclosing is to ask what one might say to help the team know you better. There's a story about George Washington that reveals the power of disclosing. Unknown to all but the most astute historians, there was a substantial movement during the waning years of the American Revolutionary War for the military to take over the civilian government and install Washington as king. At one historic point, Washington appeared before some of these military officers to condemn this affront to democracy, the cornerstone of the entire revolutionary movement. His speech, however, was falling on deaf ears. Then, at one point, as he helplessly attempted to read a missive from a member of Congress, he paused to reach for a pair of glasses, something only his closest aides had known that he needed. Then he quietly confessed to his officers: "Gentlemen, you will permit me to put on my spectacles, for I have not only grown gray but almost blind in the service of my country." The men wept. It was this statement of vulnerability alone that was thought to have nipped the movement in the bud: How could the men ignore this selfless commander who reminded them that he was one of them?

Testing, the fourth reflective skill, is an open-ended query, directed toward the group as a whole, that attempts to uncover new ways of thinking and behaving. In using testing, the facilitator may ask the group to consider its own process or may attempt to explore underlying assumptions previously taken for granted. In testing, the facilitator is trying to promote a process of collective inquiry. Some of the component skills are asking for a process check, playing devil's advocate, or acting out a scenario to explore an option. As an example, rather than offer another opinion to help a group resolve an impasse, the facilitator might suggest that group members cease defending their positions for a moment and turn to a discussion about ways to resolve the impasse.

Finally, in *probing,* the facilitator mobilizes the group or a member by making a direct inquiry, typically to one member at a time, to find out the facts, reasons, assumptions, inferences, and possible consequences of a given suggestion or action. For example, probing might attempt to point out inconsistencies in members' reasoning patterns, perhaps helping them to uncover the assumptions and beliefs behind particular actions. In using probing, however, the facilitator needs to be careful not to interrogate or make any member feel on the spot or defensive. On the other hand, probing may initially have to make some members uncomfortable if they are asked to consider assumptions that had been hidden even from their own consciousness. As an example, consider a frank inquiry posed to a member named Frank:

> Frank, every time that I can recall when we've thought about broaching our plans with Anna, you chime in that she is someone that no one can work with and a person to be avoided at all costs. I wonder if you've had some experiences with her that you can share that would help us, and perhaps you too, understand what seems to be making Anna such an obstacle. Maybe there is a way that would make it possible for perhaps one of us, including yourself, to approach her.

9

The Action Project

Paddle your own canoe.
—Maurice Kirkpatrick

As readers may have surmised, the technique of the action project is perhaps the most consistent tool associated with work-based learning programs. Whatever theories, competencies, or practices are exposed to participants, the ultimate learning of these subjects may depend upon their trying them out in actual situations. There is benefit to having participants test their newfound skills in a simulated setting, but ultimately—as has been emphasized throughout this book—there can be no substitute for practice in the very midst of real live experience. Only then will participants know whether they can change their assumptions and behaviors online. Only then will they know whether a particular conceptual theory might help them wend their way through an operating problem or whether they may need to devise a new and alternative practice theory to help them make sense out of their actual behavior. In the following sections, I discuss a number of elements to be considered in designing the work-based action project.

Project Choice and Operation

In order to replicate real-time conditions, it is normally advised that projects have strategic value to the organization or unit within the organization that is sponsoring the project. The project should contribute meaningfully to and perhaps even challenge the goals established by the sponsoring unit. The project could entail an assignment that is already being done but perhaps in a unique or more effective manner. The Executive Leadership Institute at service giant ARAMARK, to be discussed in Chapter Eleven, uses projects to help the leadership team assess how the competitive environment is changing, in particular, to know "when to shed skins" and shift to a new segment or grow a business.[1]

Most projects are experimental in at least two ways: (1) they tend to involve doing something that has never been done before, and (2) there is no known solution to the problem, or there are at least different opinions regarding how the problem is to be solved. Another way to look at project choice is to consider problems with solutions that may evolve from any number of unpredictable circumstances and conditions, which need to be surfaced during the course of the venture. An ultimate guideline is to consider projects that otherwise might have been contracted to a consultant.

Given this description, there can be no definitive list of project topics; projects need to be tailored to the individual unit sponsoring the endeavor. However, it is possible to list some prototypical topics to give the reader a flavor for the significance of these ventures. Projects, then, have entailed such concerns as:

- Developing candidates for a merger or acquisition
- Devising a marketing plan for a new line of business
- Identifying logistical cost savings
- Developing synergies across divisions
- Integrating suppliers into the business plan
- Demonstrating the social and economic trends affecting key markets
- Combating private-label competing products
- Improving the processing of the electronic medical record
- Designing an integrated customer database
- Streamlining the customer support process
- Creating a shared business service center

- Developing a knowledge storage and transfer process
- Improving management of a company's patents
- Streamlining an invoice processing and payment system
- Enhancing the work-order process used by facilities management staff
- Creating a strategy for a new business unit
- Developing a plan for revamping or integrating service departments
- Deciding whether to invest in a new technology
- Integrating technology into work design and output
- Engaging in cross-selling across business units
- Fostering integration among business units to improve customer service
- Developing community-corporate partnerships
- Improving the corporate image of a company through a community-wide survey
- Designing a human resource intranet
- Streamlining the delivery schedule of a supplier
- Enhancing company-wide communication using information technologies
- Easing work-life conflicts through a comprehensive benefits package
- Improving customer service through focus groups
- Producing a strategy to improve sales performance
- Enhancing the commitment of temporary workers
- Devising employment alternatives to downsizing
- Developing a balanced scorecard to evaluate an organization's practices

The logic Revans used to support the use of a here-and-now project is the opportunity it affords to confront real change.[2] Revans was also concerned that the work be neither too difficult or challenging nor too easy or unchallenging. Projects should also provide milestones for assessing meaningful progress so that participants can take advantage of the reflective components in work-based learning. A useful approach is to generate milestones at appropriate junctures, perhaps at learning team meetings, where the project might be discussed. These milestones need to be clear, specific, and measurable.[3] That way, colleagues in the learning team can assess whether in fact progress has been made in the interim. For example, if Rhonda were to say that to establish a proper setting to get her project off the ground, she will need to intervene to improve the conduct of her boss, Jim, at staff meetings, that would not be as useful as saying:

> Next Friday, I plan to meet with Jim prior to our staff meeting. I plan to point out to him that though his opinions are always well thought out, he tends to dominate the meeting in terms of air time. Some of us with important contributions never get a chance to get a word in. He seems especially resistant to input from Susan, who seems reduced to a silent observer. After dialoguing with him, we might work out a way to determine if the staff meeting improves in terms of member participation. Perhaps, he might even let me model some of my newfound facilitation skills.

Notice that with this set of statements, members of the learning team will have specific items to follow up on at the next learning team meeting. They will also have qualitative measures to determine her progress; for example, did she meet with Jim, how did he respond, did he change his behavior at the meeting, what did he do that was different, did he include Susan, did he allow Rhonda to facilitate, and if so, what were her interventions and how did other staff respond?

The only way to have this type of productive dialogue is to be engaged in projects that are realistic as opposed to makeshift. Programs typically are designed to give participants the opportunity to learn from live experience, not from simulated experience. It is the confronting of unexpected occurrences consistent with real problems that underlies praxis. Consider the example of Brian Caie, writing about his experience in the action learning MBA program sponsored by the International Management Centres in Buckingham, in the United Kingdom.[4] Brian had begun the implementation phase of his project, which consisted of introducing a team briefing strategy into his company. He had gotten management committed to the process and had even begun training supervisors in its use. Then, in the space of a few months, his sponsor, the sponsor's boss, and the company president were all transferred out of the division. His new managers, though sympathetic to employee communications, felt uncomfortable supporting the team briefing approach since they played no role in its development.

Brian's project had to return to the drawing board for a subsequent relaunch. In retrospect, Brian reported that the crisis in his project led to the greatest learning from the experience:

> [The crisis] provided the opportunity to review the system, reflect on its shortcomings and improve upon the initial approach. The team briefing system ultimately put in place survives to the present day because of the care taken to implement it properly and the lessons learned in what became known as the pilot project.

The strategic value of projects cannot be overstated in the sense of their having impact on the direction of the sponsoring unit and subsequently systemically across the entire organization. They're also often linked to a prospective or ongoing change effort. Unfortunately, some projects are undertaken as planning or analysis studies. Once the analysis is completed, it is presented to an official who might decide whether to accept it or not. If the decision is "go," another individual or team might be assembled to work on the recommendations of the original project team. This form of project is not an action project, nor does it provide an opportunity for sufficient reflective practice for significant double- and triple-loop learning. Projects in work-based learning are best designed when participants know that their actions are potentially going to have an impact and thus need to be evaluated against normal, difficult operating standards. Planning studies often do not require the level of commitment that might lead to serious self- and public examination.

There is also an element of scope to action projects that requires a good deal of time and concentration. Projects often involve participants in endeavors outside their own department and may require the support and commitment of other colleagues, perhaps to form a team, as a basis for undertaking the project on a useful scale. Some participants, particularly those who have not yet had strategic responsibilities, may not have had experience with projects of significant scope and time. They might be more familiar with projects that can be accomplished quickly or that might produce short-term results. For example, in reporting on project work in a transport authority, West and Choueke noted that self-initiated projects focused on such operational issues as increasing the level of involvement in office work, adding computing facilities to alleviate workload pressures, and enhancing communication between external staff and office workers.[5] Working through more ambitious action projects, especially taking the necessary time at the outset to pose the question accurately, frame the problem, and collect data, would require more advanced skills in strategic reasoning.

Another key question in project choice centers on whether the participant in the work-based program or the sponsor should ultimately select the project. If the work is to have strategic value, there may be some sympathy in having the executive sponsoring the activity decide which problems need to be addressed or which tasks need to be done. On the other hand, learning is facilitated when it makes most sense to participants; hence, there is an argument for letting the participants choose their own projects, perhaps even for purposes of forming a community of practice.[6]

One rationale for allowing flexibility in project selection is to provide an opportunity for participants to experience double- and triple-loop learning. If there is not enough flexibility built into the project design, participants—though giving the executive sponsors what they want—may not arrive at a solution that gets at the root of an issue and may not produce much of a learning opportunity for the sponsors themselves or for their organization.

Another argument on behalf of participant choice is the straightforward view that the people directly involved in a project should have the right to determine its direction. Robert Kittrell offers two reasons for this perspective:[7]

> The first one is the most obvious; people pay attention to and follow through on projects they have had a direct say in developing and articulating. This might be known as Ownership or Enlightened Self-Interest.
>
> The second one is known as Personal Responsibility. It comes from our fundamental job as educators to enlighten people so that they are in a position to help themselves. This means challenging those we work with to identify, face, and address those core problems and/or challenges that keep them or their organization from advancing toward a worthwhile future goal or mission.
>
> It is working to develop within them the courage to learn not only from what they are doing, but more importantly to question (not why they are doing what they are doing, but) the basis on which they have chosen as they have, and how the projects they selected connect to their hopes and aspirations for the future, be it personally or professionally or organizationally.

Where project choice ensues after the formation of a learning team, team members may have to decide on which problem or set of problems in the organization to focus. In this case, there are three questions that the members may wish to consider once they derive a list of possible projects:

1. "*Who knows?*" Which members of the team know not only about the problem but also about the opportunities and inherent difficulties it will present to the team.

2. "*Who cares?*" Who among the team and within the organization feels sufficiently strongly about the issue to do something about it.

3. "*Who can?*" The team typically wishes to tackle something that will effect change or progress, in which case, some members may need to be allied with senior staff who have both the power and motivation to sponsor and to endorse the change effort.

The issue of project selection raised here is critical in work-based learning, for it poses the question of whether the objectives and benefits of the program extend to the organization or only to the individual. The obvious answer is that it needs to be both. The word *learning* in work-based learning does not suggest individual learning alone. Through project work that stretches the boundaries of methods to elicit and then confront organizational problems, the organization learns new ways to examine its fundamental goals and processes. Nevertheless, individuals undertaking the project are not pawns in a system; rather, they are unique individuals who wish to develop and to enrich their own professional and personal lives. Thus, projects require the imprint of human creativity. They should evolve as participants who plan and manage them evolve. They need not be overly pre-designed. Morgan and Ramirez noted that "the more one designs the process in advance, the less opportunity for self-organization according to the insights which emerge."[8]

So the bottom line seems to be this: keep the executive sponsors involved, make sure the project is of real value to the organization, but build in enough flexibility for not only participants' buy-in but also for their shaping of the project. According to David Ashton, former chief executive of Cable & Wireless College, this shouldn't be an onerous task since most managers and executives enjoy working on real stretching problems of direct relevance to the business.[9] On the other hand, they do need structure and support to surface and reinforce their learning agendas.

Executives are very involved in the action learning Results Based Leadership (RBL) program at Southern Company, the Atlanta-based public utilities holding company.[10] Top managers from the subsidiaries nominate the participants for the program, taking into consideration diversity of function to bring fresh perspectives to the business problem assigned to the teams. An executive committee, called the leadership pipeline development council, is responsible for the project teams. Each team's sponsor is a vice president from various business divisions. The teams work on key business issues affecting their divisions. Meanwhile, the sponsors, eager to take advantage of the teams' expertise, provide resources to the projects, such as in-house subject experts, who can provide them with the information and tools to jump-start their work.

Project Presentations

The criticality of project choice and operation is matched by the importance of project presentations. Having worked on an assignment of value for a significant period, at least in the case of most projects, participants are given an opportunity to present their results. Although most programs call for such presentations at the conclusion of the experience, an action learning program sponsored at the Oxford University Press included an interim presentation to the publishing services board.[11] In those instances when participants are asked to make a presentation as a capstone to the experience, although there are likely to be some who have lost energy and are no longer motivated to present their findings, the typical scenario finds participants quite eager to make a presentation. The key questions on project presentations tend to be just these two:

1. Who should attend the presentations?
2. How should they be done?

Who should attend? There is little question that the direct sponsors of the project should attend the project presentations, but there is also sympathy for having even higher-ups attend, especially where the project has had a strategic impact on the organization as a whole. There are two constraints in having officers present if they are not sponsors. First, the project may not have a direct bearing on their operation and thus they may not be an interested party. Second, executive presence may inhibit the presentation, causing it to look more like a briefing than a learning experience.

How should they be done? Although the presentation of one's project should have a celebratory element to it, it is also best viewed as an opportunity to share one's learning from the experience as well as to present results and make recommendations. It is an opportunity for all members and related stakeholders in the work-based learning program to reflect on the experience as part of a learning community; therefore, there should at least be a balance between "show and substance." What needs to be avoided is glossing over project results that were less than satisfactory for fear of executive retaliation. On the other hand, participants should not completely avoid an element of "sell" in their presentation. After all, they have worked hard on their project and they want it to succeed. Part of the learning in the action project is knowing how to manage the political dynamics in the organization in order to give their project a good chance to move to the next level of full implementation.

In a work-based learning program in a major northeast utility company, with which I have served as a learning facilitator, senior executives from the division sponsoring the project not only attend the formal project presentations, they also sit in on a session devoted to individual and team learning. Executives from other divisions are invited both to the session on learning and to the formal presentations when their area of expertise pertain to the substantive nature of the project.

In another setting, the projects receive a high level of visibility because of their sponsorship by the top management team, including the CEO. Members of the top group, in addition to the sponsor, attend the presentations if they fall within their functional purview. Occasionally, they bring their business unit heads if they might be interested in the project team's recommendations. The teams realize and appreciate the critical nature of their work, given this level of scrutiny. However, it also adds a fair degree of anxiety, especially prior to the presentation. Since the program is designed for talent development, presentations tend to be most engaging when they evolve into a free and open exchange about both the merits of the project and the learning generated for each individual participant, for the team as a whole, and prospectively for the unit contemplating the recommendations specified.

Project Composition

Projects may be initiated as individual ventures or may be staffed by a team of participants from the same organization or even occasionally by cross-site participants. Even if undertaken as an individual endeavor, the project may inevitably involve other people in the organization or external to the organization (vendors, customers, and so forth). Oftentimes project participants will recruit others to form a team to help them work on a project, even though the other members may not be formally participating in the work-based learning program. Microsoft, for example, maintains an expert network that stores knowledge competencies and personal profiles to help teams find individuals with particular expertise necessary for staffing software development projects.[12] Occasionally, the project might be initiated with the help of either internal or external consultants.

Another project variant is to have a team from the program actually engage in the project while also meeting as a learning team. The team may be constituted of employees from the same department or may be entirely cross-departmental or even cross-divisional. Cross-functional teams are encouraged where practical because they expose participants to different ways of thinking and enlighten them to knowledge processes outside their own boundaries.

If the work-based program administrators decide on the use of a project team, they may need to determine if they should involve participants of different skill levels. In an action learning study of small- to medium-sized enterprises, the researchers were able to examine this question because they observed action learning sets of predominantly inexperienced managers and others with a mixture of experience and no experience.[13] They found that the mixed sets actually benefited both types of managers. The inexperienced managers were able to exploit the wisdom of the veterans. At the same time, the experienced managers reported a high degree of satisfaction from being able to share with others some of the valuable lessons from their own experience, as in a mentoring capacity.

It might be noted that if the format is team- and project-based, individuals must take responsibility to ensure that they are working on a specific component of the overall group venture. Otherwise, individual initiative and learning may be lost within the team effort. It is for this reason that some project exponents believe that individual projects tend to produce greater individual learning as compared with group projects.

I believe there is ultimately no one best way to constitute a project team. There is perhaps a natural efficiency in having a team work on a project while also meeting as a learning team. Further, there is a benefit in having team members mutually observe and offer constructive feedback on each other's actual job performance. Reflections on plans, assumptions, and practices can be more spontaneous and immediately contextualized. However, it may not be practical for an organization to release an entire group to work on one project.

The scope of project activity, therefore, must also be considered as a program feature. Not only must an organization decide whether to release a full team to work on a project, but it also may need to decide how many projects to have going at any one given time. For example, it is possible to suffer *action project overload*.[14] This can occur if management becomes distracted by the frequent requests for information, interviews, customer visits, and the like, which are associated with project requirements. For example, projects often send out members to obtain information from organizational or unit databanks or directly from top management. Although managerial staff are generally happy to accommodate such requests, there are limits to how much distraction from one's current job one can tolerate. Since projects have been characterized as typically strategic in character, there is also a need to retain sufficient staffing to do the tactical and operating work of the company, especially in instances when projects are being undertaken on a full-time basis. Some of these decisions on project composition will depend on the size of the organization as well as on its learning orientation.

Finally, a relatively new issue in project composition is the question of constituting *external* action projects, or projects made up of managers from different organizations. Such an approach seems to be very applicable at senior levels, where top managers may not have anyone with whom to share personal and confidential problems. There is also a strategic side to external projects, which gives top managers an opportunity to discuss business topics of mutual concern, be it trends analysis, marketing and distribution strategy, talent management and retention, or even mergers and acquisitions. The Home Office, Britain's principal criminal justice agency, and the Association of Chief Police Officers organized a yearlong action learning program for senior police officers, focusing on illegal drug activity in thirty-seven districts.[15] Participants were purposely divided into cross-regional sets to promote interagency information sharing. Participants were universally enthusiastic about the program because of the opportunity to exchange knowledge that was put to immediate use, such as improving cross-force activity against drugs, identifying gaps in suspicious activity reporting systems, or funding the financial investigation of suspects.

Project Location

A controversial topic in project development is whether the project should be conducted at the participant's very work site or at a different location, typically in the same organization (there are also experiments in which someone may "volunteer" services for another organization, perhaps a nonprofit agency). Although there tends to be immediate payoff for the work unit if individuals remain at their work site, the opportunity for long-term learning for the individual and potentially for the organization may be enhanced where the project occurs off-site or minimally alternates between settings. Yet the practicality of having a staff member acquire new skills and ideas in the classroom component of the program and then bring them back simultaneously into the actual work setting is hard to pass up. Further, in such instances, the sponsoring management can be assured that there will be the highest degree of possible transfer of new skills into the home environment. Indeed, De Loo and Verstegen contend that action learning participants are otherwise likely to hold back their employment of newly learned competencies because of potential discouragement within a culture otherwise unprepared for their introduction.[16]

Besides payoff and practicality, there is yet another reason to support project placements within familiar surroundings. This would be the case of staffing projects using different hierarchical levels, although project designers may wish to ensure that managers and direct reports not work together. Yet some staff do not necessarily have the opportunity in their daily assignments to work with higher levels of management as equals. Complicated dynamics occur in this setting and can be instructive and even at times liberating to disassemble. For example, lower-ranking members might find an immediate impulse to defer decision making to the higher-ranking members, and the latter may be inclined to delegate the "work" to the lower ranks.[17] At times, it is also more challenging to work with peers, with whom one is familiar, than with strangers, with whom one can start fresh with new roles, new expectations, and new assignments. The spirit of the project team should be to allow members to develop their own levels of responsibility and contribution apart from prior duties and ranks. Furthermore, discrepancies in commitment and participation need to be managed, regardless of past reputation or performance.

There are, on the other hand, a number of arguments to be made in favor of alternative or unfamiliar sites. Without the benefit of input from different cultures, we may develop what Hayes and Allinson refer to as "strategic myopia."[18] This is a form of single-loop learning that goes only so far as correcting the prevailing mental models within the organization. However, we occasionally need to examine our underlying assumptions and principles in order to respond to strategic challenges in a new light. Hence, if one considers the places where people work to be *culturally ordered*, with their own unwritten rules about what's important, then working in a different location can encourage new ways of thinking about otherwise familiar problems and provide breadth of experience.[19] Tyre and von Hippel found that engineers who went to sites to observe a problem firsthand learned about many unexpected occurrences of problems that they never could have fathomed in their back-home site.[20]

Working in alternative sites may also reveal unexpected insights or provide opportunities to reframe problems as knowledge and experience increase. Alternative sites can also help diffuse the knowledge that is embedded in one site into other parts of the organization. As one thinks about the use of alternative sites, projects can be categorized as performing one's already mastered job responsibilities in the new site or as assuming entirely new duties. In the former instance, the new unit obtains whatever skills and knowledge the participant transfers from his or her prior workplace, while the participant experiences the dynamic of adapting his or her typical job duties or even professional responsibilities to a different culture. The exercise of new duties in a different location offers the potential for literally "unfreezing" all of one's assumptions about work, releasing the participant to a totally new experience, both in terms of task and environment.

Project Administration Issues

Once project groups are formed, program administrators need to decide whether or not they should be funded. Some programs believe that funding should become a constraint on project development like any other constraint that the group has to overcome. If the project is to be considered worthwhile, the team might need to solicit resources from the relevant stakeholders, convincing them of its value. On the other hand, seed money might initially be needed to get the project off the ground. Worthwhile projects inevitably require expenditures, be they for travel, communications, survey work, report preparation, and the like.

The duration of projects is often debated in the literature, but there is no optimal time frame. Some programs support lengthy projects of six months to a year, as in the case of ARAMARK's Executive Leadership Institute or SUPERVALU's Work-Based Learning program. Some are mid-range, as in UBS's twelve- to fifteen-week business challenge component of its ASCENT talent development program.[21] Others can be quite short, in the four- to six-week range. The shorter time frames support full-time participation, whereas the long ones tend to require participants to work on their projects in addition to their regular jobs. The longer programs are also deemed to provide more conceptual development and in-depth experience but suffer the risk of loss of participant intensity and supervisory support.[22]

Projects can also take on a life of their own once the program is over. In fact, full implementation of a project, once it has been completed through the program, may represent the highest form of success. It indicates that the team's work has been so critical that it requires institutionalization within the unit or organization. Projects, then, should incorporate within their presentation a plan for full implementation of their findings and recommendations. The property and casualty insurer, the Chubb Corporation, runs an action learning Global Executive Program focusing on strategic innovation and critical thinking. In a recent instance, following the approximately eighteen-week program, three SBU-related project teams remained intact for three to six months after the program formally ended to experiment further with their business models and to ensure a successful handoff to their respective SBU.[23]

Where work-based learning programs are provided apart from academic accreditation, there may be some resistance on the part of participants to commit their learning and substantive outcomes to writing. However, sponsors minimally expect some report of recommendations from project teams. If credit is given for project work as part of an academic qualification, normally a full report is expected, which would meet the dual standards of academic rigor and workplace practicality. The report could be team-based or individual-based. An individualized assessment has been conducted as part of a university Advanced Certificate in Health Service Management offered through the Lancashire School of Health and Postgraduate Medicine in Preston, United Kingdom.[24] There are four components:

1. A work-based report, including a diagnostic analysis of the participant's practice and recommendations aimed at improving the practice

2. A focused analysis of a particular practice issue, such as change management, patient reform, managing quality, or organizational culture

3. A work-based project that builds on the first piece of work and looks in depth at ways of improving a specific aspect of the practice

4. A presentation outlining the skills and knowledge acquired during the program

Besides the recommendations for action steps in the domain of the project, project reports may also contain some conventional academic elements, such as a literature review and an accounting of the data collection methods used to undertake any research components. In the Boston College Leadership for Change program, with which I am affiliated, the project accounts for one half of the qualification of twelve graduate credits awarded upon successful completion of the program. Leadership for Change is described as a graduate-level executive development program to enhance individual, organizational, and societal leadership. There are ten criteria used in assessing the project work. They are presented here as questions posed to the participants to help them prepare their final project report:

1. *What was your purpose?* What problem were you attempting to solve or opportunity to exploit? What benefits did your project provide? Why is your project important to you personally, to your team, to your organization, and to the broader social environment?

2. *What was the intellectual basis of your initiative?* What ideas led you to the point where you could complete your project? Cite the relevant literature (including readings from our modules and from other sources) that have given you the necessary background. What prior work had you done in this area?

3. *What was your methodology and intervention strategy?* What techniques did you apply in order to complete your project (for example, what data did you collect or what interviews did you conduct)? What was the context that led you to choose this particular methodology and strategy?

4. *What was the impact of your project?* What, if anything, has changed as a result of your effort? Be sure to include multiple bottom-line measures of cost savings or efficiencies that occurred.

5. *Having done this project, what conclusions did you reach, and why?* What was your logic? Demonstrate how your strategies, conclusions, and policy recommendations follow logically from the evidence.

6. *Did you engage in reflective practice?* Have you been a reflective practitioner, viewing your insights and opinions as hypotheses to be tested? Have you submitted your assumptions to the inquiry of others? Have you encouraged others to reflect on their own work?

7. *Have you integrated theory and practice?* How have you put information from your readings, the modules, and your experience to use? In reflecting on your actions, how have you revised your theories?

8. *In what ways have you been creative and innovative?* Does your project show original, innovative thought and expression? How have you addressed problems in creative ways?

9. *How has your project demonstrated your leadership effort and ability?* What obstacles have you had to overcome personally and institutionally? How do you now view leadership as a practice?

10. *How does your project contribute to the "common good"?* Have
    traditional (stockholder) and nontraditional (community)
    stakeholders been served by your work? How does your project
    follow from and expand upon the models of change you have
    experienced in the LC program?

In order to prepare participants for the project, the Leadership
for Change program also encourages them to prepare a prospectus
of their project at its outset. By writing a brief prospectus, participants become more comfortable with the program's expectation
about writing, although they are encouraged to journalize throughout the entire experience. In addition, committing the project to a
prospectus form tends to make it a reality and gives it the vitality
often needed to get it off the ground. The instructions for the initial project prospectus follow:

Instructions for a Project Prospectus

**Please prepare and submit the following for your next learning team meet-
ing. You may wish to bring sufficient copies to share with each of your
team members. The prospectus should be at least 6 pp. in length.**

Provide a *title* and *topic* of your proposed work. Summarize your *research problem* in a sentence or two. Then, elaborate on the *level of analysis* at which your
subject matter and project implementation are focused. Finally, say which *type*
of project this is: intervention, research, concept, or policy analysis.

Furnish a *rationale* or explanation of the importance of the work to you personally, and if relevant, to your team, to your organization, to the societal/global environment.

If there is any previous research or analysis that has been done on topics related
to your project, either within your organization or outside of it, provide a review
of *relevant sources*. Don't forget to use sources already examined in prior modules.
Say how you are adding to knowledge in your topic area or to the knowledge base
from which decisions are made in your organization.

What *concepts*, *variables*, and/or *indicators* are you using to measure behavior,
opinion, or outcomes. How are you defining "success," "meaningful change,"
and/or "leadership"?

Instructions for a Project Prospectus, Cont'd.

If you will be undertaking an *intervention*, discuss your initial plan for action; the change agent role you might assume as well as the sponsor and target roles; how you plan to overcome resistance to change, including concerns about threat or embarrassment; and how the evaluation is to be conducted.

If applicable to your project, explain your *data collection strategy* (surveys, observation, interviewing, etc.). Describe in detail how you are going to gain access to information and to people. If you need to *sample* some population, how will you draw your sample? What will the *setting* for the research be? How long will it take? How will data be *processed* and analyzed? How much will it *cost* (in money or other resources) to complete your project?

Finally, what will you learn from doing this project? Describe any personal transformation you hope will occur. What are the benefits to your organization? How are these to be measured in terms of the "*dual bottom line*"?

While most programs not affiliated with academic institutions do not need the level of detail specified here, their requirements for project work should be communicated at the outset. Besides some of the requirements already discussed, the following issues might be addressed:[25]

- Project deliverables (over and above any report)
- Expectations of support from one's sponsor and supervisor
- Acceptable parameters regarding customer contacts
- Target audience
- Loss of client
- Duration
- Provision of supplementary resources such as workshops
- Intersection with other learning activities, such as assessments
- Methods to communicate program participation
- Effect on participants' daily responsibilities
- Responsibility for implementing recommendations
- Continuity of the group after the project is completed

The Challenge of Action Projects

If structured well, projects can have a meaningful impact within the organization, but at the same time, they can cause confusion and resentment. Knowing some of the pitfalls of action projects in advance can help program administrators plan them to achieve salutary ends.

By their very nature, action projects are a challenge to the status quo. All affected management, frequently the entire organization, need to be apprised of their unique nature. Even if well publicized, however, there is an inevitable threat to individuals whose roles or responsibilities might be challenged by the recommendations forthcoming from the project. Hence, it has to be made clear at the outset of any work-based learning program involving projects that although the program will not threaten anyone's employment security, it may result in different ways to organize the work of the organization. Further, most projects are not typically designed to reengineer anyone's current job; rather, they tend to be future- and change-oriented activities that affect entire operations and strategies. They are what might be termed *white space* endeavors. Nevertheless, since they look at ways to anticipate and cope with future organizational challenges, they may indeed invoke risks to present operating conditions. In the end, they are designed to help *everyone* in the organization prepare for the future.

This raises a larger question. Work-based learning may become a political undertaking in that it could very well bear on questions of power and social relationships in the organization as a whole. Are executives capable of making themselves vulnerable to unexpected answers? Do they want the entire organization, including them, to be involved in learning? One way to incur buy-in from executives is to involve them at the outset and to apprise them of work-based learning's potential destabilizing effects. In a work-based leadership development program at a global biopharmaceutical services company, the projects in the first year of operation were actually sponsored by the CEO and COO.[26] At George and Harding, a medium-sized construction company based in Bournemouth, United Kingdom, the chairperson became very involved in a middle-management action learning program to promote innovation and culture change, including nominating the candidates. The participants subsequently reported that they began to see this chairperson as more approachable and also became more comfortable presenting their proposals to other directors. On his part, the chairperson became very appreciative that the participants were now willing to debate matters of policy with him. The program was also reported to have made it easier for him to understand the abilities, commitment, and strategic orientation of the company's new talent.[27]

Participants who have experienced work-based learning tend to report having gone through a much deeper and more holistic exercise than ever anticipated.[28] In a way, as Weinstein warns, work-based learning can even be considered subversive within the context of conformist organizations because of what it values:[29]

- It examines everything.
- It stresses listening.
- It emphasizes questioning.
- It fosters courage.
- It incites action.
- It abets reflection.
- It endorses democratic participation.

At the same time, one could argue that projects should be managed in a way that leverages whatever the prevailing culture allows. For instance, in learning how to manage effectively, one needs to learn how to sell a project proposal to both one's peers and senior management, and that part of the learning process should be to learn how to be effective in local environments and, in particular, how to frame proposals.[30] Furthermore, although projects might start off as local ventures, the outcomes of work-based learning flow into the surrounding environment. Participants begin to question things beyond their local context.

Projects—at least if they are to have strategic impact—do not operate in a vacuum. Indeed, work-based learning is not typically designed as a one-time, individual learning opportunity. Most designers see it as having organizational learning implications. In that sense, it can end up as a subversive activity in organizations that expect conformity to a party line.

Projects in work-based learning are most effective when participants are given responsibility to pursue and follow through on the problems they confront. Project success, when defined as a learning opportunity for the sponsoring unit or organization, is dependent on releasing the talent and experience on the part of the individual or team involved. Projects gradually take on a life of their own and at times even diverge from the question originally posed to the team. What tends to be consequential to participants is a sense that no matter what they discover in their study, they will have the opportunity to see the project through to its natural conclusion, even if it means challenging the status quo. Project recommendations need not be automatically accepted. Team members just need to know that their recommendations will get a fair hearing by their sponsors even when they conflict with existing norms and plans. Work-based action projects, then, require an organizational culture of risk taking and openness, which permits occasional surfacing of ineffectual rules and practices. There is no place for reflective practice in a closed culture. Work-based learning works best when all organizational members, including those at the top, agree to submit even their governing values to scrutiny.

10

Managing and Evaluating
Work-Based Learning

> A man found an old shoe ticket in a desk drawer he
> was cleaning out. He couldn't remember the pair of
> shoes it represented but it had to be several years
> old. Out of curiosity, he took the shoe ticket to
> work and on his way home that night, he stopped
> by the shoe shop. Without saying a word, he handed
> the ticket to the old cobbler. The old man studied
> the ticket for a minute, shuffled into the back room,
> and soon returned, saying: "They'll be ready next
> Wednesday."

Having considered the building blocks of work-based learning, we now need to turn our attention to program management so that we can put these ideas into practice. We must also learn how to measure our performance against our goals in order to establish further goals for mutual learning. In work-based learning, as we know, the practice of learning is continuous.

A Guide for Program Managers

Work-based learning as a management development practice is unlikely to evolve on its own. Normally, it requires some *structure* because it is technically a program. If successful, it might evolve into a standard way of operating within an organization. For example, team- or project-based organizations have some of the rudiments already in place of what we might term a work-based learning culture.

However, the teams or project groups are typically work teams, as we have defined them, and not also learning teams.

Initiating work-based learning will require the presence of a program manager, whose job it is to set up and launch the work-based learning initiative within the organization. The program manager is responsible for recruiting the participants, the learning team facilitators, teachers (if there is an instructional component to the program), and the sponsors of the projects. Teachers and facilitators might be recruited initially from outside providers; however, internal staff could be trained to take on some of these roles, especially facilitation. In fact, facilitators might be drafted and trained from prior cohorts of the program.

I have used the term *sponsor* to refer to the supervisor of the unit within the organization who provides the project and endorses the work of the participant. Some programs, however, refer to this role as that of the *client,* whereas the sponsor may be the individual's supervisor, who enlists the employee for participation in the program. In instances when participants work on a project in their own work site, these roles are one and the same. I prefer to hold to the definition of sponsor as the role that provides the project. In this case, sponsors and program managers often need to negotiate adjustments in the participants' schedules with supervisors, especially in instances when projects require time away from the job or when current job assignments are inevitably affected.

Besides these natural tasks, program managers also coordinate the various assignments and project opportunities attending to the program. They are often involved in negotiating the nature of the project and ensuring that all parties—participants, sponsors, supervisors—are satisfied with its selection and ongoing operation. This can only occur if the parties maintain regular communication with one another. The program manager also needs to be sure that the mutual objectives for the project be supported by all constituencies and that there is agreement on the parameters of the endeavor as well as its time requirements. One guideline that can be used to manage possible disputes between the parties—and in keeping with the overall philosophy endorsed in this book for work-based learning programs—is to remind people that learning is a first priority; hence, the participant needs to have a genuine commitment to the venture as a learning opportunity yet also produce something of value.

In order to engender support from sponsors, it may be advisable to consider an informal contracting process.[1] Before the participants begin their projects, they would spend some time with their sponsor, who would review their project proposal in detail. The parties would ensure that the project be beneficial to both the participant and the unit in which it will be carried out. Participants and sponsors might develop an action plan for the first month of the program. Action plans would then be revised on a monthly basis after learning team meetings.

Program managers would also do well to spend some time with sponsors prior to the program to ensure that they understand the program's mission and methods and to solicit their support.[2] Preliminary contact can also generate and refine project ideas. In the Susan Vogt Leadership Fellows program, coordinated by the Boston Consortium for Higher Education (a network of top administrators among Boston's world-renowned institutions of higher learning), sponsors are asked to consider a number of prospective roles, especially during the year of the fellowship:

- Role model expectations for a successful project.

  Encourage fellows to use their new learning in situations back on the job.

  After the initiative, help create opportunities for participants to continue developing skills.

  Establish success criteria that are (1) project-oriented and (2) learning-oriented.

    Examples: the project's cross-campus shared function should save x dollars due to synergies in distribution.

    Participant will show demonstrated improvement in handling conflict in her unit and in being more responsive to feedback from her staff.

- Create an open, supportive, and challenging environment for the initiative.

    Be willing to have your own assumptions about the organization, the culture, and the project challenged.

    Treat mistakes by participants as opportunities for them to learn.

- Lend support in the form of resources and commitment.

    Explicitly ask what your fellow needs.

    Coordinate with senior administrators regarding the project.

    Encourage your fellow to accept responsibility.

    Ensure that the managers and peers of the participants support the time commitment.

    Establish a working agreement with your fellow's facilitator and coach regarding how you will work together to support your fellow.

Program managers need to play a central role in organizing an evaluation of the work-based learning experience. Although I shall elaborate on measurement later in this chapter, some of the critical evaluation components include: identifying criteria that can be used in defining program performance, establishing a base of comparison with either other programs or with current conditions prior to the program, and using the evaluation results to improve both the effectiveness and credibility of the program. Program managers also need to ensure that the views of all internal and external constituencies are considered when evaluation criteria are developed.[3]

Perhaps the best way to manage a work-based learning program in which there are multiple stakeholders is to arrange for a partnership in the administrative structure. For example, an advisory board could be set up that represents the various constituencies, all of whom would have a role in designing the critical features of the program. The board would continue to meet throughout the program to advise on policy-related matters as they evolve. For example, how should the program adapt to a sponsoring company being acquired by a company not affiliated with the program? How might the program respond when a program participant leaves or takes an extended absence from the program? How should the program handle a request for a project extension or even a project adaptation that falls outside the original project brief?

Program managers need to ensure that facilitators or set advisers are sufficiently trained to handle the administrative, political, and social challenges confronted within a learning team. They also need to schedule a variety of operating features and support mechanisms during the life of the project, be they ongoing learning team meetings; mentorships or other developmental functions; technical assistance, including occasional workshops or classes; and of course final project presentations. Although most programs expect participant teams to provide written recommendations to the sponsor of their project, many also require oral presentations, as I suggested in the last chapter, and ask that participants talk about their learning from the work-based learning experience as well as about the more substantive outcomes.

Program managers may be involved not only in managing a current cycle of work-based learning programs but also in managing numerous program cycles over a period of years. In such an instance, it is important that current project groups have access to prior endeavors to help them build on past accomplishments as well as to avoid "reinventing the wheel." Program managers can introduce an important service by creating a project database, which would provide a record of all past projects. Besides including a complete description of the project and its results (or current status if its recommendations are still in the implementation phase), the database should also list the names of key contact persons who would be available to share information with current program participants.

Managing Academic Affiliations

Some work-based learning programs intersect with formal providers, such as action researchers from colleges and universities or management consultants, to help them get started. There are controversial elements in work-based learning when viewed from a pure academic perspective. For example, work-based learning considers managerial problems or performance deficiencies as viable elements of the curriculum. Further, instructional components are preferably introduced "just-in-time;" that is, structured to respond to current professional needs. Strict academics may also object that work-based learning programs do not provide sufficient breadth of subject coverage and mistakenly rely on business criteria as a basis to assess academic performance.[4]

Work-based learning's intersection with academic institutions also becomes controversial when its proponents claim that it should be associated with academic qualification, or minimally, an industry-recognized credential. The educational institution needs to be assured that any program meet rigorous academic standards, whereas the employer needs assurance that the program has prepared its novices to enter or contribute to the field in question with the highest attainable quality standards. Academic qualification will typically require an assessment that through diverse means—testing, supervisory evaluation, individual portfolio, learning contract—can identify the necessary learning outcomes, the level at which these outcomes are being achieved, the criteria for achieving the outcomes, and evidence of their achievement.[5] In work-based learning in particular, the volume of learning activity needs to be established to support the accreditation. Although the ultimate award of credit rests with the university, other parties, such as the employing organization, program deliverers, and associated consultants and facilitators, have their respective interests to sustain.[6]

By reducing on-campus time, accredited work-based learning can be responsive to the needs of adult learners who have multiple responsibilities in their lives. It accredits the process of learning rather than the work product.[7] Nevertheless, higher educational institutions need to establish the relevance between learning achieved in work and academic qualifications. They need to document the conceptual content, competencies, and learning outcomes involved. When they provide certification, as noted in the *Accreditation of Prior Work Based Learning* report from the United Kingdom's National Health Service, it's like certifying that "a fish is fresh, without being able to see it, smell it, or know the source from which it has arisen!"[8]

An example of the use of accredited work-based learning, as reported by Miles, is a part-time program in biomedical sciences at the University of Westminster.[9] A sixth of the curriculum was based on accredited work-based learning. The students were employed as trainees in laboratories across the southeast of England. Each student produced a portfolio of evidence, demonstrating achievement of twenty-five learning outcomes. Working with an on-site tutor, students received steady feedback on their progress and also had to demonstrate achievement of learning based on assessment criteria set by the tutor and the university.

Program managers need to make the case that work-based learning arises from a different intellectual tradition than standard training programs. For example, it questions the view that such fields as management can be known in advance using systematic logic. The world of management practice is as much chaotic as ordered, and no matter how hard managers try to apply universal criteria or use advanced analytical techniques, they confront everyday idiosyncrasies that defy categorization. Work-based learning derives from a tradition that values interdependence among diverse stakeholders and perspectives in order to account for the changing circumstances, values, and needs of practicing managers.

Managing the Top

Typically, program managers serve as a link between the program and top management and thus carry out the critical role of gaining and sustaining the top team's support of work-based learning practice. In this way, they serve as an ambassador of the logic of learning as a reflective practice and help assimilate this logic or approach within the psyche of the organization itself. Work-based learning projects typically do not provide quick fixes to problems. They might even reveal new ways of approaching particular processes or markets.

In this way, they can be potentially threatening to current job incumbents. As has been emphasized throughout this book, work-based learning typically requires a mind-set that accepts the inevitability of risk and change within the organization. If the organization has not accepted this mind-set, the program manager needs to prepare all parties emotionally as well as strategically for this change in the way things are done, and this includes not just top management but operating management as well.

Lack of support from executives or from supervisors can constitute a recipe for failure. Work-based learning projects should not be designed as "skunkworks," which operate in isolation. By design, they operate in a context—the context of the surrounding culture. That culture and the systems that underlie it need to be at least partially supportive of the ideology represented by work-based learning. As has been demonstrated throughout this book, this ideology is not a radical agenda. It merely espouses the value of a questioning, democratic basis of organization. Participants tend to come out of work-based learning programs more inquisitive, more challenging, more self-confident yet more exposed, and more collaborative than when they went in. Although they may feel freer to challenge organizational goals, they tend to take responsibility for the public discourse that they may engender. Hence, senior managers should find them willing to make not only their conclusions but also the reasoning behind their conclusions accessible to others in the organization.[10] They also tend to be bold in their leadership behavior; for example, they feel free to engage in upward influence and are interested in second- and third-order learning, which involves change affecting the very governing values of the organization.

It is therefore beneficial to have a surrounding culture that endorses experimentation, trust, risk taking, and an interest in reasoned change from the status quo. Sponsors and operating managers will at times need to relinquish control and risk releasing the potential of program participants, trusting that they will do what is in the best interest of the unit or company.[11]

What can happen when these conditions are unavailable? For one, department heads, fearing scrutiny of their unit because it could reveal weaknesses, might be reluctant to hand over worthwhile projects, and makeshift work could result. Even if worthwhile projects are initiated and completed, they may never be implemented on any wide scale within the organization if they are seen as threatening the turf of a director. This in turn could have an especially alienating effect on the participants who had tackled the project in good faith with hopes of broad influence.

In addition, program managers, especially those who in the past had been involved in the delivery of training, have to be prepared to face the insecurity and political risks of managing a program whose outcomes are not predictable. Classroom programs, although edifying for students, do not typically foster much internal change within the organization. They are normally dedicated to helping employees do their current jobs better, and this includes the job of management. Work-based learning, as we have seen, has the potential of mobilizing a transformation in organizational structure and operation. Participants begin to perceive how their individual learning may be tied to changes in the wider organizational culture. Hence, they may return to their jobs questioning some of the basic values, practices, and power relationships within their unit. This may create tensions within the department, especially when their questioning concerns social, political, ethical, and personal issues as opposed to mere technical matters.[12] Without sufficient support from peers and superiors, program managers are unlikely to risk their professional careers on a program that by definition is about learning and change.

Is there anything a program manager can do to "soften up" reluctant managers or executives to prepare them for work-based learning ideology, perhaps even to the point of gaining their endorsement? If preservation of the status quo is the manager's ultimate modus operandi or if the manager refuses to permit time for reflective practice, there may not be much that can be accomplished. There is no point pushing against a brick wall. However, be aware that we tend as human beings to imagine resistances as firmer than they may be. There are some strategies, therefore, that might work with resisting bosses.

First, try to link some of the components of the program to strategic initiatives to which the boss may be committed. Even further, link the program, where possible, to financial indicators of success, such as metrics of growth, profitability, and performance. Invite well-known people from other organizations or from academia who subscribe to work-based learning approaches to address your organization and speak personally to your executives. Be aware of the comfort zone of your boss and try not to make any proposal that would invade that zone. If possible, arrange to give hesitant executives a preview of the work-based learning experience. For example, executives may become more predisposed to the value of feedback and reflective processes after having experienced 360-degree feedback on their own behavioral practices. Finally, remember to nourish yourself by developing a support base around you, with whom you can reflectively practice. Introducing change is tough business from a psychological standpoint. Don Schön put it this way:[13]

> When a member of a bureaucracy embarks on a course of reflective practice, allowing himself to experience confusion and uncertainty, subjecting his frames and theories to conscious criticism and change, he may increase his capacity to contribute to significant organizational learning, but he also becomes, by the same token, a danger to the stable system of rules and procedures within which he is expected to deliver his technical expertise.

If one expects to serve in the capacity of work-based learning program administrator, here are some steps and considerations that should be applicable in most organizational settings:[14]

- Decide if you really want to do it.
- Start explaining why and what you are doing.
- Gain some support and commitment.
- Obtain agreement on the people and problems/opportunities that the program is aimed at.

- Produce a basic outline of the program (for example, objectives, estimated time and costs, resources activities).
- Present a cost-benefit analysis (in operational and financial terms).
- Produce a prospectus explaining the program.
- Agree on a budget.
- Recruit staff and resources internally and externally.
- Recruit participants and organize projects and learning teams.
- Brief everyone on the program but particularly participants, sponsors, participants' bosses, your boss(es), top management, colleagues, human resource staff.
- Bring everyone together for an orientation.
- Get going.

The Measurement of Work-Based Learning

As in any human resource intervention, work-based learning activities need to be measured and evaluated to ensure their ongoing worth. Sponsors must be apprised of the outcomes of work-based learning, and program managers and facilitators need measures to inform them how effective the ongoing program is. Assessment is thus used as a vehicle for continuous improvement. Like any intervention, work-based learning programs need to change to be responsive to their stakeholders. Once changes are recommended, measurement is also required to ensure that they have been effectively implemented.

Standard Performance Indicators

There is possible concern that without measurement, work-based learning programs will not be able to sustain the support of chief executives. CEOs tend to notice and support human resource development programs when they demonstrate that they consistently convert learning into improved business performance. CEOs are also reputed to respond most critically to financial performance measures—measures that impact the economic bottom line. Some accounts have disputed these claims, arguing that most companies view traditional accounting and financial measures as mainly reporting on the stewardship of money entrusted to management, not charting the strategic direction of the business.[15] Human resource practices, such as work-based learning programs, address the utilization of human and intellectual capital and can be viewed as a source of genuine competitive advantage for most corporations.[16] Human resource activities thus need to demonstrate how they can alleviate the obstacles to reaching an organization's strategic goals.

Nevertheless, economic benefits that can be traced back to work-based learning programs unequivocally lend them extra credibility. One way of demonstrating the impact of work-based learning would be to establish an intervening effect between the program and its financial results. A method to measure the intervening effect is to measure changes in the participants going through the program. Once those changes are measured, then the second relationship can be demonstrated between the benefits to the participants and financial results. Reflective practices, for example, are known to be essential to group development, especially in helping group members learn to appreciate contrary points of view, styles of interaction, varying levels of commitment to the team, and so forth. Effective teams in turn are known to produce consensual decisions, leading to implementable activities and effective outcomes. The outcomes—be they more efficient operations processes, reduced downtime, higher-quality products—are in turn measurable using standard financial indicators.

An example of this intervening effect is the link that Sears, Roebuck and Company would make between employee behaviors and business success.[17] At Sears, the first set of measures establish a relationship between leadership development and improved employee attitudes, especially in the area of customer relations, such as meeting customers quickly, greeting them with a smile, and calling attention to sales items. The next set of measures show how these customer behaviors lead to customer satisfaction and purchases, which in turn have enhanced store revenue and profitability.

Measurement systems such as these can go a long way toward convincing skeptical CEOs—insisting on bottom-line results—of worthwhile work-based learning practices. As noted here, however, work-based learning-type programs tend to have intermediate rather than strict bottom-line impacts. Profitability measures, for example, derive from the accumulation of improved managerial performance over time. Project results, such as improved customer service, may affect one function but not necessarily the entire organization. The main reason for the difficulty in measuring long-term impact resulting from one change is the chance for moderating effects resulting from counteractive forces elsewhere in the organization. For instance, improved customer service may be counteracted by an outdated or disjointed information system. Program administrators of work-based learning need to caution against their ability to "prove" bottom-line results.

Yet there are many ways to assess mid-level or intermediate results that can be readily seen as ultimately affecting the bottom line. For example, the careers of program graduates can be tracked to determine if their professional careers progress at a faster rate than their peers. If so, a connection could be demonstrated between the supply of talent and strategic accomplishment. Similarly, it might be useful to measure attrition rates of participants compared with their nonparticipating peers, under the assumption that program participants might reciprocate for their developmental experience with increased loyalty and commitment.[18] Once the program recruits a critical mass of managerial talent, organization-wide measurement systems might be installed. A U.S. Department of Labor study examining a number of firms' valuation levels found that those firms noted for their progressive use of employee development and process management practices had price-to-book valuation ratios significantly higher than their industry peers.[19]

Although not always necessary for organizational purposes, evaluations might be tied to academic research efforts in order to provide a firm empirical basis for the value of work-based learning.[20]

Program managers might therefore consider commissioning impact studies using more sophisticated techniques than before-and-after assessments. For example, through time series analyses, evaluators can track outcome trends. Six sigma methodology can track the interests of stakeholders through output indicators of process and performance.[21] Using randomized experiments, evaluators can estimate the extent to which a demonstration project in work-based learning differentiated outcomes between randomly assigned experimental and control groups. Finally, cost-benefit analyses can be conducted to compare program costs with estimates of the economic value of program impacts.[22]

Work-based learning's exponents claim that it can also produce institutional or cultural change since it represents a form of intra- and inter-organizational learning.[23] Over the course of time, especially when program managers attempt to collect, store, and disseminate the knowledge originating from projects, work-based learning can add to an organization's institutional memory. The sharing of knowledge and practices can transfer intelligence across generations of employees. Further, as activities seep into organizational practices, there is the genuine opportunity for shifts in culture to occur as well as performance improvements.

As for specific studies demonstrating the effectiveness of work-based learning programs, there have been steady and ample testimonies through the years. For example, Burgoyne and Stuart in the 1970s found that translation of managerial skills into practice was enhanced when participants were involved in solving real—as opposed to simulated—management problems.[24] Furthermore, Rackham and Morgan found that skill retention was augmented when managers were asked to perform new skills in specific contexts rather than when they merely acquired them generically to be applied at a later time.[25] Joyce and Showers also found greater transfer of training when programs provided opportunities for local, factual feedback on trainee performance in actual practice situations.[26] The Reed Travel Group, when part of Reed International, had calculated that its project-based action learning programs generated a return of five to ten times the investment in less than two years.[27] Shell Oil Company of the United States in the 1990s reported that its Leadership and Performance (LEAP) action learning program consistently exceeded its goal of a return of 25:1, and Motorola concluded from its own internal research that targeted (as opposed to general classroom) educational efforts could generate better than a 30:1 return within three years.[28] Enderby and Phelan, reporting on an action learning program at a major Australian bank, compared customer perceptions between branches that sponsored action learning groups and those that did not.[29] In every dimension of customer service, customers rated the action learning branches more highly. Leadership in International Management Ltd. described how a global truck company, having adopted the company's Action Reflection Learning process, saved a year's production time and earned approximately $7 million from a project team's design of an innovative parts distribution system for their operation in Poland.[30]

More recently, Forum Corporation reported the results of a sixty-day Action Learning Lab provided to a $35 billion global consumer goods company committed to shifting its strategic focus from profit maximization to top-line growth. The lab featured individual action learning projects, but each participant had a thinking partner, who, throughout the program, served as a sounding board to keep each other on track, including lessons learned. Experienced leaders also provided one-on-one coaching to the participants. Of the more than four hundred managers going through the program, 99 percent said it dealt with issues relevant to their jobs, and 92 percent reported that the experience influenced how they lead. From the business point of view, the projects produced a 9 percent reduction in shelf overfills, resulting in a $125,000 savings; a new, patentable invention; and 20 to 30 percent new-growth potential in product "share of shelf."[31]

There are several levels of measurement that can be recommended in work-based learning. In the tradition of the well-known Kirkpatrick model of evaluation, it is not enough to measure the degree of satisfaction of participants during the program.[32] We are also interested in the knowledge and skills acquired as well as the behavioral changes detected on the job. Most critical, however, are the results or outcomes of the program both in terms of project success and in terms of organizational changes that result from managerial improvement experienced by the participants.

Another way to consider the levels of measurement is through the three criteria of *effort, process,* and *performance*. Effort (also referred to as *input*) measures the resources expended on behalf of the program. Process details what the program did. Performance (or *output*) measures how well the program achieved its goals and can be evaluated both short-term and long-term.

Consider some more specific measures for each of these three criteria:

Effort

What was the cost of the program?

How many people participated?

How much time did it take (for example, in terms of participants being away from their job)?

Who sponsored the program and what were their expectations?

Process

What need is the program responding to?

How is the presenting problem being addressed?

What were the distinguishing features of the program and how should they be changed during the next iteration?

What instructional strategies and materials were used to supplement the project phase of the program?

Which projects were chosen and how?

Were learning teams or other reflective practices built into the program?

Performance (Short Term)

What competencies were addressed, changed, added?

What were the participants' reactions to the experience?

How did other stakeholders, such as the participants' supervisors, react to the experience?

Did the program meet its cost and time schedules?

Did the project produce a direct beneficial change?

Was the need that inspired the project met?

How were the learning teams received?

Performance (Long Term)

Have participants changed their managerial behavior, and did it have a salutary effect on their unit, organization?

Was there significant transformation in the participants' personal development, values, practices?

Did the program lead to career change or advancement for any participants?

Have there been residual effects from the project in other parts of the organization?

Did the program produce reflective practices not only in participants but also in the units to which they were affiliated?

Has the project evolved into a significant venture for the organization?

Did the program change any cultural norms or organizational practices?

Were changes noted in costs, revenues, or other bottom-line results?

Beyond these programmatic measures, specific features of the program need separate measurement and measurers. We wish to know how participants themselves felt about their personal development and achievements in the program, so individual assessment should be built into any evaluation system. In addition, peer assessment has become more common in the human resource field and can be very applicable in work-based learning, especially given that learning team members perhaps know one another better than any other possible assessors. Since project work is built into the process, program management might also seek evaluative data from sponsors and perhaps from the participant's manager or coworkers. Finally, if the program is tied to an academic degree, it may be advisable to use standard academic measures of achievement, which are normally assigned by faculty.

It may be very useful to obtain measures *before* as well as after the program and from a control group of individuals who did not participate in work-based learning. The use of a control group and pretesting, compared with after-program measures, are thought to achieve greater validity according to academic standards but can also provide important information to program administrators and to participants. For example, if conditions within the work site change due to program participation, we would be in a better position to credit the program rather than other factors for influencing the change. At the same time, participants should have benchmarks of their personal and managerial performance prior to the program in order to gauge any subsequent change or improvement.

The Center for Creative Leadership (CCL) uses a 360-degree assessment tool called *Reflections* to assess participant behaviors in its action learning programs using a unique retrospective *post-then* design.[33] CCL is careful to choose indicators from its Reflections Competency Library to match the leadership competencies that are being emphasized by the client's sponsors. Raters are asked to provide assessments on both individual performance and on growth in strategic organizational capabilities on the part of the unit to which the participant has been responsible. In work with such clients as Catholic Healthcare Partners and the U.S. Postal Service, some of the competencies that have shown the most degree of change from both self and observers have been the following:

- *Acting systemically* (for example, establishing collaborative relationships and alliances throughout the organization)
- *Engaging across boundaries* (for example, maintaining smooth, effective working relationships)
- *Participative management* (for example, using effective listening skills and communication to involve others)
- *Courage to take risks* (for example, taking a stand when others disagree)

Alternative Substantive Measures

As work-based learning emphasizes reflective processes, it is important to measure results that help members of the entire learning community reflect back on their own learning from the program. It is also useful to communicate these results, even though difficult at times to articulate, to those who have not experienced the process directly.[34] Measuring these substantive results may at times require indicators not typically used in conventional training programs. As we have seen, work-based learning encourages individuals and teams to create their own workplace reality through ongoing individual and public reflection. Measures may incorporate, for example, informal or incidental learning that occurs within the workplace itself rather than in the classroom.[35]

There are some general guidelines that might develop and foster such substantive measures:[36]

- Use a family of measures rather than rely on one global measure to serve as the ultimate indicator.
- Limit the number of measures.
- Develop team-oriented measures where appropriate and separate them from individual measures of performance.
- Identify measures that are accomplishment- or outcome-based as well as process-based.
- Develop some averages to track measures.

- Seek the level of precision sufficient for the purpose (you don't have to reach six sigma in every project).
- Don't be afraid to change course in midstream.
- Seek to raise standards.

Recalling prior discussions in this book about critical learning, we have seen that there have been calls for work-based learning in its many forms to likewise be more critical in its focus on measurement, especially that it assume more of an emancipatory agenda that would take into consideration the power dynamics across and within the hierarchical levels of an organization. Such an agenda would also address the social, political, cultural, economic, ethnic, and gender structures that constrain people.[37] Yet, I see the focus of work-based learning—especially in its endorsement of praxis—remaining with what Reynolds refers to as a *process* or a *dialectical dynamic*, which can review and alter misconstrued meanings found in conventional wisdom or in power relationships.[38] The degree of its emancipatory potential arises from the interest of learners in understanding how knowledge is constructed and managed. Through this process, they may derive a passion for justice, mutual respect for each other's learning, and mindfulness about hegemonic relations without feeling personally on the line for changing our world.[39] As Craig Johnson and David Spicer further suggest in their review of the action learning–based Engineering Management MBA program at Bradford University in the United Kingdom, "Workplace-centered learning produces *learning* managers as opposed to *learned* managers" [italics added].[40] As learners of this nature develop both heightened consciousness and critical mass, they may be able to produce organizational and institutional democratic reform.[41]

Patricia Inman and Sally Vernon suggest the development of narratives and dialogic approaches, such as scenarios and process maps, to capture the rich, embedded learning made available through work-based learning.[42] Narratives are comparable to journals but seek to connect the individual's accomplishments to the wider organizational culture. Scenario building and process mapping extend the narrative methodology by engaging participants in planning and consensus-building processes that invite them to reorganize their perceptions about future team-unit development and organizational growth.

Measuring the substantive outcomes from work-based learning can be grouped into four categories: (1) effects on self, (2) effects on interpersonal and team relationships, (3) effects on professional behavior, and (4) effects on projects.

Effects on the Self. Within the self domain, there are three categories of interest: academic development, personal development, and career development. Although links have been found between work-based learning and academic performance, the real academic benefit derives from the participants' increased motivation to learn and their heightened interest in learning itself.[43] Other benefits include the ability to put classroom theories into practice as well as crafting a major that aligns well with one's talent and then persisting in that major until graduation.[44]

Personal development refers to the personal and social growth of participants, and it covers a range of individual and interpersonal benefits. Among these are gains in self-esteem, increased empathetic listening, relationship building, and ethical orientation; commitment to challenge oneself; knowledge of one's preferred learning style; enhanced ability to formulate more informed actions; higher readiness to take responsibility and initiative; proclivity to share and reflect more with others; and capacity to recognize multiple perspectives.[45]

Career development refers to the evolution of life roles that people assume throughout their lives, though in the instance of graduating students, it tends to refer to their vocational choices upon the completion of full-time schooling. Career benefits have incorporated such dimensions as career identity and clarification, career decision making, job search duration, and career progress.[46]

To provide an example of specific measures that have shown good promise of revealing the deeper individual benefits embedded in work-based learning, let's consider two variables: *work self-efficacy* and *practice-based learning outcomes*. Self-efficacy can be thought of as an intervening variable affecting the ultimate outcomes of practice-based learning. It has been widely established in the literature as a critical construct within Albert Bandura's social learning theory.[47] It constitutes a judgment about one's ability to perform a particular behavior pattern. Self-efficacy expectations are considered the primary cognitive determinant of whether or not an individual will attempt a given behavior. Self-efficacy is known to have considerable explanatory power over such behaviors as self-regulation, achievement strivings, academic persistence and success, coping, choice of career opportunities, and career competency.[48] Perhaps its most noteworthy contribution is its empirical relationship to subsequent performance.[49]

Whereas self-efficacy, in general, refers to one's confidence in executing courses of action in managing a wide array of situations, work self-efficacy assesses workers' confidence in managing workplace experiences. A new work self-efficacy inventory under development at the Center for Work and Learning at Northeastern University measures a range of behaviors and practices—for example, exhibiting teamwork, expressing sensitivity, managing politics, handling pressure—attending to participants' beliefs in their command of the social requirements necessary for success in the workplace. Since efficacy is a malleable property, there are methods by which employees may achieve relative success in their jobs as well as learning within the workplace by increasing their confidence in performing many of these work-related behaviors.

Ultimately, work-based learning should be able to target learning outcomes that are specifically practice-based—in other words, that derive from learning within the practice world rather than from the classroom.[50] An outcome variable of this nature is proposed to entail three dimensions:

Engaging knowledge from experience: Engagement posits a condition that may have to exist within the participant because it characterizes a readiness to learn from experience. Accordingly, engagement precedes understanding by its appeal to participants to see their own views as tentative and to be open to the views of others.[51] Practice-based learning should accelerate the engagement process by helping participants become more critically aware of their own assumptions and defenses and inconsistencies between their espoused beliefs and their actions.

Extending knowledge from experience: The extending stage characterizes participants using the knowledge they currently have and sharing it with others to manage new or unknown situations. As in Piaget's *assimilation concept*, they attempt to use and also extend an existing cognitive structure to make sense of, systematize, and potentially improve workplace conditions.[52] They may also draw on knowledge from alternative sources, such as the institutional memory of the institution, to help them work through problem dilemmas and challenges and to recognize patterns from one situation to another.[53]

Originating knowledge from experience: In originating, participants develop the confidence to construct new knowledge, often in conjunction with fellow learners, if their command of current theory or if existing cognitive structures are inadequate within new contexts.[54] They thus make contextually relevant judgments while continuing to learn about themselves in practice.[55] They can extract principles that may apply in different cultural settings while continuing to improvise and reframe problems as they go.

Effects on Interpersonal and Team Relationships.   The learning team approach of work-based learning affords participants an opportunity to acquire enhanced teamwork or interpersonal skills. Measures of success might incorporate increased awareness of team dynamics, improved performance as a team member, ability to facilitate teams, greater patience with others, improved listening acuity, faculty in communicating one's feelings, greater sensitivity to others, better probing skills, proficiency in challenging others, adeptness in soliciting collective inquiry, and enhanced networking capability. Teams also benefit as a social system from work-based learning, resulting in possible team learning. Indicators at the team level may include fullness of member participation, creativity, equivalence of influence, balance between concern for task and support of others, degree of challenge and openness, morale, conflict management, commitment to learning, valuing of differences, and ethical consciousness.

My own research of three comprehensive executive programs using action learning verified some of these individual and interpersonal outcomes, which I noted were quite different from conventional training program results.[56] In particular, the programs developed avid questioners: practitioners who questioned not just their own work or that of their unit but also the governing values of their own organization. Johnson's research found that action learning produced both breadth of learning, in the sense of the experience touching on everyday work issues, and depth, addressing deeply rooted attitudes and beliefs.[57] Research by Harley Frank, formerly at Huddersfield University in the United Kingdom, disclosed three principal interpersonal (and personal) learning outcomes from managers' having participated in the university's master's program, based on work-based learning:[58]

1. In working on live issues, the managers began to reframe the problem and even saw themselves as part of the problem they were attempting to deal with.

2. In working through their work-based problem, they ultimately became personally transformed.

3. They experienced double-loop learning.

Consider a case from Professor Frank's work. He described the account of Maggie, a new registrar of a museum service in a large British city. The museum service comprised four separate museums plus a large art gallery. As registrar, Maggie was given the responsibility to upgrade the service's collection standards in order to qualify for national registration and receive funding aid. The enhancement of the service's collections became Maggie's project for the year. In working through this project, Maggie exemplified how a work-based learning student experiences each of the aforementioned outcomes.

1. *She became part of the problem.* Maggie reported that initially she began her project more as a consultant than as a member of the staff. She realized that to be effective she would have to adopt a role in which she would be seen more as "one of them." As she became aware of the gap that existed between the comfortable, settled, "middle-aged men with their cardigans" and her, a motivated young woman, she began to reframe the situation. She came to think of herself as being a "learning manager" in a "non-learning organization." Thinking of herself in these new terms considerably helped her to formulate new actions that she could undertake to positively influence the organization.

2. *She became transformed.* As her project evolved, she began to see that she herself was using ineffectual attributions to characterize her staff. For example, through reflective dialogue in her learning team, she became aware of her observation that her colleagues were unable and unwilling to change, graphically captured in the phrase "middle-aged men with their cardigans," waiting for retirement. Maggie noted, "Following discussion in my set, I reflected and realized I needed to look again and re-interpret my observations. I found I came to appreciate more clearly the staff's situation."

3. *She experienced double-loop learning.* In double-loop and triple-loop learning, which I introduced in Chapter Two, participants seek to inquire about the most fundamental assumptions behind their very practices. One of Maggie's interventions was to initiate an extensive training program for staff, but in order to make it useful, she had to overcome a widely shared perception that training was a "waste of time." Again, through assistance from her learning team, she reformulated training as something more than teaching and instruction. It could also serve as a tool for community building, bringing together groups and individuals in the service who had never met. Further, by rotating the training venues among the service's different museum sites, staff could be given the chance to visit

sites in the same city that many had never seen. Better working relationships evolved among the staff, and Maggie established vital contacts with both internal and external training providers and other stakeholders throughout the city.

Effects on Professional Behavior. Professional behavior or work skills are often ability-based and relate to the technical knowledge pertaining to the profession or field in question.[59] There are some competencies, however, that are generalizable across settings. For example, work-based learning methods are thoughts to point to learners who tend to be more reflective, more interdependent, and more divergent and innovative in their thinking and action.[60] Most of the research in the professional domain has been applied to settings involving management and executive development. Thus, programs are designed to have beneficial outcomes on the participant's managerial behavior. Again, although outcomes reported have tended to be specific to the function or technical area in which the participant may have chosen to concentrate, there are generic managerial indicators of benefits derived from participation in work-based learning.[61] For example, participants note that they have learned the following:

- How to organize teams better back in their work site
- How to relate better to their staff, especially to listen and take criticism
- How to critically question their colleagues on their own problems
- How to delegate more effectively, in particular, to give their staff more responsibility
- How to be more open with their coworkers
- How to behave with greater confidence with senior managers
- How to be more organized
- How to take initiative in improving conditions at work
- How to take on more responsibility in their role
- How to monitor operations more effectively

- How to effect culture change more effectively within their organization

Effects on Projects.   Perhaps the most critical feature in a work-based learning program is the project and the effect it has had on the sponsoring work unit. The measures used in this instance should apply to the business function in question and might be derived as business indicators of effort, process, and performance. If the project were to initiate quality processes, to reduce downtime, to improve customer satisfaction, or to save on costs, then the measures should flow from these respective variables. The reason for including the aforementioned indicators is to avoid an availability bias resulting from concentrating on only a few measures.[62] As suggested earlier, it might also be advisable to collect data both before and after the project to demonstrate change and improvement. If the data can be converted to quantitative metrics, the measurement process can proceed in a straightforward manner. Consider as an example a project in the domain of distribution.[63] A new system is to be put in place to cut down on the number of wrong deliveries from a retail distribution warehouse. The costs associated with wrong orders can be quantified using such indicators as these:

- Cost of picking up the wrong order and redelivering the correct order
- Staff time in stores and at the distribution center reorganizing the order
- Time attributed to sales staff in pacifying angry customers
- Time calculated for the finance staff to reinvoice and issue credit notes

Using data of this sort can lead to explicit calculations that can demonstrate the benefits from the project. However, less obvious, nonquantitative measures should not be overlooked in the measurement system. Some benefits, such as customer goodwill or staff morale, though not as readily computable, should be incorporated. There may also be hidden costs in a project of this nature that should be accounted for, such as resistance from critical stakeholders or loss of staff commitment if there were to be pressure to achieve immediate targets.

A measurement system should be designed initially based upon the goals of the project and then adapted as the project unfolds. Any decision regarding the number of measures should follow the well-known canon that one should measure everything that matters and not much else! The key is to provide project stakeholders with timely and reliable information that would be relevant to the ongoing development of the project. Intangible factors, such as morale and satisfaction, should be included along with standard performance indicators. In some instances, *proxy indicators* or unobtrusive measures will need to be devised in place of the less tangible variables. An example of an unobtrusive measure is growth in resources attached to the project over and above its budgeted expenses. Successful projects generate support that can be measured in the amount of resources, physical and human, that are allocated to it. Another unobtrusive measure is the survival of the project beyond the work-based learning program. This measure suggests that successful projects take on a life of their own. Similarly, in the instance of measuring the overall success of a work-based learning program, one might use the willingness to pay for a repeat performance as an appropriate proxy.

The more direct measures can be divided into the three criteria already presented (effort, process, performance), but let's refer to them using the systems theory references of input, process, and output. Consider the following example of a project in the domain of order entry:[64]

The project was initiated in the order entry (OE) department as a result of what appeared to be a growing number of complaints about orders picked up by the customer service department. The participant undertaking the project was asked by the OE manager to find out if in fact the number of complaints was accelerating, what the source of these complaints was, and what the implications were. The project unfolded as a research undertaking for the participant, who designed a plan to interview staff, survey customers, assess records, and observe the department in operation. Although the analysis constituted the bulk of the project in this case, a more extensive project or a follow-up to the diagnosis would require the planning and implementation of some specific interventions to solve the problems identified, not only in order entry but also in related departments.

The measures that might be used for the project phase include some of the following:

Input

Number of orders changed as a percentage of total orders over a specified monthly period

Number of complaints received by product, severity, and reason (that is, order incorrect, order incomplete, order damaged on delivery, order unduly delayed)

Process (Internal)

Number of complaints processed per hour by product, severity, and reason

Number of orders processed that were considered illegible

A detailed description of the order entry job as its relates to complaint handling as reported by order entry clerks, with any variances noted

Process (External)

Assessment of phone system downtime and problems based upon records over a monthly period

Assessment of mail delivery system over the same monthly period

Sales forecast for the month in question

Shipping errors occurring during the month in question

Output

Cost of complaint handling in terms of time and labor

Cost of complaints in terms of refunds, replacements, and lost sales

Percentage of complaints not resolved on first inquiry,
within twenty-four hours

Customer satisfaction index (from direct mailing to
complainants)

It is important to keep in mind that outputs from work-based
learning cannot always jibe with standard financial indicators since
we are often measuring knowledge, an intangible asset. Intangible
assets constitute the difference between the market value of a company and its official net book value. They embody the competence
of its employees and their contribution to the success of the organization through such vehicles as R&D, customer and supplier relations, concepts and "know-how," and image. Measuring outputs in
knowledge and learning is very possible but requires the development of nonstandard measures of performance. Consider as an example the indicators Sveiby has developed in the domain of
customer relations for some Swedish professional service firms such
as Scandia, PLS-Consult, and Celemi.[65] These measures could be
adopted as part of project activities, for instance, in the area of market outreach.

Sveiby recommends that firms first categorize customers into
such domains as those who can contribute to and extend the firm's
image, those who can provide references to other prospective customers, those who provide challenging and growthful assignments,
and those who provide learning opportunities for junior staff.

Once customers are so categorized, a number of output measures
have been developed beyond the conventional customer satisfaction index, including:

- Sales and profitability per customer type
- Size of customer base
- Devoted customer ratio
- Frequency of repeat orders
- Proportion of junior time spent with competence-enhancing
  customers

11

Work-Based Learning Program Applications

Frank Leahy, the legendary football coach of Notre
Dame, would occasionally rely on theory to get his
point across. At one practice, dissatisfied with the level
of play, he picked up an object and said to his players:
"All right men, let's return to the fundamentals. Let's
say this is a football." One of the linemen, taking notes
in the back of the room fervently yelled out, "Wait a
minute, Coach. Not so fast!"

This last chapter is devoted purely to practical applications of the
methods detailed in the book. In particular, for those who wish to
undertake a program of work-based learning in their organization,
I have prepared a prototype program at the outset of the chapter. I
then provide some examples, especially in the developing world, on
how to apply work-based learning in global programs. I also address
the issue of multicultural sensitivity when attempting to apply
work-based learning methods abroad. We finish with three comprehensive examples of work-based learning programs that make
use of many of the principles and practices outlined in this book.

Prototype Program

I would like to demonstrate a prototypical learning program, combining some of the collective learning types of the model of work-based
learning and applying them to the domain of executive education
(see Table 11.1). In any orientation, which precedes program launch,

it is important that the executive team of the organization, as suggested in the last chapter, commit itself to executive development using a work-based learning approach rather than the conventional structured classroom model. The program should also be designed in an environment that supports learning as a basic tenet of the culture. Further, senior staff should demonstrate their support of the program by being actively involved, whether by promoting the value of the program in their communications or by participating as sponsors of projects, mentors, module speakers, instructors, or participants.

Even in conventional training programs, senior executives and their staffs have begun to play more of a role in the instructional domain. For example, in launching a new enterprise strategy containing a revised worldwide code of conduct, Caterpillar used a cascade strategy involving *leaders as teachers*.[1] The teaching strategy began with the CEO and five top executives teaching six hundred directors over two days in six locations around the world. The six hundred directors then taught other managers who in turn taught their employees, thereby spreading the strategy throughout the organization.

No two programs need to look alike from one organization to another since the features of work-based learning are dependent on such conditions as the readiness level of the learners, the strengths and preferences of the sponsors and facilitators, or the past practices of the sponsoring unit or organization. As a rule of thumb, however, if the learners are uninitiated, it is more threatening to expose them to their tacit assumptions than to have them articulate their explicit beliefs. This is especially the case if the assumptions under review might expose learners to their psychological defenses or to their emotional or personal reactions to others. Hence, programs might start by having participants, perhaps through a seminar series, study some novel domains of professional practice, exposing them to some new skills and competencies that (1) they can immediately put to use in their current job and (2) they will find helpful in the development of their subsequent work-based learning experiences. For example, they might consider different perspectives of leadership or learn how the organization might like to transition to a team-based

Table 11.1. A Prototype Work-Based Learning Program for Executive Development

	Orientation	Seminar Series	Learning Teams	Projects	Community of Practice	Presentation
Purpose	Recognition of value of work-based learning philosophy	Exposure to competencies to use on the job and to support work-based projects	Opportunity to place new theories into practice and obtain the support of a learning team	Practice of leadership concepts in projects that supply strategic value to organization	Merger of learning teams and work teams to undertake worthwhile projects while working toward higher levels of insight and performance	Opportunity for project teams to present findings and learning to sponsors
Approximate time frame	One day prior to program or through communications	Two hours/week for six to ten weeks	Cycles of two hours/week for six to twenty-four weeks	Daily for two to three weeks or one day/week for four to six months	Daily for two to three weeks or one day/week for four to six months or continually	One to two days
Sample activities	Communication from senior management to support recruitment into program	Perspectives on leadership, research methods, journal writing, e-portfolios, mentorship	Debriefing of real-time experiences, testing of theories-in-use, learning how to publicly reflect	Individuals working in such projects as globalization of HR or IT functions or quality processes, while continuing to meet in learning teams	Current work teams now versed in action learning and action science techniques, complete short- or long-term projects while developing themselves as a high-performing supportive unit	Teams make a presentation of their projects to sponsors and to other interested senior executives, noting challenges, accomplishments, and learning, both acquired and yet to be acquired

culture. In support of subsequent modules of the program, participants might study both how to collect and how to analyze data. This might include a crash course on the use of quantitative and qualitative research methods. Although the discussion at this point might safely begin at the conceptual level, there should also be opportunities for participants to practice some of the new skills introduced, using experiential methods.

Citibank, under senior human resource executive, Larry Phillips, developed a Business Manager Leadership action learning program that started off with a learning seminar. During this seminar, six skills, thought to be critical in preparing the participating executives for the program, were presented:[2]

- Strategy
- Service quality and handling
- Strategic cost management
- Risk management
- Technology management
- People management

In time, the focus can shift from the experiential level to one in which reflections might be offered regarding the use of the ideas in practice. Participants might even be encouraged to bring in experiences from their own jobs to verify or challenge some of the theories under review. During these components, participants should be encouraged to continually observe themselves and others in practice and try to become sensitive to why they act in certain ways. In particular, they should try to notice what tacit theories are actually used in practice, how these theories match against the new theories introduced in the program, and whether people actually behave consistently with whatever theories they espouse.

It may be difficult for some participants to engage in these reflective components without the assistance of a partner or mentor. These *developmental roles* can be critical in encouraging participants to try out new workplace behaviors and learn from their experiences. They are particularly helpful where learning teams are not available to participants on any ongoing basis. The LeaderLab, referred to in Chapter Seven, deployed three helper roles—a process adviser represented by a staff professional, who meets with the participants in person and by phone during the three-month experience; in-course change partners, who work with one another to experiment with and reflect on classroom experiences; and back-home change partners, who help the participants transfer off-site lessons back into the work site.[3]

Another complementary tool to help participants reflect more on their individual development is the journal or portfolio (see Chapter Seven). Journal writing provides an opportunity for participants to break their habitual ways of thinking and acting through reflective withdrawal and reentry.[4] Journals help participants distill lessons from experience and help them track their learning, be it from important lessons, trends, or patterns.[5] What makes the journal or portfolio effective is the discipline it imposes on participants to systematically reflect on their experiences. It also has an anticipatory function in that it allows the participant to visualize experiences before embarking on them.

Perhaps the most propitious way to engage in public reflection and to assess how effectively new theories are being used in practice is to solicit the support of a learning team. Learning teams or action learning sets give participants a chance to debrief their real-time experiences.[6] The experience of working in learning teams was also described in depth in Chapter Seven. Learning teams tend to meet periodically, for example, on a monthly basis, and serve as a supporting mechanism for both individual and project development.

Program development can advance to the next collective level of activity in which participants are asked to deliberately work together to practice some of the new ideas introduced. One way to foster this type of learning is to work on action projects in the sponsoring organization. As was detailed in Chapter Nine, projects are designed to be challenging, to be experimental, and to have strategic value to their sponsoring unit. The identification of projects can be handled through sponsorship or through self-selection. A learning consortium group made up of six major companies in a large New England city uses a focus group methodology to prioritize the most critical issues for the participating executives to study. Group members come together on a monthly basis to discuss the chosen topic, while attempting to carry out changes in their back-home corporate environment precipitated by their learning experience in the group.

Plans and actions undertaken in action projects are subjected to inquiry about their effectiveness. Participants are also typically invited to present their project. Besides a presentation of results, however, participants may be required to prepare a project report detailing the learnings and competencies addressed in the experience as well as any constraints that may have blocked proposed interventions.

General Electric's John F. Welch Leadership Center at Crotonville has been a pioneer in action learning in the United States. Although it provides an array of probing courses and modules, its action learning segments, through such programs as the Business Manager Course (BMC) or the Executive Development Course (EDC), are known for their assembling promising managers and executives into teams to work on a specific assignment critical to GE. The assignments vary by topic from year to year, and although sponsors get a completed project at the end of the courses, the focus at GE has always been on learning. Among its innovations in work-based learning, participants would receive briefings on pertinent market, customer, and financial information. Crotonville would also lay the foundation for the projects by providing in the first weeks of the program state-of-the-art concepts in key substantive domains, ranging from strategic marketing and financial planning to competitive analysis and organizational change. GE also initiated developmental action planning within the action learning experience through a feedback instrument referred to as the Leadership Effectiveness Survey (LES). Finally, just as they did when Jack Welsh was CEO, participants in the BMC and EDC, at the conclusion of the programs, make their recommendations in a presentation to current CEO, Jeffrey Immelt.[7]

Project groups need not assemble organizational strangers to work on problems outside their work area. Intact work teams can participate in development programs to help them become more of a community of practice (CoP). CoPs recognize that their very effectiveness rests on the ability of its members to learn from one another. Participants in such groups not only learn to observe and experiment with their own collective tacit processes in action, but while doing so, they seek to improve their own performance. There are many team-building methods available to help intact groups work toward higher levels of insight and performance. Teaching participants how to become process observers of their own interactions can accelerate development by exposing team members to each other's potential contributions as well as to the team's overall needs.

If the learning community is willing, members can continue to engage their collective consciousness through the process known as *action science*.[8] More than the other learning types, it calls for the deliberate questioning of existing perspectives and interpretations and thus seeks to make explicit the constituent elements of our assumptive worlds. The practices of action science can vary in personal risk from scenario analysis, wherein participants explore the actions of hypothetical characters, to critical incidents, wherein they have the opportunity to face the assumptions framing their own practice through an analysis of events in their lives that are remembered for their emotional significance.[9] For example, participants may be asked to describe an event that made them feel a real "high" of satisfaction and fulfillment and one that made them feel a real "low" of dissatisfaction and disappointment. Repertory grids and metaphor analysis can also be used to help participants bring to the surface their otherwise tacit personal constructs.[10]

The Susan Vogt Fellowship program, sponsored by The Boston Consortium for Higher Education (TBC), referred to in the last chapter, provides elements of both communities of practice and action science in its methodology. The purpose of the Vogt Fellowship is to encourage academic administrators to serve their own staffs as intermediaries of mutual learning and mutual action. Through a year-long process of personal and professional development, a process of collaborative leadership cascades not only throughout the departments and organizations of the fellows but also between their institutions. The program features both didactic modules and individual projects sponsored by senior executives. Fellows meet in learning teams, in which they serve as sounding boards to one another and also challenge each other on their individual and collective tacit processes in action. Each learning team is staffed by a trained facilitator, who reinforces open disclosures by fellows of project dilemmas and of interpersonal blockages occurring within the team. At times, the facilitators will engage the fellows in real-time experiments or rehearsals of current and forthcoming engagements, using such tools as action science's *ladder of inference*. The fellows gradually establish communities of practice that stretch beyond school boundaries and last well beyond the completion of the program. Through this form of collaboration, they unlock any knowledge and generate social capital that in turn they share with the entire consortium of universities within TBC. As one fellow stated in his learning journal prior to completing the program:[11]

> I have forged connections with colleagues that I would not have ordinarily had time for. It has increased my confidence in my own preparation, learning, and judgment. I am eager to go forward and extend this experience into my work environment.

Global Programs

Although most experiments in work-based learning have taken place in the West, it is an approach that has applications for the world at large. Nevertheless, work-based learning needs to be adapted to observe the customs and predispositions toward learning in the new cultures in which it might be introduced.

Experiments in the Developing World

In developing countries, public enterprises are often the engines of development, so it is not surprising that most work-based learning experiments concentrate on developing managerial and business practices in the public sector and among nongovernmental organizations (NGOs). The Khanya-African Institute for Community Driven Development promotes community-driven development and sustainable livelihoods throughout Africa, using action learning and other compatible supplementary processes, such as knowledge management, action research, personal work planning, and evaluation.[12] The Centre for Socio-Eco-Nomic Development (CSEND) in Geneva, Switzerland, has developed management capability programs for many emerging economies, such as in Slovenia, China, and Bolivia. Most of the programs, according to their directorate, are based upon action research and action learning principles as a vehicle for facilitating system transformation and for developing the personal competencies of change agents. In tandem with these two development processes, CSEND also co-creates new institutional arrangements in order to embed action research and action learning methodologies within the larger social system.

Working with their clients' host training institutions, CSEND's work-based learning projects were undertaken having wide policy implications. Examples of such projects in China were:

- Conducting a needs analysis for Chinese training institutions
- Determining how to manage the training of Chinese civil servants
- Improving the competence of county magistrates in decision making, coordination, and organization
- Establishing an intrinsic motivational mechanism within Chinese state enterprises

Examples of such projects in Slovenia were:

- Improving the efficiency of administrative procedures for licensing businesses

- Rationalizing the procedure for obtaining new telephone lines by the Slovene Telekom Office
- Improving the methods for selecting and financing scientific research projects by the Ministry of Science and Technology
- Reorganizing the human resource management function in the Ministry of Transportation and Communication

Work-based learning is at the heart of a community of learners, called GAN-Net, representing global action network directors, researchers, funders, and other stakeholders committed to addressing urgent global social, economic, and environmental issues.[13] Global Action Networks, or GANs, are intersectoral structures that foster linkages among diverse organizations committed to societal change in such areas as employment, nutrition, HIV/AIDS, microenterprise, corruption, climate change, and sustainable fishing and forestry. GAN-Net coordinates activities to promote learning and innovation among GANs. One of its projects has been to establish a community of practice, incorporating some fifty diverse GAN leaders, using what are called *generative dialogic change processes*. The generative change (GC) community engages in multi-stakeholder dialogues that are generative because participants experience a mutual shift in awareness regarding their relationship to others and to the project at hand. For example, they have focused on such issues as an irrigation project in Nepal, a "shuttle dialogue" in Northern Ireland; a peace initiative in the province of Sulu, the Philippines; the development of Millennium Development Goals in Mauritania; and a national dialogue on education in Guatemala.

The core protocol for implementing change within the GC community of practice is the support of action learning initiatives that create spaces for collective reflection within and across the multiple areas of activity. The community synthesizes the learning that emerges and then formulates guiding questions for subsequent inquiry. Through these work-based learning processes, the GC community has attempted to create a space for fundamental system change by examining the deep structures behind existing relationships and by co-creating positive outcomes for all involved stakeholders.

Although there are opportunities for wide application of work-based learning principles in developing countries, educational policymakers wishing to undertake experiments in work-based learning are advised to proceed cautiously. In order to be careful about possible implicit ethnocentrism, cautions could also be advised for organizational subcultures within the developed world. The principal concern is that in many cultures, learners are viewed as (and may even view themselves as) passive and dependent, whereas teachers are active and authoritative.[14] In such environments, learners have difficulty with pedagogical approaches such as work-based learning, which ask them to take responsibility for their own learning and self-reflect. In a similar vein, teachers find it difficult to let go of their control of the learning process for fear that it would undermine their authority. Indeed, in some cultures there is wide deference to those with presumed expert authority. Moreover, there is also tremendous respect for book knowledge over knowledge emanating from work itself.

Some of the work-based learning developmental approaches, such as mentorships, multisource feedback, and individual development plans, require considerable contextual adaptations. A cross-cultural study on the effectiveness of 360-degree feedback—in particular its process for originating, distributing, and sharing feedback data and the willingness of ratees to accept and act upon such data—found its practices to be culturally dependent.[15] For example, the Malaysian participants, as compared with the Israeli, Filipino, and U.S. managers, showed consistent declines in self-awareness and skill development, resulting in lower subordinate ratings. The authors' explanation for the difference was that the 360-degree feedback process is likely to be most effective in cultures low on power distance—that maintain relatively narrow social stratification within the society—and individualistic rather than collectivistic in their cultural values. Other studies have found that individuals in high power distance cultures are reluctant to provide information to someone who is not a superior or to assess someone apart from one's work group.[16]

Roland Yeo also reported on a three-year experiment using reflective–action learning groups (RALG) in a Singaporean institution of higher education.[17] The RALGs were designed to give faculty a learning space to safely question their own observations and insights, especially relative to their teaching practices, and to question the academic practices of their own institution using double-loop learning. Although the experiment was judged to be successful in exposing staff to meaningful teaching practices, most of the lower-ranking faculty could not see the immediate effects of RALG and found it added responsibility to their daily work. Further, some of the reflective practices cannot be deemed consistent with action science principles originating in the United States. For example, discussions were based on a specific topic in line with a theme set by the deputy director of academic affairs. And although the participants felt safe exploring issues with one another, there seemed to have been an emphasis on order and deference. In the words of one participant, "The discussions help us to internalize and put things in the right perspective; for example, are we on the right or wrong track?"

Mike Marquardt and Lichia Yiu have offered some very specific cautions in using work-based learning in the non-Western world.[18] Nevertheless, they don't advise barring ongoing experimentation with some of this book's principles and practices but rather that they be introduced while keeping in mind some of our inherent Western-based assumptions.[19] Let's consider three specific instances: learning teams, projects, and public reflection.

Learning teams: In constituting learning teams, we tend to mix people of differing ages, genders, and roles. The inherent philosophy of such teams recognizes such Western values as egalitarianism and informality and such practices as offering different perspectives and promoting give-and-take among members. In most other cultures, however, mixing people of different status groups may disturb their sense of hierarchy, their respect of differences, and the role of power and authority in the workplace. Further, formality among the different statuses in groups may be the expected communication mode.

In one of Yiu's action learning interventions to improve the effectiveness of management training among China's economic and administrative cadres, she found that learning team members were much more prone to share their questioning insights with their learning team facilitator than with one another. Meanwhile, facilitators were observed as having a more paternalistic, nurturing, and less confrontational style, compared with their Western counterparts and were more comfortable working on challenging personal issues with members individually than with the team as a whole.

Projects: As we have seen, action projects tend to focus on real organizational problems within real time frames. The project team is advised to assume authority to act within its sphere of responsibility. Yet in some non-Western cultures, having a group take on a managerial task might reflect poorly on the manager, who might lose face if having to admit an inability to handle the problem himself or herself. In addition, the sharing of personal difficulties might be seen as culturally crass. Having someone outside one's immediate environment work on an internal problem might also be seen as an unnecessary incursion.

Public reflection: Public reflection, by promoting a thinking about one's thinking, calls for public examination of the most fundamental assumptions and premises behind our practices. Co-participants in work-based learning are viewed as learning resources who can help us bring things into perspective and draw out our questioning insight. In some cultures, however, a manager's authority, professional competence, and information are seen as personal possessions. He or she may be reluctant to share information. Moreover, questioning one another, especially pointing out a weakness to those of superior status, would be seen as disrespectful or insulting. One also does not wish to be seen asking a foolish question. There is also value, within some Asian countries for example, to withholding one's feelings and thoughts and to respect personal boundaries by not prying into the feelings and thoughts of others.

Work-based learning programs thus need cultural modifications to be successful. Yiu and her colleague, Professor Raymond Saner, found they had to make the following modifications to the earlier cited training program to adapt it to the Chinese culture:

1. The native instructional team performed more effectively after receiving personal coaching in work-based learning.

2. Considerable attention needed to be devoted to identify individuals with sufficient psychological consciousness and interpersonal skills to deal with the social processes inherent in learning teams.

3. Reflection was introduced focusing more on tasks and methodology than on individual challenges and relationships.

4. Senior supervisors supported projects after experiencing a training program of their own with its own learning objectives, and after having more personal contact with the trainers.

Transformation in non-Western cultures toward more reflective practices is possible, especially as these practices are contextually adapted. In some instances, the practice may just require a reframing. Thinking of a question as a challenge may be reframed as a sign of interest or curiosity, even a gift. Consider the example of the work of Arphorn Chuaprapaisilp, who combined action research with the Buddhist teaching known as *Satipatthana* to transform nursing education at the Department of Medical Nursing, Prince of Songkla University, in Thailand.[20] Chuaprapaisilp reported that there are few work-based learning components in clinical teaching in Thailand and instead that content learning and academic excellence are stressed. Chuaprapaisilp's intervention entailed moving the traditional approach to learning—based on observing, remembering, and copying—to a critical approach represented by reflection on experience. According to the new approach, known as the Critical Experiential Learning Model, teachers initially created a democratic learning atmosphere wherein they clarified together with their students the objectives, structures, processes, roles, and assumptions in the conduct of the students' subsequent clinical work. The model included a process of gaining emancipation through experience such that teachers and students together challenged existing structures, identified contradictions, established clear communication, and engaged in the reflective process of Satipatthana, or mindfulness. Satipatthana promotes contemplation of the body, feelings, mental states, and mental events. Chuaprapaisilp points out that in Buddhist terminology, productive *contemplation*, supported by *virtue*, will ultimately lead to *wisdom*. The Critical Experiential Learning Model, according to Chuaprapaisilp, not only demonstrated that participants in this Eastern culture were able to improve their learning practices but it also demonstrated that such practices could enhance the quality of nursing care.

In contrast to the view that work-based learning is potentially inaccessible to the developing world, a branch of action learning, sometimes referred to as the *Southern School*, suggests that any deficiency of learner proactivity in the Third World is as much due to oppression as to adherence to cultural values. Freire, for example, believed that learning starts when people can begin to construct their own reality as opposed to receiving the wisdom of the dominant culture; therefore, learning is very much tied to the process of empowerment.[21] Fals-Borda and Rahman delve into the relationship between knowledge and power, arguing that control over the production of knowledge can further isolate disenfranchised groups from those in intellectual power who maintain a monopoly over the supply of knowledge, just as the wealthy maintain a monopoly over material resources.[22] In this case, work-based learning also has a political dimension, calling for collaboration between participants from privileged groups, who have academic or conceptual knowledge, and those among the economically disadvantaged, who have experiential knowledge.

Multinational Sensitivity

Work-based learning is ideally designed to help organizations develop their cross-cultural sensitivity, a competency that has become critical in our age of the global marketplace. Many of our national corporations are looking to establish a global identity and strategy for their businesses. Accordingly, they are interested in expanding beyond domestic markets, especially as local demand becomes satiated. Not only are they seeking new markets for their products and services, but they are also intent on acquiring new resources, be it physical or labor. However, global expansion requires much more than "showing up." Multinational pathfinders need to develop a sensitivity in working across boundaries. They need to know how to develop trusting relationships with officials from host countries. This includes more than learning how to speak their language. It also requires addressing those subtle cultural differences that exist below the surface.

In one U.S. multinational that relied on short-term action learning projects, a team was sent over to Western Europe to develop ways to increase the company's share of the lighting market. There were questions about whether the market was ready for a new player or whether the company could actually change the market. To get a handle on these questions, the team went into the field and began to interview customers, suppliers, and other stakeholders. Their interviews touched on a wide range of issues from consumer preferences, tax laws, currency fluctuations, and legislation, to the nuances of language. Reporting on this and comparable global projects, Dotlich and Noel suggested that the experience taught program participants that globalization was "not a matter of *where* the company did business but *how*. . . . Being a global company is a mindset rather than a location. . . . [The program helped] future leaders come to terms with the subtleties and ambiguities that come with a global marketplace."[23]

Nancy Adler believes that a great deal of cross-cultural miscommunication stems from misperception, especially caused by stereotypes, subconscious cultural blinders, lack of self-awareness, and projected similarity.[24] Without direct exposure to the other culture, one tends to use one's own meaning to make sense out of the other person's reality. Adler tells the story of a Japanese businessman who wants to tell his Western client that he is uninterested in a particular sale. To be polite, the Japanese businessman says, "That will be very difficult." The client interprets this statement to mean that there are still unresolved problems but that they can be overcome. He responds by asking how his company can help solve the problem. The Japanese businessman, meanwhile, is mystified since he believes he has sent the message that the sale is off.

Americans are often surprised to discover that they are often seen by foreigners as hurried, overly explicit, quite hard working, law abiding, and often too inquisitive. They may come across as businesslike and inauthentic. Miscommunication caused by such impressions needs to be addressed, or it may have unintentional consequences that could affect relationships and ultimately business performance.

One benefit of work-based learning is that it requires direct exposure on the part of participants to other cultures when projects take place in other parts of the world. Further, global teams can be used to constitute these projects. Such teams can give participants a broad understanding of the company's international business, can open up informal networks of communication throughout the organization, and can provide a unique opportunity for employee development. Using social learning theory, Black and Mendenhall argue that cultural sensitivity is best learned from experience because individuals use the consequences of their experiences to shape current and future behavior.[25] Having exposure to projects in other cultures gives work-based learning participants a chance to make sense of their interactions—teaching them, for example, what is appropriate and inappropriate in these settings or which behaviors to execute or suppress. The resulting cross-cultural experience is not simulated as in a classroom exercise but is real, emanating from the rough-and-tumble of actual practice in the field. Participants gain experience in a number of ways, be it from on-site interviews inquiring about the viability of a project prospectus or from having to sell the findings from a project to a local management.

Nortel Networks Corporation, the Toronto-based multinational telecommunications equipment manufacturer, formerly Northern Telecom Ltd., used global executive teams in the early 1990s to initiate its globalization efforts and to change mind-sets. Teams met for nine-month periods, and about five teams were active at any given time. One of the teams included two salespeople from the United States, a country manager from France, an R&D professional from Canada, a manufacturing manger from England, and a senior HR professional from Canada. The team's charge was to determine the best strategy for externalizing product development. Consequently, members traveled to Europe, the Far East, and North America to benchmark best practices and put their recommendations together.[26]

The experience of working with a global, cross-cultural team can present participants with critical lessons in intercultural competence. Intercultural competence entails the ability to analyze communication behavior within a new culture, resulting in an ability to respond to messages *as if from within* that culture.[27] Working with learning teams, Smith and Berg found that there are three processes that can lead early on to growing intercultural competence.[28] First, the team members need to learn how to learn together. As members think of situations in which they had the opportunity to learn something of value but did not, they gradually learn to be more patient with each other when group crises occur. For example, they begin to recognize that some environments are not hospitable to productive group life.

Second, members need to explore their interdependence, which can be accomplished by exploring each other's unique cultural contributions. As they reflect upon the sociopolitical issues within their respective cultures, for example, they may begin to recognize their connectedness. Finally, they also need to learn to work through their differences as they consider cultural norms that are sacred to each respective culture. In this way, they can deal with the inevitable polarities embedded within the group environment, such as confrontation versus conciliation, or individuality versus collectivism. In the former case, some members may believe that it is preferable to confront conflicts or irritations directly, where others may strive to accommodate differences. In the latter instance, some members may be culturally disposed to preserve the centrality of the individual, whereas others may expect individuals to subordinate themselves to the well-being of the group.

In a learning team affiliated with a university-based action learning program that is highly multicultural, one of the members reflected on her experience in the learning team:

> Learning teams constitute a fertile environment where people can develop the ability to diagnose important differences and appreciate cultural diversity. Being part of a team with members from all over the world has allowed me to reconsider certain personal aspects and forced me to become more adaptable according to the team's needs. From different eating habits and vegetarian preferences to working schedules and family issues, a team will always remind you that you cannot be self-centered and that there are different people with various needs in their lives which you have to respect.

Consider next the challenge that general manager Michael Burchett faced when opening the Four Seasons Resort in Bali, Indonesia. Blunt senior managers (like him) from Australia and from other Western societies had to learn how to manage, but even more importantly, how to empower indirect, subtle, and exceptionally polite Indonesians. According to Burchett, expatriate senior managers perceived the local managers as not being sufficiently direct with their staff—that is, as not managing.[29] Meanwhile, the managers were frustrated with senior management because they felt they weren't letting them manage in their own way. The expatriates countered that they had to help them learn to "manage" by instructing them in detail. This in turn led the managers to believe that they were being talked down to.

The reflective elements of work-based learning can help senior managers like Burchett and his staff overcome these cultural barriers by exposing them to their implicit cultural biases and assumptions. In the safety of the learning team, for example, they can explore with their peers from different cultures how their social constructions of reality differ based upon their cultural upbringing and predispositions. Whether in one's own culture or in a global environment, work-based learning can serve as a first step in helping people learn to anticipate and work through the complex human conditions faced in our twenty-first-century organizations.

Comprehensive Case Examples

As a culmination of the many principles and practices recounted throughout this book, let's consider three examples of work-based learning in action.

ARAMARK

Lynn McKee, Executive Vice President of Human Resources for ARAMARK, supplies our first comprehensive example. ARA-MARK, founded in 1959 as Automatic Retailers of America, is today a globally managed services company, having core businesses in food, hospitality, facility, and uniform services. Named to *Fortune Magazine's* list of "America's Most Admired Companies," ARA-MARK, since 1998, has consistently been ranked as one of the top three most admired companies in its industry, as evaluated by peers and industry analysts. The company was also ranked first in its industry in the 2007 Fortune 500 survey.

Although the company achieved an adequate level of success in the early 1990s, revenues and earnings growth were beginning to flatten. The executive staff saw its challenge as transforming the company into a growth enterprise. From a human resource perspective, it had to identify the skills and competencies necessary to make this transformation and then infuse them into the organization, starting with its senior leadership.

Accordingly, ARAMARK—in conjunction with the Pennsylvania State University Executive Programs—created an Executive Leadership Institute (ELI) in 1993 to conceive and implement a shared vision for growth for the company and to bring to fruition its executive education initiatives. It divided its efforts into three components: education, personal development, and action projects.

In the education domain, the ELI recruits a world-class faculty to deliver customized courses over a six-month period. The personal development process for each ELI participant features in-depth interviews with a management psychologist; 360-degree feedback from superiors, peers, and subordinates; and the preparation of a development plan based on the results of these processes.

Turning to the action project component, assignments are made during the first class session. Projects are undertaken concurrent with participants' ongoing job duties. Compatible with work-based learning principles, projects deal with real, challenging business issues and provide ample opportunity for professional and personal growth and development. Each ELI cohort is made up of five teams of six participants per team, with the membership being cross-functional and cross-business unit. The object is to equip the project with fresh eyes and to get participants out into the businesses to help them learn more about the company as a whole. At the conclusion of the experience, project teams make a presentation complete with strategic recommendations.

After the first meeting, project teams schedule their subsequent meetings on their own and decide how they will maintain contact throughout the six-month project period. McKee reports that they meet on an as-needed basis, using whatever communication format is most appropriate. For instance, they might dialogue online; they'll use conference calls; or they might meet face-to-face, especially when they can combine it with attendance at regional or national business meetings of the business unit that they happen to be studying.

In terms of project selection, recommendations for project work from line departments first go to a central pool. Selected senior managers review all recommendations, ensuring that there is substantive variety, balance across business units, and minimal redundancy. ELI staff then, in conjunction with business unit managers, prepare a statement of the project, which in many instances is supported by supplemental information, often in the form of a briefing book. Projects are then assigned to select teams. Each team is also assigned a trained coach.

As an example of a typical project, one team was assigned to critically evaluate the strategic and tactical options for the Vending Division route business. As a division of the Business Services

Group, ARAMARK's vending services maintains a route-based distribution to its client base, primarily business and industry, hospitals, and universities. The project team began by deciding to reframe vending as the *unattended refreshment business*. Interviews and surveys were administered to internal and external stakeholders, including competitors. The approach gradually developed by the team was to consider establishing vending as an independent line of business and thus distinct from business services. This would permit other ARAMARK businesses to manage and sell vending services to their existing clients with support from experts in the newly reformulated Vending Division.

The team next recommended that Vending consider consolidating its operation with ARAMARK/Cory Refreshment Services. A route-based distribution business, Cory focused primarily on small businesses and dealt with white-collar customers as opposed to Vending's solid blue collar base. The benefits projected by the team, which later came to fruition, were reduction in capital costs—such as the need for fewer vehicles, more efficient distribution, reduction in labor costs as support staff could be shared, and consolidated technology.

McKee has shared evaluation data from the ELI, revealing remarkable results. For example, 50 percent of ELI alumni said that their expectations were exceeded, and the other 50 percent said it met their expectations. As for the action projects, fully 98 percent said that the projects provided a meaningful opportunity to apply models and insights to a real ARAMARK issue; 99 percent felt that they gained personal benefit from participating in the project; and 98 percent said they gained insights that could be applied to their own current business environment. Lynn also attributes ELI as having played a critical role not just in the company's growth but also in its transformation to a collaborative culture that values partnerships, teamwork, and innovation.

Penn State Executive Education Professor Albert Vicere was also interviewed about ELI since he was there at the outset and has been consulted in its progression ever since. Vicere characterizes the program in this way:[30]

Because of the nature of ARAMARK's business—low margin, trans-action-based, cash flow as king, profitability as a driving force—the culture of the company at the time was very hierarchical. There was-n't a lot of push back; there wasn't a lot of dialogue. What ELI did was to provide a platform for discussion, and once people got a taste of that, a lot more of it started happening. [ELI participants learned] they could have impact. They could be challenging each other; learning from each other.

SUPERVALU

A second comprehensive example of the use of work-based learning is a program of the same name at SUPERVALU. Since its acquisi-tion in 2006 of the retail properties of Albertsons, SUPERVALU has become the third-largest grocery retailing company in the United States, with a nationwide network of some twenty-five hundred re-tail stores. It also complements its retail focus with the nation's largest grocery supply chain operation.

In 2001, the head of its Leadership Development and Organi-zational Effectiveness group and his successor believed that the only meaningful way to provide for internal leadership growth was through a talent development process using work-based learning. Their plans were subsequently endorsed by the top leadership of SUPERVALU, especially by the incoming chief executive officer. In conjunction with then Professor of Management at Boston Col-lege, Joe Raelin, they devised a unique seven-month program that at the time of this writing was in its sixth annual cohort group. Some thirty participants are asked to participate each year, and most are director- and middle-level mangers, representing all the major corporate functions. Divided into project teams, which also function as learning teams, they are assigned to address key strate-gic business issues selected by the executive staff. The projects nor-mally fall outside the participants' area of expertise.

The project teams meet virtually at least weekly and in person four to five times over the full span of the program, when the full community of participants is assembled in what are called *learning conferences*. When brought together as a learning team, the teams meet every two weeks and focus exclusively on personal, professional, and team development with the aid of a trained internal facilitator.

Some of the themes addressed in past projects have been ethnic marketing, extreme price formats, store remodels, distribution leadership, and least cost path. Fifty percent of the projects have been implemented so far, and a number are still active. Teams function "leaderfully," meaning that all participants share the leadership role.

As for accomplishing the original goal of promoting from within and solidifying the company's bench strength, the program has exceeded expectations. The retention rate of all participants has been 91 percent, and the promotion rate for the early cohorts was 49 percent, and for the later cohorts so far, it has been 22 percent.

The current program director has also reported on additional paybacks from SUPERVALU's work-based learning program. Participants acquired vital skills without the expense of job rotations, transfers, or relocation costs. They received broader exposure to all aspects of the company's business. Meanwhile, the projects that were completed successfully would otherwise have been resourced through other means or may not have been funded at all. She also commented on the unique reflection component of the program's learning teams:

> For many, it was a new concept. They learned to give and receive feedback on their individual learning. They also engaged in journaling, one-on-one's, coaching from their facilitator, and team feedback. It forced them to slow down and learn from their actions. Sometimes it was painful but it was always eye-opening and a huge growth opportunity.

Finally, the program director has credited the work-based learning program with providing the company with a brilliant means to help integrate the two entities forming the post-acquisition SUPERVALU, especially from a cultural point of view. It is a challenge for a company to assimilate a new culture, particularly when the resulting organization is four times its prior size—in employment terms. The current cohort, which is made up of both major constituents to the acquisition, has broken down barriers, created new social networks and communities of practice, and formed a single core identity not only because the projects are resolutely cross-sectoral but also because of the program's emphasis on collaborative learning.

AstraZeneca

AstraZeneca is one of the world's leading pharmaceutical companies and is active in over one hundred countries, delivering a flow of new medicines that make a difference in the lives of patients.[31] Angela Hyde, Vice President for Global Learning and Development, has been a strong advocate of using real organizational dilemmas and opportunities as an arena for learning. In particular, she has used a variant of work-based learning, known as Action Reflection Learning (ARL), co-developed by Leadership in International Management, Ltd. (LIM) and the MiL Institute in Sweden.

One of Hyde's greatest challenges has been designing a program that would effectively develop and integrate the top six hundred leaders of the merged AstraZeneca, formed in 1999 through the merger of Astra AB of Sweden and Zeneca group PLC of the United Kingdom. Within the first two years following the merger, the Growing Our AstraZeneca Leaders (GOAL) programs were launched, featuring thirty-two programs, averaging twenty participants per program. Each program had two modules, four Business Challenge Groups (BCGs), and four coaches—one for each BCG. The coaches facilitated large group sessions as well as the work of the BCGs. Each program spanned four to six months, allowing the BCGs to meet between the modules. Prior to each program, the participants completed a 360-degree feedback instrument that served as a foundation for enriching their individual development plans. The larger group sessions provided a forum to illuminate some of the key dilemmas and transitions AstraZeneca was facing as it became a new enterprise.

GOAL ensured that participants from both former Astra and Zeneca participated and that different functions and regions of the world were represented. As these were the six hundred most senior leaders across the company, most of them led sizeable organizations. Most of the business challenges brought to the program focused on such topics as organizational effectiveness, change management, leading across borders, and team alignment. Each challenge was deemed to be current, within the participant's direct control or influence, important to the success of the merger, and supported by the participant's supervisor.

Ernie Turner, President of LIM and one of the consultants working with Hyde in developing GOAL, reported on the case of one of his BCG participants. Robert (a fictitious name) had recently been appointed the manager of a global clinical team, and as a result of the merger, he acquired a new boss "overnight," along with a new team with members from the United States, the United Kingdom, and Sweden. This challenge produced a number of questions that Robert wanted to work on in his team, but the members encouraged him to narrow his questions down to the one that was uppermost in his mind and perhaps critical to the success of the others. He quickly selected the question: "How can I develop a trusting relationship with my new boss who just arrived from a different company other than Astra or Zeneca?"

Ernie suggested an ARL technique of having each team member, using sticky notes, write down as many open-ended rather than leading questions that each could think of, using "I" instead of "you." So, instead of a question like, "Why don't you set some norms with your boss?" which is both leading and actually a recommendation in the guise of a question, it could be something more like, "What have I tried in the past in other relationships with prior bosses that helped me make those relationships really work?" The open "I" question is friendlier than the directive "you" question, so it tends to produce less defensiveness and offers many more potential solutions.

The team tried this approach and within five minutes of a Stop/Reflect/Write/Report silent period, the members generated over sixty questions related to developing a trusting relationship with one's boss. Robert was not asked to answer these questions, nor did he have to write them down. He only had to listen as all of the members read their question before giving the sticky note to Robert. His task was to organize these questions, figure out where he wanted to begin, and report back to the team at the next telecom or face-to-face meeting.

This process had a powerful effect on the team. Everyone was surprised with the range and number of questions that were collectively generated in such a short period. They discovered the art and power of framing challenging yet friendly questions. Since all participants had a chance to share their questions, there was no competition to jump in and control the conversation. It was a relaxed and appreciative atmosphere conducive to learning. And everyone participated.

Similar approaches were used successfully throughout the BCG experience. A secondary benefit was an appreciation for different parts of the business brought to life by the participants' challenges. The team also took time along the way to reflect on the process and how team members could apply this coaching process back home. Several of them tried the same process out in meetings with their own teams.

Through the support and challenge of their peers and coaches, the majority of the participants were able to resolve their business challenges. More importantly, they developed an appreciation and respect for their colleagues who came from different functions, cultures (national and international), and geographical locations. A living network emerged, forming bonds that later served to open doors and solve problems for years to come. Ernie Turner believes that the GOAL Program was the principal reason why the AstraZeneca merger has been so successful. Subsequent leadership programs have been applying similar ARL principles and practices using real business and organizational challenges as the cornerstones for developing line managers, enterprise leaders, and HR business partners.

Among the principles of work-based learning that were brought out by Action Reflection Learning through the GOAL program were:

1. *Reflection.* By building in time to think before speaking, the introverts were allowed the time they needed to be clear on what they wanted to say, and the extraverts had time to edit their thoughts—both of these vital to good listening.

2. *Relevance.* The business challenges were real and current (they were not old case studies), and they evolved with time.

3. *Awareness.* The 360-degree instrument plus frequent feedback raised the level of self-awareness of the participants and thus laid the foundation for continual self-development using Individual Development Plans.

4. *Communities of Practice.* The BCGs became greatly valued learning communities. Many continued well after the program.

5. *Facilitated Learning.* The learning coaches helped create a safe environment and brought new concepts, tools, and just-in-time feedback to individuals, to the BCGs, and to the large group.

6. *Tacit Learning.* While the learning coaches created a receptive environment and introduced helpful processes, most of the wisdom came from the participants; it was their challenges, their questions, and their insights that really made the program work.

7. *Challenging Mental Models.* The diversity in program participation along with learning coach encouragement provided ample fodder for participants to have their mental models constantly challenged.

8. *Holistic Learning.* Through the informal and incidental exchanges over meals and breaks, as well as through the formal design, the staff ensured that everyone brought their whole selves into the program.

Notes

Chapter One

1. See G. Bateson. *Steps to an Ecology of Mind*. New York: Ballantine, 1972; and R. Revans, *The Origins and Growth of Action Learning*. New York: McGraw-Hill, 1982.
2. S. I. Meisel & D. S. Fearon, "Leading Learning." pp. 180–209 in S. A. Cavaleri and D. S. Fearon (eds.), *Managing in Organizations That Learn*. Cambridge, MA: Blackwell, 1996.
3. P.A.C. Smith, "Action Learning and Reflective Practice in Project Environments That Are Related to Leadership Development." *Management Learning*, 32(1), 31–48, 2001.
4. K. Ohmae, *The Mind of the Strategist*. New York: McGraw-Hill, 1982.
5. D. A. Kolb, *Experiential Learning as the Source of Learning and Development*. Upper Saddle River, NJ: Prentice Hall, 1984.
6. P. Honey & A. Mumford, *Manual of Learning Styles* (3rd ed.). Maidenhead, U.K.: Peter Honey Publications, 1992.
7. E. Langer, *The Power of Mindful Learning*. Reading, MA: Addison-Wesley, 1997.
8. J. A. Raelin, "Toward an Epistemology of Practice." *Academy of Management Learning and Education*, 6(4), 2007.
9. C. Lévi-Strauss, *The Savage Mind*. Chicago: University of Chicago Press, 1966.
10. P. B. Vaill. *Learning as a Way of Being*. San Francisco: Jossey-Bass, 1997.

Chapter Two

1. J. D. Adams, "The Hurrier I Go the Behinder I Get." *Vision/Action*, 12(1), 7–11, 1993.
2. S. M. Rinpoche, "Slow Down, You Move Too Fast." *Shambhala Sun*, March 2005, retrieved May 1, 2007, from http://www.shambhalasun.com/index .php?option=com_content&task=view&id=2110.
3. S. E. Berryman, "Apprenticeship as a Paradigm for Learning." pp. 25–40 in J. E. Rosenbaum et al. (eds.), *Youth Apprenticeship in America: Guidelines*

for Building an Effective System. Washington, DC: William T. Grant Foundation Commission on Youth and America's Future, 1992.

4. B. Jordan, "Modes of Teaching and Learning: Questions Raised by the Training of Traditional Birth Attendants." Report No. IRL87–0004. Palo Alto, CA: Institute for Research on Learning, 1987.

5. For a full discussion of the three forms of learning, see M. Visser, "Deutero-Learning in Organizations: A Review and a Reformulation." *Academy of Management Review*, 32(2), 659–667, 2007. For the original work on the subject, see G. Bateson, *Steps to an Ecology of Mind*. San Francisco: Chandler, 1972; and C. Argyris & D. Schön, *Theory in Practice: Increasing Professional Effectiveness*. San Francisco: Jossey-Bass, 1974.

6. See, for example, P. Freire, *Pedagogy of the Oppressed*. New York: Seabury Press, 1970; and J. Burgoyne & V. E. Hodgson, "Natural Learning and Managerial Action: A Phenomenological Study in the Field Setting." *Journal of Management Studies*, 20, 387–399.

7. R. L. Ackoff, *The Democratic Corporation*. New York: Oxford University Press, 1994.

8. Quoted in "The Learning Organization: CE Roundtable." *Chief Executive*, no. 101, 57–64, March 1995.

9. C. A. Twigg, "The Need for a National Learning Infrastructure." *Educom Review*, 29(4, 5, 6), 1994.

10. K. L. Hughes & D. T. Moore, "Pedagogical Strategies for Work-Based Learning." Paper presented at the 1999 Meeting of the American Educational Research Association, Montreal, April 1999.

11. J. S. Bruner, "The Social Context of Language Acquisition." *Language and Communication*, 1(2/3), 155–178, 1981.

12. This is the basis for social cognitive learning theory. See, for example, A. Bandura, *Social Foundations of Thought and Action: A Social Cognitive Theory*. Upper Saddle River, NJ: Prentice Hall, 1986.

13. D. Schön, *The Reflective Practitioner: How Professionals Think in Action*. New York: Basic Books, 1983.

14. J. S. Brown & P. Duguid, "Organizational Learning and Communities of Practice: Towards a Unified View of Working, Learning and Organization." *Organization Science*, 2(1), 40–57, 1991.

15. See, for example, J. W. Martineau & K. M. Hannum, *Evaluating the Impact of Leadership Development: A Professional Guide*. Greensboro, NC: Center for Creative Leadership, 2003; and G. Hernez-Broome & R. L. Hughes, "Leadership Development: Past, Present, and Future." *Human Resource Planning*, 27(1), 24–32, 2004.

16. K. Holmgren, "Pursuing the Corporate Voice: Engaging External Business Partners in Curricular Innovation." *MBA Innovation*, p. 12, Summer 2006.

17. S. Tannenbaum & G. Yukl, "Training and Development in Work Organizations." *Annual Review of Psychology*, 43, 399–441, 1992.

18. K. E. Sveiby, *The New Organizational Wealth*. San Francisco: Berrett-Koehler, 1997.

19. R. O. Brinkerhoff & S. J. Gill, *The Learning Alliance: Systems Thinking in Human Resource Development*. San Francisco: Jossey-Bass, 1994.

20. D. Stamps, "Communities of Practice: Learning Is Social. Training Is Irrelevant?" *Training*, 34(2), 34–42, 1997.

21. A. A. Vicere, M. W. Taylor, & V. T. Freeman, "Executive Development in Major Corporations: A Ten-Year Study." *Journal of Management Development*, 13(1), 4–22, 1994.

22. See, for example, C. Bunning, "Turning Experience into Learning." *Journal of European Industrial Training*, 16(6), 7–12, 1992.

23. R. Gerber, "How Do Workers Learn in Their Work?" *Learning Organization*, 5(4), 168–175, 1998.

24. G. Salaman & J. Butler, "Why Managers Won't Learn." *Management Education and Development*, 21, 183–191, 1990.

25. N. Rabb, "Becoming an Expert in Not Knowing." *Management Learning*, 28(2), 161–175, 1997.

26. E. E. Lawler III, D. A. Nadler, & C. Cammann, *Organizational Assessment*. Hoboken, NJ: Wiley, 1980; and C. Argyris & R. S. Kaplan, "Implementing New Knowledge: The Case of Activity-Based Costing." *Accounting Horizons*, 8(3), 83–105, 1994.

27. J. A. Raelin, "Individual and Situational Predictors of Successful Outcomes from Action Learning." *Journal of Management Education*, 21(3), 368–394, 1997; and J. A. Raelin & M. Lebien, "Learn by Doing." *HR Magazine*, 38(2), 61–70, 1993.

28. J. A. Raelin, "The Effects of Graduate Management Action Learning Environments on Public Reflectiveness in Managerial Practice." *Management Research News*, 14(7/8/9), 43–48, 1991.

29. G. Salaman & J. Butler, "Why Managers Won't Learn." *Management Education and Development*, 21, 183–191, 1990.

30. N. Adler & A. B. (Rami) Shani, "In Search of an Alternative Framework for the Creation of Actionable Knowledge: Table-Tennis Research at Ericsson." In W. Pasmore and R. W. Woodman (eds.), *Research in Organizational Change and Development* (Vol. 13., pp. 43–79). Greenwich, CT: JAI, 2001.

Chapter Three

1. J. C. Redding & R. F. Catalanello, *Strategic Readiness*. San Francisco: Jossey-Bass, 1994.

2. P. B. Vaill, *Learning as a Way of Being*. San Francisco: Jossey-Bass, 1997.

3. A. L. Flood, "The Business of Business Is Learning." Address to the Canadian Payments Association, Vancouver, Canada, April 26, 1993.

4. J. Hayes & C. W. Allinson, "Cognitive Style and the Theory and Practice of Individual and Collective Learning in Organizations." *Management Learning*, 51(7), 847–871, 1998.

5. A. J. DiBella, E. C. Nevis, & J. M. Gould, "Understanding Organizational Learning Capability." *Journal of Management Studies*, 33, 361–379, 1996.

6. C. W. Choo, *The Knowing Organization*. New York: Oxford University Press, 1998.

7. K. E. Weick, *The Social Psychology of Organizing* (2nd ed.). New York: Random House, 1979.

8. A. D. Meyer, "Adapting to Environmental Jolts." *Administrative Science Quarterly*, 27(4), 515–537, 1982.

9. N. M. Dixon, "A Practical Model for Organizational Learning." *Issues and Observations*, 15(2), 1–4, 1995.

10. C. Hendry, "Understanding and Creating Whole Organizational Change Through Learning Theory." *Human Relations*, 49(5), 621–641, 1996.

11. R. M. Grant, "Prospering in Dynamically-Competitive Environments: Organizational Capability as Knowledge Integration." *Organization Science*, 7, 375–387, 1996.

12. C. Argyris, *Reasoning, Learning and Action*. San Francisco: Jossey-Bass, 1982.

13. L. Baird, J. Henderson, & S. Watts, "Learning from Action: An Analysis of the Center for Army Lessons Learned (CALL)." *Human Resource Management*, 36(4), 385–395, 1997.

14. D. R. Tobin, *The Knowledge-Enabled Organization*. New York: AMACOM, 1988.

15. M. Egan, "Creating a Knowledge Bank." *Strategic Human Resource Review*, 2(2), 30–34, 2003.

16. J. Hibbard, "Knowing What We Know." *Information Week*, no. 653, 46–64, October 20, 1997.

17. M. Halper, "Everyone in the Knowledge Pool." *Computerworld Global Innovators*, December 8, 1997.

18. C. O'Dell & C. J. Grayson, "If Only We Knew What We Know: Identification and Transfer of Internal Best Practices." *California Management Review*, 40(3), 154–174, 1998.

19. M. Polanyi, *The Tacit Dimension*. New York: Doubleday, 1966.

20. D. Schön, *The Reflective Practitioner: How Professionals Think in Action*. New York: Basic Books, 1983; and K. L. Dreyfus & S. E. Dreyfus, *Mind Over Machine*. New York: Free Press, 1986.

21. L. T. Hoshmand & D. E. Polkinghorne, "Redefining the Science-Practice Relationship and Professional Training." *American Psychologist*, 47(1), 55–66, 1992.

22. W. Orlikowski, "Improvising Organizational Transformation over Time: A Situated Change Perspective." *Information Systems Research*, 7, 63–92, 1986; and H. Tsoukas, *Complex Knowledge: Studies in Organizational Epistemology*. New York: Oxford University Press, 2005.

23. G. Morgan & R. Ramirez, "Action Learning: A Holographic Metaphor for Guiding Social Change." *Human Relations*, 37(1), 1–28, 1983.

24. A. Nehamas, *Nietzsche: Life as Literature*. Cambridge, MA: Harvard University Press, 1985.

25. J. A. Raelin, *The Clash of Cultures: Managers Managing Professionals*. Boston: Harvard Business School Press, 1991.

26. K. E. Sveiby, *The New Organizational Wealth*. San Francisco: Berrett-Koehler, 1997.

27. S. Gherardi, D. Nicolini, & F. Odella, "Toward a Social Understanding of How People Learn in Organizations." *Management Learning*, 29(3), 273–297, 1998.

28. R. Newton & M. J. Wilkinson, "When the Talking Is Over: Using Action Learning." *Health Manpower Management*, 21(1), 34–39, 1995.

29. D. Botham, "Action Learning and the Programme at the Revans Centre." University of Salford, U.K., Unpublished manuscript, 1997.

30. B. Rogoff, *Apprenticeship in Thinking*. New York: Oxford University Press, 1990.

31. A. de Geus, "The Living Company." *Harvard Business Review*, 75(2), 51–59, 1997.

32. P. Coughlan, A. Harbison, T. Dromgoole, & D. Duff, "Continuous Improvement Through Collaborative Action Learning." *International Journal of Technology Management*, 22(4), 285–302, 2001.

33. See Y. Boshyk (ed.), *Action Learning Worldwide: Experiences of Leadership and Organizational Development*. New York: Palgrave, 2002.

34. A. Gregg-Logan, "Business Driven Action Learning Catches on All Over the World." Distance-Educator.com, retrieved May 29, 2007, from http://www.distance-educator.com/ecourses/Article6809.html.

35. R. Jacobs, "Getting the Measure of Management Competence." *Personnel Management*, 21(6), 32–37, 1989; and H. M. Schroder, *Managerial Competencies: The Key to Excellence*. Dubuque, IA: Kendall/Hunt, 1989.

36. R. Albanese, "Competence-Based Management Education." *Journal of Management Development*, 8(2), 66–76, 1989.

37. R. Boyatzis, *The Competent Manager: A Model for Effective Performance*. Hoboken, NJ: Wiley, 1982.

38. E. A. Powers, "The AMA Management Competency Programs: A Development Process." *Exchange: The Organization Behavior Teaching Journal*, 8(2), 16–20, 1983.

39. J. A. Raelin & S. Cooledge, "From Generic to Organic Competencies." *Human Resource Planning*, 18(3), 24–33, 1995.

40. C. Woodruffe, "Competent by Any Other Name." *Personnel Management*, 23(9), 30–33, 1991.

41. M. Pedler, J. Burgoyne, & T. Boydell, *A Manager's Guide to Self Development*. New York: McGraw-Hill, 1978.

42. T.W.H. Ng & D. C. Feldman, "The School-to-Work Transition: A Role Identity Perspective." *Journal of Vocational Behavior*, 71(1), 114–134, 2007.

43. For more detail on experiential education programs, see, for example, J. Eyler & D. E. Giles, *Where Is the Learning in Service-Learning?* San Francisco: Jossey-Bass, 1999; P. L. Linn, A. Howard & E. Miller (eds.), *Handbook for Research in Cooperative Education and Internships*. Mahwah, NJ: Erlbaum, 2004; and the Web site http://www.work-basedlearning.org,

created by the Conference Board with financial support from the U.S. Department of Education.

44. See, for example, R. Wilson, *Invisible No Longer: Advancing the Entry-Level Workforce in Health Care*, Boston: Jobs for the Future, 2006; and the Web site, http://www.jobs2careers.org/, accessed on May 28, 2007.

45. V. Swallow, "Learning on the Job: Accredited Work Based Learning." *Emergency Nurse*, 8(6), 35–39, 2000.

46. M. A. Hamilton & S. F. Hamilton, "When Is Work a Learning Experience." *Phi Delta Kappan*, 78(9), 682–689, 1997.

47. K. M. Hollenbeck, "School-to-Work: Promise and Effectiveness." *Upjohn Institute Employment Research*, 4(2), 5–6, 1997.

48. A. R. Damasio, *Descartes' Error: Emotion, Reason, and the Human Brain*. New York: Putnam, 1994; H. Letiche & R. Van Hattem, "Self and Organization: Knowledge Work and Fragmentation." *Journal of Organization Change Management*, 13(4), 93–107, 2000; and A. Styhre, "Knowledge as a Virtual Asset: Bergson's Notion of Virtuality and Organizational Knowledge." *Culture and Organization*, 9(1), 15–26, 2003.

49. R. M. Freeland, "The Third Way." *Atlantic Monthly*, 294(3), 141–147, 2004.

50. J. M. Braxton, "Reflections on a Scholarship of Practice." *Review of Higher Education*, 28(2), 285–293, 2005.

51. See, for example, Association of American Medical Colleges. *Physicians for the Twenty-First Century. Report of the Project Panel on the General Professional Education for the Physician*. Washington, DC: Association of American Medical Colleges, 1998; R. Maccrate, *Legal Education and Professional Development: An Educational Continuum Report of the Task Force on Law Schools and the Profession: Narrowing the Gap*. Washington, DC: American Bar Association, Section of Legal Education and Admission to the Bar, 1992; and H. Mintzberg, *Managers Not MBAs: A Hard Look at the Soft Practice of Managing and Management Development*. San Francisco: Berrett-Koehler, 2004.

52. M. Bastedo, "General Education." In J. Forest & K. Kinser (eds.), *Higher Education in the United States* (pp. 273–276). Santa Barbara: ABC-CLIO, 2002; and S. M. Glynn, L. P. Aultman, & A. M. Owens, "Motivation to Learn in General Education Programs." *Journal of General Education*, 54(2), 150–170, 2005.

53. J. A. Raelin, "Individual and Situational Predictors of Successful Outcomes from Action Learning." *Journal of Management Education*, 21(3), 368–394, 1997.

54. C. Bunning, "Turning Experience into Learning." *Journal of European Industrial Training*, 16(6), 7–12, 1992.

55. P. Honey & A. Mumford, *Manual of Learning Styles* (3rd ed.). Maidenhead, U.K.: Peter Honey Publications, 1992.

56. L. T. Eby & G. H. Dobbins, "Collectivist Orientation in Teams: An Individual and Group-level Analysis." *Journal of Organizational Behavior*, 18, 275–295, 1997.

57. E. Antonacopoulou, "Mathophobia and Philomathia: A New Perspective and Its Implications for Management Education." Paper presented at the 1995 Annual Meeting of the Academy of Management, Vancouver, Canada, August 7, 1995.

58. K. Weinstein, *Action Learning: A Journey in Discovery and Development*. New York: HarperCollins, 1995.

59. A. Bandura, *Social Foundations of Thought and Action: A Social Cognitive Theory*. Upper Saddle River, NJ: Prentice Hall, 1986.

60. J. A. Raelin, "Toward an Epistemology of Practice." *Academy of Management Learning and Education*, 6(4), 2007.

61. C. Bunning, "Turning Experience into Learning." *Journal of European Industrial Training*, 16(6), 7–12, 1992.

62. P. Honey, "Establishing a Learning Regime." *Organisations and People*, 1(1), 6–9, 1994.

63. J. A. Raelin, *Creating Leaderful Organizations: How to Bring Out Leadership in Everyone*. San Francisco: Berrett-Koehler, 2003.

64. C. L. Pearce & J. A. Conger, *Shared Leadership: Reframing the Hows and Whys of Leadership*. Thousand Oaks, CA: Sage, 2002.

65. See C. L. Pearce & H. P. Sims Jr., "Vertical Versus Shared Leadership as Predictors of the Effectiveness of Change Management Teams: An Examination of Aversive, Directive, Transactional, Transformational, and Empowering Leader Behaviors." *Group Dynamics: Theory, Research, and Practice*, 6(2), 172–197, 2002.

66. M. Ackerman, V. Pipek, & V. Wulf (eds.), *Sharing Expertise: Beyond Knowledge Management*. Cambridge, MA: MIT Press, 2003.

67. For a review of participative group processes, see K. Lewin, *Field Theory in Social Science: Selected Theoretical Papers* (D. Cartwright, ed.). New York: HarperCollins, 1951; D. Cartwright & A. Zander (eds.), *Group Dynamics: Research and Theory*. Evanston, IL: Row, Peterson and Company, 1953; W. G. Dyer, *Team Building: Issues and Alternatives*. Reading, MA: Addison-Wesley, 1987; and D. R. Forsyth, *Group Dynamics* (4th ed.). Pacific Grove, CA: Brooks/Cole, 1999.

68. S.W.J. Kozlowski, S. M. Gully, E. Salas, & J. A. Cannon-Bowers, "Team Leadership and Development: Theory, Principles, and Guidelines for Training Leaders and Teams." In M. M. Beyerlein, D. A. Johnson, & S. T. Beyerlein, (eds.), *Advances in Interdisciplinary Studies of Work Teams* (Vol. 3, pp. 173–209). Greenwich, CT: JAI Press, 1996.

69. J. R. Hackman, *Groups That Work (and Those That Don't)*. San Francisco: Jossey-Bass, 1990.

70. B. L. Kirkman & B. Rosen, "Powering Up Teams." *Organizational Dynamics*, 28(3), 48–66, 2000.

71. K. Fisher, *Leading Self-Directed Work Teams*. New York: McGraw-Hill, 1993.

72. H. Kelleher, "A Culture of Commitment." *Leader to Leader*, 4, 20–24, Spring 1997.

73. C. Argyris & D. A. Schön, *Organizational Learning. A Theory of Action Perspective*. Reading, MA: Addison-Wesley, 1978; and W. B. Reddy & K. Jamison (eds.), *Team Building*. San Diego: University Associates, 1988.

74. R. Hiemstra & R. G. Brockett (eds.), *Overcoming Resistance to Self-Direction in Adult Learning*. San Francisco: Jossey-Bass, 1994.

75. C. Argyris & D. A. Schön, *Theory in Practice: Increasing Professional Effectiveness*. San Francisco: Jossey-Bass, 1974; and J. Mezirow, *Transformative Dimensions of Adult Learning*. San Francisco: Jossey-Bass, 1991.

76. W. Isaacs, *Dialogue and the Art of Thinking Together*. New York: Doubleday, 1999.

77. D. L. Laurie, *The Real Work of Leaders*. Cambridge, MA: Perseus, 2000.

78. See, for example, J. Habermas, *The Theory of Communicative Action* (Vol. 1: *Reason and the Rationalization of Society*). (Trans. T. McCarthy). Boston: Beacon Press, 1984; J. D. Ford & L. W. Ford, "The Role of Conversations in Producing Intentional Change in Organizations." *Academy of Management Review*, 20(3), 541–570, 1995; and W. Isaacs, *Dialogue and the Art of Thinking Together*. New York: Doubleday, 1999.

79. P.A.C. Smith, "Action Learning and Reflective Practice in Project Environments That Are Related to Leadership Development." *Management Learning*, 32(1), 31–48, 2001.

80. H. G. Gadamer, *Truth and Method*. New York: Continuum, 1975; and N. Phillips & C. Hardy, *Discourse Analysis: Investigating Processes of Social Construction*. Thousand Oaks, CA: Sage, 2002.

81. L. Beaty, T. Bourner, & P. Frost, "Action Learning: Reflections on Becoming a Set Member." *Management Education and Development*, 24, 350–367, 1993.

82. K. Weinstein, *Action Learning: A Journey in Discovery and Development*. New York: HarperCollins, 1995; and M. Reynolds & R. Vince, "Critical Management Education and Action-Based Learning: Synergies and Contradictions." *Academy of Management Learning and Education*, 3(4), 442–456, 2004.

83. E. Wenger, *Communities of Practice: Learning, Meaning, and Identity*. Cambridge, U.K.: Cambridge University Press, 1998.

84. J. Habermas, *Knowledge and Human Interests*. (Trans. J. Shapiro). Boston: Beacon Press, 1971.

85. W. Peace, "The Hard Work of Being a Soft Manager." *Harvard Business Review*, 79(12), 99–104, 2001.

86. J. Garrick & S. Clegg, "Stressed-Out Knowledge Workers in Performative Times: A Postmodern Take on Project-Based Learning." *Management Learning*, 32(1), 119–134.

87. H. Wilmott, "Critical Management Learning." In J. Burgoyne & M. Reynolds (eds.), *Management Learning: Integrating Perspectives in Theory and Practice* (pp. 161–171). Thousand Oaks, CA: Sage, 1997.

88. L. Anderson & R. Thorpe, "New Perspectives on Action Learning: Developing Criticality." *Journal of European Industrial Training*, 28(8/9), 657–668, 2004.

89. M. Alvesson & H. Willmott, "On the Idea of Emancipation in Manage-
    ment and Organization Studies. *Academy of Management Review*, 17,
    432–464, 1992.

90. See, for example, J. Habermas, *Theory and Practice*. London: Heinemann,
    1974; and E. Fromm, *To Have or to Be?* New York: HarperCollins, 1976.

91. P. Tosey & J. Nugent, "Beyond the Threshold: Organizational Learning at
    the Edge." In J. Holford, C. Griffin, & P. Jarvis (eds.), *Proceedings of the
    Lifelong Learning: Rhetoric and Public Policy Conference* (pp. 271–276). Sur-
    rey, U.K.: University of Surrey, 1997; H. Wilmott, "Critical Management
    Learning." In J. Burgoyne & M. Reynolds (eds.), *Management Learning:
    Integrating Perspectives in Theory and Practice* (pp. 161–176), London: Sage,
    1997; V. Fournier & C. Grey, "At the Critical Moment: Conditions and
    Prospects for Critical Management Studies." *Human Relations*, 53(1), 7–32,
    2000; and D. Meyerson & D. M. Kolb, "Moving out of the 'Armchair':
    Developing a Framework to Bridge the Gap Between Feminist Theory
    and Practice." *Organization*, 7(4), 553–571, 2000.

92. See, for example, J. Habermas, *Knowledge and Human Interests* (Trans.
    J. Shapiro). Boston: Beacon Press, 1971; J. A. Raelin, "Public Reflection
    as the Basis for Learning." *Management Learning*, 32(1), 11–30, 2001; and
    J. A. O'Neil & V. J. Marsick, *Understanding Action Learning*. New York:
    American Management Association, forthcoming.

93. R. Heifetz, *Leadership Without Easy Answers*. Cambridge, MA: Belknap
    Press, 1994.

94. R. D. Lakes, *Critical Education for Work: Multidisciplinary Approaches*. Nor-
    wood, NJ: Ablex, 1994; and A. Nash, "Participatory Workplace Educa-
    tion." In P. Campbell & B. Burnaby (eds.), *Participatory Practices in Adult
    Education* (pp. 185–196). Mahwah, NJ: Erlbaum, 2001.

95. R. Gutierrez, "Change in Classroom Relations: An Attempt That Signals
    Some Difficulties." *Journal of Management Education*, 26(5), 527–549,
    2002.

96. S. D. Brookfield, "Tales from the Dark Side: A Phenomenography of
    Adult Critical Reflection." *International Journal of Lifelong Education*,
    13(3), 203–216, 1994; D. Buckingham, "Critical Pedagogy and Media Ed-
    ucation: A Theory in Search of Practice." *Journal of Curriculum Studies*,
    28(6), 627–650, 1996; and M. Reynolds, "Grasping the Nettle: Possibili-
    ties and Pitfalls of a Critical Management Pedagogy." *British Journal of
    Management*, 9, 171–184, 1999.

97. L. Caron & K. Fisher, "Raising the Bar on Criticality: Students' Critical
    Reflection in an Internship Program." *Journal of Management Education*,
    30(5), 700–723, 2006.

98. C. Rigg & K. Trehan, "Reflections on Working with Critical Action
    Learning." *Action Learning: Research and Practice*, 1(2), 149–165, 2004.

99. P. Reason, *Participation in Human Inquiry*. Thousand Oaks, CA: Sage,
    1994; A. Nash, "Participatory Workplace Education." In P. Campbell &
    B. Burnaby (eds.), *Participatory Practices in Adult Education* (pp. 185–196).

Mahwah, NJ: Erlbaum, 2001; and T. J. Fenwick, "Toward a Critical HRD in Theory and Practice." *Adult Education Quarterly*, 54(3), 193–209, 2004.

Chapter Four

1. E. Wenger, *Communities of Practice: Learning, Meaning, and Identity*. Cambridge, U.K.: Cambridge University Press, 1998.
2. V. W. Mott, "Knowledge Comes from Practice: Reflective Theory Building in Practice." *New Directions for Adult and Continuing Education*, no. 72, 57–63, Winter 1996.
3. D. Schön, *The Reflective Practitioner: How Professionals Think in Action*. New York: Basic Books, 1983.
4. Ibid.
5. R. J. Bernstein, *The Restructuring of Social and Political Theory*. Philadelphia: University of Pennsylvania Press, 1976; O. Hanfling, *Logical Positivism*. New York: Columbia University Press, 1981; and P. M. Rosenau, *Postmodernism and the Social Sciences*. Princeton, NJ: Princeton University Press, 1992.
6. D. Bell, *The Coming of Post-Industrial Society*. London: Heinemann, 1974.
7. R. Cooper & G. Burrell, "Modernism, Postmodernism, and Organizational Analysis: An Introduction." *Organization Studies*, 9, 91–112, 1988.
8. A. S. Lee, "Integrating Positivist and Interpretive Approaches to Organizational Behavior." *Organization Science*, 2, 342–365, 1991.
9. K. Popper, *The Logic of Scientific Discovery*. New York: Basic Books, 1959.
10. R. I. Sutton & R. M. Staw, "What Theory Is Not." *Administrative Science Quarterly*, 40, 371–384, 1995; and K. Rajagopalan, "On the Theoretical Trappings of the Thesis of Anti-Theory; or Why the Idea of Theory May Not, After All, Be All That Bad: A Response to Gary Thomas." *Harvard Educational Review*, 68(3), 335–352, 1998.
11. J. Van Maanen, "Some Notes on the Importance of Writing in Organization Studies." Harvard Business School Research Colloquium, 27–33. Boston: Harvard Business School, 1989; and G. Thomas, "What's the Use of Theory?" *Harvard Educational Review*, 67(1), 75–104, 1997.
12. B. Bledstein, *The Culture of Professionalism: The Middle Class and the Development of Higher Education in America*. New York: Norton, 1978; and J. M. Braxton, "Reflections on a Scholarship of Practice." *Review of Higher Education*, 28(2), 285–293, 2005.
13. J. Lave, "The Practice of Learning." In S. Chaiklin and J. Lave (eds.), *Understanding Practice: Perspectives on Activity and Context* (pp. 3–34). Cambridge, U.K.: Cambridge University Press, 1996.
14. M. Polanyi, *The Tacit Dimension*. New York: Doubleday, 1966.
15. N. Pleasants, "Nothing Is Concealed: De-centering Tacit Knowledge and Rules from Social Theory." *Journal for the Theory of Social Behaviour*, 26(3), 233–255, 1996.

16. G. Ryle, "Knowing How and Knowing That." *Aristotelian Society Proceedings*, 46, 1–16, 1945.

17. J. R. Anderson, *The Architecture of Cognition*. Cambridge, MA: Harvard University Press, 1983.

18. R. W. Wright, "The Effects of Tacitness and Tangibility on the Diffusion of Knowledge-Based Resources." In *Proceedings of the 1994 Academy of Management Annual Meeting*, Dallas, 1994.

19. R. F. Reilly, "Teaching Relevant Management Skills in MBA Programs." *Journal of Business Education*, 57(4), 139–142, 1982.

20. I. Nonaka, "The Knowledge-Creating Company." *Harvard Business Review*, 69(6), 96–104, 1991.

21. D. A. Shirley & J. Langan-Fox, "Intuition: A Review of the Literature." *Psychological Reports*, 79, 563–584, 1996.

22. G. Gregory, "Developing Intuition Through Management Education." In T. Atkinson & G. Claxton (eds.), *The Intuitive Practitioner: On the Value of Not Always Knowing What One Is Doing* (pp. 182–195). Buckingham: Open University Press, 2000.

23. A. S. Reber, "Implicit Learning and Tacit Knowledge." *Journal of Experimental Psychology: General*, 3, 219–235, 1989; and E. Dane & M. G. Pratt, "Exploring Intuition and Its Role in Managerial Decision Making." *Academy of Management Review*, 32(1), 33–54, 2007.

24. H. Collins, "Bicycling on the Moon: Collective Tacit Knowledge and Somatic-Limit Tacit Knowledge." *Organization Studies*, 28, 257–262, 2007.

25. S. G. Arnal & S. Burwood, "Tacit Knowledge and Public Accounts." *Journal of Philosophy of Education*, 3(3), 377–391, 2003.

26. M. Polanyi, *The Tacit Dimension*. New York: Doubleday, 1966; and A. S. Reber, "Implicit Learning of Synthetic Languages: The Role of Instructional Set." *Journal of Experimental Psychology: Human Learning and Memory*, 2, 88–94, 1976.

27. J. H. Howard & M. Ballas, "Syntactic and Semantic Factors in the Classification of Nonspeech Transient Patterns." *Perception and Psychophysics*, 29, 431–439, 1980; and P. Lewicki, *Nonconscious Social Information Processing*. Orlando, FL: Academic Press, 1986.

28. D. A. Kolb, J. S. Osland, & I. M. Rubin, *Organizational Behavior: An Experiential Approach*. Upper Saddle River, NJ: Prentice Hall, 1995.

29. D.A. Kolb & M. S. Plovnick, "The Experiential Learning Theory of Career Development." In J. Van Maanen (ed.), *Organizational Careers: Some New Perspectives* (pp. 65–87). Hoboken, NJ: Wiley, 1977.

30. R. Thorpe, "An MSc by Action Learning: A Management Development Initiative by Higher Degree." *Management Education and Development*, 19(1), 68–78, 1988.

31. P. Maclagan, "Ethical Thinking in Organizations." *Management Learning*, 26(2), 159–177, 1995.

32. J. Dewey, *Democracy and Education*. Toronto: Macmillan, 1916.

33. M. Polanyi, *The Tacit Dimension*. New York: Doubleday, 1966.
34. C. Argyris & D. A. Schön, *Theory in Practice: Increasing Professional Effectiveness*. San Francisco: Jossey-Bass, 1974.
35. D. G. Long, *Learner Managed Learning*. New York: St. Martin's Press, 1990.
36. P. Lewicki, T. Hill, & M. Czyzewska, "Nonconscious Acquisition of Information." *American Psychologist*, 47, 796–801, 1992.
37. N. A. Hayes & D. E. Broadbent, "Two Modes of Learning for Interactive Tasks." *Cognition*, 28, 249–276, 1988; and R.E.A. Green & D. R. Shanks, "On the Existence of Independent Explicit and Implicit Learning Systems: An Examination of Some Evidence." *Memory and Cognition*, 21, 304–317, 1993.
38. A. S. Reber, "Implicit Learning and Tacit Knowledge." *Journal of Experimental Psychology: General*, 3, 219–235, 1989.
39. J. Gold, R. Thorpe, J. Woodall, & E. Sadler-Smith, "Continuing Professional Development in the Legal Profession: A Practice-Based Learning Perspective." *Management Learning*, 38(2), 235–250, 2007.
40. J. Viljoen, D. Holt, & S. Petzall, "The MBA Experience: Participants' Entry Level Conceptions of Management." *Management Education and Development*, 21(1), 1–12, 1990.
41. C. Argyris & D. A. Schön, *Organizational Learning. A Theory of Action Perspective*. Reading, MA: Addison-Wesley, 1978; V. J. Marsick, "Learning in the Workplace: The Case for Reflectivity and Critical Reflectivity." *Adult Education Quarterly*, 38(4), 187–198, 1988; and J. A. Raelin, "Theory and Practice: Their Roles, Relationship, and Limitations in Advanced Management Education." *Business Horizons*, 36(3), 85–89, 1993.
42. A. Bandura, *Social Foundations of Thought and Action*. Upper Saddle River, NJ.: Prentice Hall, 1986.
43. A. Bandura, *Social Learning Theory*. Upper Saddle River, NJ: Prentice Hall, 1977.
44. P. M. King & K. S. Kitchener, *Developing Reflective Judgment*. San Francisco: Jossey-Bass, 1994.
45. J. Mezirow, *Transformative Dimensions of Adult Learning*. San Francisco: Jossey-Bass, 1991.
46. J. Broughton, "Beyond Formal Operations: Theoretical Thought in Adolescence." *Teachers College Record*, 79(1), 87–97, 1977.
47. J. Mezirow, "A Critical Theory of Adult Learning and Education." *Adult Education*, 32(1), 3–24, 1981.
48. R. J. Bernstein, *The Restructuring of Social and Political Theory*. Philadelphia: University of Pennsylvania Press, 1976; O. Hanfling, *Logical Positivism*. New York: Columbia University Press, 1981; and P. M. Rosenau, *Postmodernism and the Social Sciences*. Princeton, NJ: Princeton University Press, 1992.
49. L. T. Hoshmand & D. E. Polkinghorne, "Redefining the Science-Practice Relationship and Professional Training." *American Psychologist*, 47(1), 55–66, 1992.

50. R. Putnam, "Transforming Social Practice: An Action Science Perspective." *Management Learning*, 30(2), 177–187, 1999.

51. D. Sutton, "Further Thoughts on Action Learning." *Journal of European Industrial Training*, 13(3), 32–35, 1989.

52. S. Toulmin, *Cosmopolis, The Hidden Agenda of Modernity*. New York: Free Press, 1990; and H. Willmott, "Breaking the Paradigm Mentality." *Organization Studies*, 14, 681–719, 1983.

53. R. W. Paul, *Critical Thinking*. Santa Rosa, CA: Foundation for Critical Thinking, 1992.

54. S. Vazquez, *The Philosophy of Praxis*. Atlantic Highlands, NJ: Humanities Press, 1977; G. N. Kitching, *Karl Marx and the Philosophy of Praxis*. New York: Routledge, 1988; J. A. Raelin, "The Role of Facilitation in Praxis." *Organizational Dynamics*, 35(1), 83–95, 2006.

55. L. T. Hoshmand & D. E. Polkinghorne, "Redefining the Science-Practice Relationship and Professional Training." *American Psychologist*, 47(1), 55–66, 1992.

56. J. A. Raelin, "A Model of Work-Based Learning." *Organization Science*, 8(6), 563–578, 1997.

57. S. Brookfield, "Self-Directed Learning, Political Clarity, and the Critical Practice of Adult Education." *Adult Education Quarterly*, 43, 227–242, 1993.

Chapter Five

1. J. A. Conger & B. Benjamin, *Building Leaders: How Successful Companies Develop the Next Generation*. San Francisco: Jossey-Bass, 1999; and C. Johnson & D. P. Spicer, "A Case Study of Action Learning in an MBA Program." *Education and Training*, 48(1), 39–54, 2006.

2. G. Korey & Y. Bogorya, "The Managerial Action Learning Concept: Theory and Application." *Management Decision*, 23(2), 3–11, 1985; and J. A. Raelin, "Individual and Situational Predictors of Successful Outcomes from Action Learning." *Journal of Management Education*, 21(3), 368–394, 1997.

3. J. S. Brown & P. Duguid, "Organizational Learning and Communities of Practice: Towards a Unified View of Working, Learning and Organization." *Organization Science*, 2(1), 40–57, 1991.

4. M. Pedler, *Action Learning for Managers*. London: Lemos & Crane, 1996; M. J. Marquardt, *Action Learning in Action*. Palo Alto, CA: Davies-Black, 1999; L. Yorks, J. O'Neil, & V. J. Marsick (eds.), *Advances in Developing Human Resources: Action Learning: Successful Strategies for Individual, Team and Organizational Development*. San Francisco: Berrett Koehler, 1999; Y. Boshyk (ed.), *Action Learning Worldwide: Experiences of Leadership and Organizational Development*. New York: Palgrave, 2002.

5. I. Nonaka, "A Dynamic Theory of Organizational Knowledge Creation." *Organization Science*, 5(1), 14–37, 1994.

6. B. Garratt, "The Power of Action Learning." In M. Pedler (ed.), *Action Learning in Practice* (2nd ed., pp. 45–61). Aldershot, U.K.: Gower, 1991.

7. R. V. Revans, *The Origin and Growth of Action Learning.* Brickley, U.K.: Chartwell-Bratt, 1982; and R. V. Revans, *ABC of Action Learning.* London: Lemos and Crane, 1998.

8. C. Argyris & D. A. Schön, *Organizational Learning II.* Reading, MA: Addison-Wesley, 1996.

9. D. Coghlan & T. Brannick, *Doing Action Research in Your Own Organization.* Thousand Oaks, CA: Sage, 2001.

10. V. J. Marsick, "Action Learning and Reflection in the Workplace." In J. Mezirow (ed.), *Fostering Critical Reflection in Adulthood: A Guide to Transformative and Emancipatory Learning* (pp. 23–46). San Francisco: Jossey-Bass, 1990

11. H. Tsoukas & N. Mylonopoulos, "Introduction: Knowledge Construction and Creation in Organizations." *British Journal of Management,* 15(1), 1–9, 2004.

12. K. Weinstein, *Action Learning: A Journey in Discovery and Development.* London: HarperCollins, 1995; R. W. Revans, *ABC of Action Learning.* London: Lemos and Crane, 1998; V. J. Marsick & J. O'Neill, "The Many Faces of Action Learning." *Management Learning,* 30(2), 159–176, 1999; V. Willis, "Inspecting Cases: Prevailing Degrees of Action Learning Using Revans' Theory and Rules of Engagement as Standard." *Action Learning: Research and Practice,* 1(1), 11–27, 2004; and M. Pedler, J. Burgoyne, & C. Brook, "What Has Action Learning Learned to Become?" *Action Learning: Research and Practice,* 2(1), 49–68, 2005.

13. M. Pedler (ed.), *Action Learning in Practice* (2nd ed.). Aldershot, U.K.: Gower, 1991; and K. Weinstein, *Action Learning: A Journey in Discovery and Development.* New York: HarperCollins, 1995.

14. R. L. Ackoff, *Creating the Corporate Future.* Hoboken, NJ: Wiley, 1981.

15. See, for example, D. L. Dotlich & J. L. Noel, *Action Learning: How the World's Top Companies Are Re-Creating Their Leaders and Themselves.* San Francisco: Jossey-Bass, 1998; A. A. Vicere, "Changes in Practices, Changes in Perspectives: The 1997 International Study of Executive Development Trends." *Journal of Management Development,* 17(7), 526–543, 1998; M. J. Marquardt, *Action Learning in Action.* Palo Alto, CA: Davies-Black, 1999; R. M. Fulmer, P. A. Gibbs, & M. Goldsmith, "Developing Leaders: How Winning Companies Keep on Winning." *Sloan Management Review,* 42(1), 49–59, 2000; Y. Boshyk (ed.), *Action Learning Worldwide: Experiences of Leadership and Organizational Development.* New York: Palgrave, 2002; C. L. Davey, J. A. Powell, J. E. Powell, & I. Cooper, "Action Learning in a Medium-Sized Construction Company." *Building Research and Information,* 30(1), 5–15, 2002; and G. Hernez-Broome & R. L. Hughes, "Leadership Development: Past, Present, and Future." *Human Resource Planning,* 27(1), 24–32, 2004.

16. E. T. Hall, *Beyond Culture*. New York: Doubleday, 1977.

17. I. McGill & L. Beaty, *Action Learning: A Practitioner's Guide*. London: Kogan Page, 1992.

18. C. Johnson, "The Essential Principles of Action Learning." In Electronic Conference, "New Approaches to Management Education and Development (NAMED)." Bradford, U.K.: MCB University Press, 1997.

19. P. Smith, "Second Thoughts on Action Learning." *Journal of European Industrial Training*, 12(6), 28–31, 1988; and D. Sutton, "Further Thoughts on Action Learning." *Journal of European Industrial Training*, 13(3), 32–35, 1989.

20. J. A. Raelin, "The Persean Ethic: Consistency of Belief and Action in Managerial Practice." *Human Relations*, 46(5), 575–621, 1993.

21. M. Boaden, "A Pilot Action Learning Set for NHS R&D Managers." *Action Learning: Research and Practice*, 1(2), 247–253, 2004.

22. T. F. Dunne, "Feeding a Growing Team: Action Learning as Fertilizer." *Action Learning: Research and Practice*, 1(2), 231–237.

23. J. R. Katzenbach & D. K. Smith, *The Wisdom of Teams: Creating the High-Performance Organization*. New York: HarperBusiness, 2003.

24. W. H. Drath & C. J. Palus, *Making Common Sense*. Greensboro, NC: Center for Creative Leadership, 1994.

25. R. R. Nelson & S. G. Winter, *An Evolutionary Theory of Economic Change*. Cambridge, MA: Belknap Press, 1982; D. Bohm, *Unfolding Meaning*. Loveland, CO: Foundation House, 1985; and S. Scribner, "Thinking in Action: Some Characteristics of Practical Thought." In R. Sternberg & R. K. Wagner (eds.), *Practical Intelligence: Nature and Origins of Competence in the Everyday World* (pp. 13–30), Cambridge, U.K.: Cambridge University Press, 1986.

26. E. Wenger, *Communities of Practice: Learning, Meaning, and Identity*. Cambridge, U.K.: Cambridge University Press, 1998.

27. E. Wenger, R. McDermott, & W. M. Snyder, *Cultivating Communities of Practice*. Boston: Harvard Business School Press, 2002.

28. J. L. Badaracco, *The Knowledge Link: How Firms Compete Through Strategic Alliances*. Boston: Harvard Business School Press, 1991; and C. W. Choo, *The Knowing Organization*. New York: Oxford University Press, 1998.

29. A. De Geus, "Learning Together for Good Decision Making." *Reflections*, 8(1), 28–35, 2007.

30. K. Labich, "Elite . . . ." *Fortune*, 90–99, February 19, 1996.

31. J. Janov, "Creating Meaning: The Heart of Learning Communities." *Training and Development*, 49(5), 53–59, 1995.

32. P. Berger & T. Luckmann, *The Social Construction of Reality*. New York: Anchor Books, 1967; and L. G. Bolman & T. E. Deal, *Reframing Organizations: Artistry, Choice, and Leadership* (2nd ed.). San Francisco: Jossey-Bass, 1997.

33. R. Boody, K. East, L. M. Fitzgerald, M. L. Heston, & A. M. Iverson, "Talking Teaching and Learning: Using Practical Argument to Make Reflective Thinking Audible." *Action in Teacher Education*, 19(4), 88–101, 1998.

34. T. A. Stewart, "The Invisible Key to Success." *Fortune*, August 5, 173–176, 1996.

35. E. Wenger, "Clarica's Agent Network: A Community of Practice Among Independent Sales Agents Who Sell the Products of a Canadian Insurance Company." A Case Study, September 2002. Retrieved June 8, 2007, from http://www.ewenger.com/pub/index.htm.

36. J. M. Ryder & R. E. Redding, "Integrating Cognitive Task Analysis into Instructional Systems Development." *Educational Technology Research and Development*, 41(2), 75–96, 1993.

37. A. D. Fisk & J. K. Gallini, "Training Consistent Components of Tasks: Developing an Instructional System Based on Automatic/Controlled Processing Principles." *Human Factors*, 31, 453–463, 1989.

38. E. Wenger, R. McDermott, & W. M. Snyder, *Cultivating Communities of Practice*. Boston: Harvard Business School Press, 2002.

39. J. E. Orr, "Sharing Knowledge, Celebrating Identity: Community Memory in a Service Culture." In D. S. Middleton & D. Edwards (eds.), *Collective Remembering* (pp. 169–189), Thousand Oaks, CA: Sage, 1990.

40. R. R. Nelson & S. G. Winter, *An Evolutionary Theory of Economic Change*. Cambridge, MA: Belknap Press, 1982.

41. S. Scribner, "Thinking in Action: Some Characteristics of Practical Thought." In R. Sternberg & R. K. Wagner (eds.), *Practical Intelligence: Nature and Origins of Competence in the Everyday World* (pp. 13–30), Cambridge, U.K.: Cambridge University Press, 1986.

42. D. Bohm, *Unfolding Meaning*. Loveland, CO: Foundation House, 1985.

43. R. L. Daft & K. E. Weick, "Toward a Model of Organizations as Interpretation Systems." *Academy of Management Review*, 9, 284–295, 1984.

44. J. S. Brown & P. Duguid, "Organizational Learning and Communities of Practice: Towards a Unified View of Working, Learning and Organization." *Organization Science*, 2(1), 40–57, 1991.

45. J. Wertsch, *Vygotsky and the Social Formation of Mind*. Cambridge, MA: Harvard University Press, 1985; F. Blackler, "Knowledge and the Theory of Organizations: Organizations as Activity Systems and the Reframing of Management." *Journal of Management Studies*, 30, 863–884, 1993; and S. Gherardi, D. Nicolini, & F. Odella, "Toward a Social Understanding of How People Learn in Organizations." *Management Learning*, 29(3), 273–297, 1998.

46. J. Lave & E. Wenger, *Situated Learning: Legitimate Peripheral Participation*. Cambridge, U.K.: Cambridge University Press, 1991.

47. E. Wenger, *Communities of Practice: Learning, Meaning, and Identity*. Cambridge, U.K.: Cambridge University Press, 1998.

48. K. Handley, T. Clark, R. Fincham, & A. Sturdy, "Researching Situated Learning: Participation, Identity and Practices in Client-Consultant Relationships." *Management Learning*, 38(2), 173–191.

49. J. S. Valacich & C. Schwenk. "Devil's Advocacy and Dialectical Inquiry Effects on Face-to-Face and Computer-Mediated Group Decision Making."

Organizational Behavior and Human Decision Process, 63(2), 158–173, 1995; and G. DeSanctis & P. Monge, "Introduction to the Special Issue: Communication Processes for Virtual Organizations." *Organization Science,* 10(6), 693–703, 1999.

50. S. G. Straus & J. A. Miles, "The Effects of Videoconference, Telephone, and Face-to-Face Media on Interviewer and Applicant Judgments in Employer Interviews." *Journal of Management,* 27(3), 363–381, 2001.

51. P. Hildreth, C. Kimble, & P. Wright, "Communities of Practice in the Distributed International Environment." *Journal of Knowledge Management,* 4(1), 27–38, 2000.

52. D. Stamps, "Communities of Practice: Learning Is Social. Training Is Irrelevant?" *Training,* 34(2), 34–42, 1997.

53. L. Chidambaram, "Relational Development in Computer-Supported Groups." *MIS Quarterly,* 20(2), 143–163, 1996; M. E. Warkentin, L. Sayeed, & R. Hightower, "Virtual Teams Versus Face-to-Face Teams: An Exploratory Study of a Web-Based Conference System." *Decision Sciences,* 28(4), 975–996, 1997; and P. J. Hinds & D. E. Bailey, "Out of Sight, Out of Sync: Understanding Conflict in Distributed Teams." *Organization Science,* 14(6), 615–632, 2003.

54. R. Edwards, "Enhancing Learning Support for Master's Dissertation Students: A Role for Action Learning Online?" Paper presented at the Higher Education Academy's BEST Conference, Edinburgh, April 8–10, 2002.

55. D. L. Coutu, "Trust in Virtual Teams." *Harvard Business Review,* 76(3), 20–21, 1998.

56. A. M. Townsend, S. M. DeMarie, & A. R. Hendrickson, "Virtual Teams: Technology and the Workplace of the Future." *Academy of Management Executive,* 12(3), 17–29, 1998; and D. J. Pauleen, "Leadership in a Global Virtual Team: An Action Learning Approach." *Leadership and Organization Development Journal,* 24(3), 153–162, 2003.

57. A. Rossett (ed.), *The ASTD E-Learning Handbook: Best Practices, Strategies, and Case Studies for an Emerging Field.* New York: McGraw-Hill, 2002; L. L. Martins & F. W. Kellermanns, "A Model of Business School Students' Acceptance of a Web-Based Course Management System." *Academy of Management Learning and Education,* 3(1), 7–26, 2004; L. Dubé, A. Bourhis, & R. Jacob, "The Impact of Structuring Characteristics on the Launching of Virtual Communities of Practice." *Journal of Organizational Change Management,* 18(2), 145–166, 2005; and D. DeWolfe Waddill, "Action E-learning: An Exploratory Case Study of Action Learning Applied Online." *Human Resource Development International,* 9(2), 157–171, 2006.

58. C. D. Cramton, "Finding Common Ground in Dispersed Collaboration." *Organizational Dynamics,* 30(4), 356–367, 2002.

59. S. L. Jarvenpaa & D. E. Leidner, "Communication and Trust in Global Virtual Teams." *Organization Science,* 10(6), 791–815, 1999.

60. W. J. Orlikowski, K. Okamura, & M. Fujimoto, "Shaping Electronic Communication: The Metastructuring of Technology in the Context of Use." *Organization Science*, 6(4), 423–444, 1995; and P. Mosher, "Building and Managing Cross-Functional Teams." *Workforce Performance Solutions*, 1(2), 44–47, 2005.

61. Private communication from Don Haggerty, October 26, 2004.

62. B. E. Mennecke, J. A. Hoffer, & B. E. Wynne, "The Implications of Group Development and History for Group Support System Theory and Practice." *Small Group Research*, 23(4), 524–572, 1992; and T. Gear, R. Vince, M. Read, & A. L. Minkes, "Group Enquiry for Collective Learning in Organisations." *Journal of Management Development*, 22(2), 88–102, 2003.

63. R. O. Briggs, V. Ramesh, N. C. Romano Jr., & J. Latimer, "The Exemplar Project: Using Group Support Systems to Improve the Learning Environment." *Journal of Educational Technology Systems*, 23(3), 277–291, 1994–1995.

64. M. Halper, "Everyone in the Knowledge Pool." *Computerworld Global Innovators*, December 8, 1997; and Y. Malhotra & D. Galletta, "Role of Commitment and Motivation in Knowledge Management Systems Implementation: Theory, Conceptualization, and Measurement of Antecedents of Success." *In Proceedings of the 36th Annual Hawaii International Conference on Systems Sciences, IEEE*, pp. 1–10, January 6–9, 2003.

65. J. S. Brown & E. S. Gray, "The People Are the Company." *Fast Company, Premier Issue*, 78–82, 1995; and E. Wenger, R. McDermott, & W. M. Snyder, *Cultivating Communities of Practice*. Boston: Harvard Business School Press, 2002.

66. T. H. Davenport, D. W. De Long, & M. C. Beers, "Successful Knowledge Management Projects." *Sloan Management Review*, 39(2), 43–57, 1998.

67. B. B. Bunker & B. T. Alban, *Large Group Interventions*. San Francisco: Jossey-Bass, 1997.

68. M. R. Weisbord & S. Janoff, *Future Search*. San Francisco: Berrett-Koehler, 2000.

69. N. M. Dixon, "The Hallways of Learning." *Organizational Dynamics*, 25(4), 23–34, 1997.

70. D. L. Cooperrider & D. Whitney, *Appreciative Inquiry: A Positive Revolution in Change*. San Francisco: Berrett-Koehler, 2005.

71. D. Axelrod, "Getting Everyone Involved: How One Organization Involved Its Employees, Supervisors, and Managers in Redesigning the Organization." *Journal of Applied Behavioral Science*, 28, 499–509, 1992.

72. H. Owen, *Open Space Technology: A User's Guide*. San Francisco: Berrett-Koehler, 1997.

73. F. Emery, "Participative Design: Effective, Flexible and Successful, Now!" *Journal for Quality and Participation*, 18(1), 6–9, 1995.

74. M. Herzig & L. Chasin, *Fostering Dialogue Across Divides*. Watertown, MA: Public Conversations Project, 2006.

75. M. Emery & R. E. Purser, *The Search Conference: Theory and Practice: A Powerful Method for Planning Organizational Change and Community Action*. San Francisco: Jossey-Bass, 2004.

76. C. Spring & C. Garfield, *Wisdom Circles: A Guide to Self Discovery and Community Building in Small Groups*. New York: Hyperion, 1999.

77. J. Brown & D. Isaacs, *The World Café: Shaping Our Futures Through Conversations That Matter*. San Francisco: Berrett-Koehler, 2005.

78. Ibid.

79. C. Thirapantu, "The People's Assembly in Thailand: The Quest for a Sustaining Energy for Societal Change." Retrieved June 13, 2007, from http://www.theworldcafe.com/stories/thailand.htm.

80. A. Kleiner & G. Roth, "How to Make Experience Your Company's Best Teacher." *Harvard Business Review*, 75(5), 172–177, 1997.

81. N. M. Dixon, "The Hallways of Learning." *Organizational Dynamics*, 25(4), 23–34, 1997.

82. P. N. Senge, *The Fifth Discipline: The Art and Practice of the Learning Organization*. New York: Currency/Doubleday, 1994.

83. C. Argyris & D. A. Schön, *Organizational Learning. A Theory of Action Perspective*. Reading, MA: Addison-Wesley, 1978.

84. R. Putnam, "Transforming Social Practice: An Action Science Perspective." *Management Learning*, 30(2), 177–187, 1999.

85. D. Schön, *The Reflective Practitioner: How Professionals Think in Action*. New York: Basic Books, 1983.

86. J. Habermas, *Knowledge and Human Interests*. Boston: Beacon Press, 1971.

87. G. Lakoff & M. Johnson, *Metaphors We Live By*. Chicago: University of Chicago Press, 1980; and G. Bateson, *Steps to an Ecology of Mind*. San Francisco: Chandler, 1972.

88. J. Wolff, "Hermeneutics and the Critique of Ideology." *Sociological Review*, 23, 811–828, 1975.

89. R. M. Bokeno, "The Work of Chris Argyris as Critical Organization Practice." *Journal of Organizational Change Management*, 16(6), 633–649, 2003.

90. G. Burrell, "Modernism, Postmodernism and Organizational Analysis 4: The Contribution of Jürgen Habermas." *Organization Studies*, 15(1), 1–19, 1994.

91. R. Vince & L. Martin, "Inside Action Learning: An Exploration of the Psychology and Politics of the Action Learning Model." *Management Education and Development*, 24, 205–215, 1993.

92. C. Argyris & D. A. Schön, *Theory in Practice: Increasing Professional Effectiveness*. San Francisco: Jossey-Bass, 1974.

93. C. Argyris, *Reasoning, Learning and Action*. San Francisco: Jossey-Bass, 1982.

94. J. Mezirow, "A Critical Theory of Adult Learning and Education." *Adult Education*, 32(1), 3–24, 1981.

95. W.M.K. Trochim, "Concept Mapping: Soft Science or Hard Art?" *Evaluation and Program Planning*, 12(1), 87–110, 1989.

96. C. Eden, "Cognitive Mapping: A Review." *European Journal of Operational Research,* 36(1), 1–13, 1988; and M. Hofman, "Facilitating Multi-Disciplinary Teams Through Cognitive Mapping." Unpublished thesis, Nijenrode University, Breukelen, The Netherlands, 1997.

97. A. S. Huff, *Mapping Strategic Thought.* Hoboken, NJ: Wiley, 1990.

98. P. B. Checkland, "Achieving `Desirable and Feasible' Change: An Application of Soft Systems Methodology." *Journal of the Operational Research Society,* 36(9), 821–831, 1985.

99. C. Eden, "Using Cognitive Mapping for Strategic Options Development and Analysis (SODA)." In J. Rosenhead (ed.), *Rational Analysis for a Problematic World* (pp. 21–42). Hoboken, NJ: Wiley, 1989.

100. K. E. Watkins & T. J. Shindell, "Learning and Transforming Through Action Science." *New Directions for Adult and Continuing Education,* no. 63, 43–55, Fall 1994.

101. E. A. Keen, *A Primer in Phenomenological Psychology.* Lanham, MD: University Press of America, 1975.

102. See especially E. de Bono, *De Bono's Thinking Course.* New York: Facts on File, 1994.

103. E. de Bono, *Six Thinking Hats.* Boston: Back Bay Books, 1999.

104. See, for example, C. Argyris, R. Putnam, & D. M. Smith, *Action Science: Concepts, Methods, and Skills for Research and Intervention.* San Francisco: Jossey-Bass, 1985.

105. C. Argyris, "Action Science and Intervention." *Journal of Applied Behavioral Science,* 19(2), 115–140, 1983.

106. N. A. Wishart, J. J. Elam., & D. Robey, "Redrawing the Portrait of a Learning Organization: Inside Knight-Ridder, Inc." *Academy of Management Executive,* 10(1), 7–20, 1996.

Chapter Six

1. E. W. Taylor, "Building upon the Theoretical Debate: A Critical Review of the Empirical Studies of Mezirow's Transformative Learning Theory." *Adult Education Quarterly,* 48(1), 34–59, 1997.

2. D. Hollenbach, "Is Tolerance Enough? The Catholic University and the Common Good." *Conversations,* 13, 5–15, Spring 1998.

3. J. Habermas, *The Theory of Communicative Action,* Vol. 1: *Reason and the Rationalization of Society* (Trans. T. McCarthy). Boston: Beacon Press, 1984.

4. C. Argyris & D. A. Schön, *Theory in Practice: Increasing Professional Effectiveness.* San Francisco: Jossey-Bass, 1974; and J. A. Raelin, "The Persean Ethic: Consistency of Belief and Action in Managerial Practice." *Human Relations,* 46(5), 575–621, 1993.

5. B. Bright, "Reflecting on `Reflective Practice.'" *Studies in the Education of Adults,* 28(2), 162–184, 1996.

6 N. M. Ferry & J. M. Ross-Gordon, "An Inquiry into Schön's Epistemology of Practice: Exploring Links Between Experience and Reflective Practice." *Adult Education Quarterly*, 48(2), 98–112, 1998.

7. C. Bereiter & M. Scardamalia, *Surpassing Ourselves*. Chicago: Open Court, 1993.

8. D. Schön, *The Reflective Practitioner: How Professionals Think in Action*. New York: Basic Books, 1983; and N. M. Ferry & J. M. Ross-Gordon, "An Inquiry into Schön's Epistemology of Practice: Exploring Links Between Experience and Reflective Practice." *Adult Education Quarterly*, 48(2), 98–112, 1998.

9. E. Goffman, *Frame Analysis: An Essay on the Organization of Experience*. New York: HarperCollins, 1974; R. D. Benford & D. A. Snow, "Framing Processes and Social Movements: An Overview and Assessment." *American Review of Sociology*, 26, 611–639, 2000; and G. Musson, L. Cohen, & S. Tietze, "Pedagogy and the 'Linguistic Turn:' Developing Understanding through Semiotics." *Management Learning*, 38(1), 45–60, 2007.

10. E. Wenger, *Communities of Practice: Learning, Meaning, and Identity*. Cambridge: Cambridge University Press, 1998.

11. E. W. Taylor, "Building upon the Theoretical Debate: A Critical Review of the Empirical Studies of Mezirow's Transformative Learning Theory." *Adult Education Quarterly*, 48(1), 34–59, 1997.

12. I. Rimanóczy, "What Does It Mean to Be a Learning Coach?" Leadership in International Management Ltd., 1997. Retrieved June 8, 2007, from http://limglobal.net/Readings/Articles/The%20Learning%20Coach%20 English%20-%20I%20Rimanoczy.doc.

13. L. Vygotsky, *Thought and Language* (Trans. A. Koulzin). Cambridge, MA: MIT Press, 1988; and D. Holman, K. Pavlica, & R. Thorpe, "Rethinking Kolb's Theory of Experiential Learning in Management Education." *Management Learning*, 28(2), 135–148, 1997.

14. H. Wilmott, "Managing Education: Provocations to a Debate." *Management Learning*, 25(1), 105–136, 1994.

15. R. Jackall, "Moral Mazes: Bureaucracy and Managerial Work." *Harvard Business Review*, 61(5), 118–130, 1983.

16. L. G. Bolman & T. E. Deal, *Reframing Organizations: Artistry, Choice, and Leadership* (2nd ed.). San Francisco: Jossey-Bass, 1997.

17. M. Hammer & S. A. Stanton, "The Power of Reflection." *Fortune*, 136(10), 291–296, 1997.

18. M. C. Jensen, "Non-Rational Behavior, Agency Costs, and Organizations." Paper presented at the Boston-Cambridge Seminar on Economics of Organizations, Harvard Business School, Boston, May 9, 1997.

19. P. C. Pitcher, *The Drama of Leadership*. Hoboken, NJ: Wiley, 1997.

20. A. Giddens, *Modernity and Self-Identity: Self and Society in the Late Modern Age*. Cambridge: Polity Press, 1991.

21. A. W. Gouldner, *The Coming Crisis of Western Sociology*. London: Heinemann, 1970.

22. M. Markovic, "Dialectic Today." In M. Markovic & G. Petrovic (eds.), *Praxis* (pp. 3–44). Boston: D. Reidel, 1979; W. Heydebrand, "Organizational Contradictions in Public Bureaucracies: Toward a Marxian Theory of Organizations." In A. Etzioni & E. Lehman (eds.), *A Sociological Reader on Complex Organizations* (pp. 56–73). New York: Holt, 1980; M. Kihl, "Integrating Planning Theory and Practice." *Policy Studies Journal*, 23(3), 551–554, 1995; and J. Braaten, "The Succession of Theory and the Recession of Practice." *Social Theory Practice*, 18(1), 81–111, 1992.

23. B. Bright, "Reflecting on 'Reflective Practice.'" *Studies in the Education of Adults*, 28(2), 162–184, 1996; J. A. Raelin, "A Model of Work-Based Learning." *Organization Science*, 8(6), 563–578, 1997; M. Merleau-Ponty, *Causeries 1948*. Paris: Editions du Seuil, 2002; and A. Strati, "Sensible Knowledge and Practice-Based Learning." *Management Learning*, 38(1), 61–77, 2007.

24. H. A. Giroux, *Ideology, Culture and the Process of Schooling*. London: Falmer Press, 1981.

25. P. Freire, *Pedagogy of the Oppressed*. New York: Seabury Press, 1970.

26. I. Shor, *Empowering Education: Critical Teaching for Social Change*. Chicago: University of Chicago Press, 1992; M. E. Boyce, "Teaching Critically as an Act of Praxis and Resistance." *Electronic Journal of Radical Organizational Theory*, 2(2), 2–9, 1996; and M. D. McMaster, *The Intelligence Advantage: Organizing for Complexity*. Boston: Butterworth-Heinemann, 1996.

27. J. M. Jermier, "Introduction: Critical Perspectives on Organizational Control." *Administrative Science Quarterly*, 43, 235–256, 1998.

28. A. Huxley, *Brave New World* (originally published in 1932). New York: HarperCollins, 1969.

29. P. Johnson & J. Duberley, *Understanding Management Research*. Thousand Oaks, CA: Sage, 2000; and D. O'Donnell, D. Mcguire, & C. Cross, "Critically Challenging Some Assumptions in HRD." *International Journal of Training and Development*, 10, 4–16, 2006.

30. C. Rigg & K. Trehan, "Reflections on Working with Critical Action Learning." *Action Learning: Research and Practice*, 1(2), 149–165, 2004.

31. J. L. Kinchloe & P. L. McLaren, "Rethinking Critical Theory and Qualitative Research." In N. K. Denzin & Y. S. Lincoln (eds.), *Handbook of Qualitative Research* (pp. 138–157). Thousand Oaks, CA: Sage, 1994.

32. M. Twain, *The Adventures of Huckleberry Finn*. New York: Grosset & Dunlap, 1948.

Chapter Seven

1. J. R. Mercer, "Action Learning: A Student's Perspective." *Industrial and Commercial Training*, 22(2), 3–8, 1990.

2. L. Beaty, T. Bourner, & P. Frost, "Action Learning: Reflections on Becoming a Set Member." *Management Education and Development*, 24, 350–367, 1993.

3. H. Frank, "Another Review of the Revans Centre Seminar." *Link-Up with Action Learning,* 1(4), 21–22, 1998.

4. K. Weinstein, "The Power, and Dilemma, of Honesty: Action Learning for Social Entrepreneurs." *Action Learning: Research and Practice,* 2(2), 213–219, 2005.

5. A. Lauriala, "Reformative In-Service Education for Teachers (Rinset) as a Collaborative Action and Learning Enterprise: Experiences from a Finnish Context." *Teaching and Teacher Education,* 14(1), 53–66, 1998.

6. L. Beaty, T. Bourner, & P. Frost, "Action Learning: Reflections on Becoming a Set Member." *Management Education and Development,* 24, 350–367, 1993.

7. J. Luft, *Of Human Interaction.* Palo Alto, CA: National Press Books, 1969.

8. L. Beaty, T. Bourner, & P. Frost, "Action Learning: Reflections on Becoming a Set Member." *Management Education and Development,* 24, 350–367, 1993.

9. M. Meehan & J. Jarvis, "A Refreshing Angle on Staff Education: Action Learning at Britvic Soft Drinks." *People Management,* 2(14), 38, 1996.

10. K. Weinstein, "The Power, and Dilemma, of Honesty: Action Learning for Social Entrepreneurs." *Action Learning: Research and Practice,* 2(2), 213–219, 2005.

11. Ibid.; and A. Mumford, "Effective Learners in Action Learning Sets." *Employee Counseling Today,* 8(6). 5–12, 1996.

12. E. Schein, *Process Consultation,* Vol. 1. Reading, MA: Addison-Wesley, 1967.

13. J. A. Raelin, "Public Reflection as the Basis for Learning." *Management Learning,* 32(1), 11–30, 2001.

14. Ibid.

15. D. Rigano & J. Edwards, "Incorporating Reflection into Work Practice." *Management Learning,* 29(4), 431–446, 1998.

16. I. Progoff, *At a Journal Workshop.* New York: Dialogue House Library, 1975.

17. D. Rigano & J. Edwards, "Incorporating Reflection into Work Practice." *Management Learning,* 29(4), 431–446, 1998.

18. W. Carr & S. Kemmis, *Becoming Critical: Education, Knowledge, and Action Research.* London: Falmer Press, 1986; and D. Boud, R. Keogh, & D. Walker (eds.), *Reflection: Turning Experiences into Learning.* New York: Nichols, 1985.

19. E. Sadler-Smith & E. Shefy, "Developing Intuitive Awareness in Management Education." *Academy of Management Learning & Education,* 6(2), 186–205, 2007; and R. J. Sternberg, *Cognitive Psychology.* Orlando, FL: Harcourt Brace, 1999.

20. C. Argyris, "The Executive Mind and Double-Loop Learning." *Organizational Dynamics,* 11(2), 5–22, 1982; see also an adaptation in P. M. Senge, A. Kleiner, C. Roberts, R. Ross, & B, Smith, *The Fifth Discipline Fieldbook: Strategies and Tools for Building a Learning Organization.* New York: Doubleday, 1994.

21. A. L. Cunliffe, "On Becoming a Critically Reflexive Practitioner." *Journal of Management Education*, 28(4), 407–426, 2004.

22. C. Hogan, "Creative and Reflective Journal Process." *Learning Organization*, 2(2), 4–17, 1995; and R. Loo, "Journaling: A Learning Tool for Project Management Training and Team-Building." *Project Management Journal*, 35(4), 61–66, 2002.

23. J. McKernan, "Some Developments in the Methodology of Action Research: Studied Enactments." In C. J. Colins & P. J. Chippendale (eds.), *Proceedings of the First World Congress on Action Research and Process Management*, Vol. 1, *Theory and Praxis Frameworks* (pp. 43–56), Brisbane: Acorn, 1991.

24. A. L. Cunliffe, "On Becoming a Critically Reflexive Practitioner." *Journal of Management Education*, 28(4), 407–426, 2004.

25. C. Hogan, "Creative and Reflective Journal Process." *Learning Organization*, 2(2), 4–17, 1995.

26. See, for example, I. Progoff, *At a Journal Workshop*. New York: Dialogue House Library, 1975; T. Ranier, *The New Diary*. Los Angeles: Tarcher, 1978; T. Fulwiler (ed.), *The Journal Book*. Portsmouth, NH: Boynton/Cook, 1987; J. Lukinsky, "Reflective Withdrawal Through Journal Writing." In J. Mezirow and Associates (eds.), *Fostering Critical Reflection in Adulthood* (pp. 213–234). San Francisco: Jossey-Bass, 1990; C. Hogan, "Creative and Reflective Journal Process." *Learning Organization*, 2(2), 4–17, 1995; and L. Capacchione, *The Creative Journal: The Art of Finding Yourself*. Franklin Lakes, NJ: New Page Books, 2002.

27. D. Elder, "Learning with Online Portfolios." *e.learning age*, 20–22, February 2003; M. S. Heath, *Electronic Portfolios: A Guide to Professional Development and Assessment*. Worthington, OH: Linworth, 2004; and S. Carliner, "E-Portfolios" *TD*, 59(5), 70–74, 2005.

28. N. Strudler & K. Wetzel, "The Diffusion of Electronic Portfolios in Teacher Education: Issues of Initiation and Implementation." *Journal of Research on Technology in Education*, 37(4), 411–433, 2005.

29. R. Fagin, D. Hand, & K. Boyd, "Electronic Portfolios for Aggregating and Disaggregating Data: Measuring a Transformed Life." In S. Van Kollenburg (ed.), *Promoting Student Learning and Effective Teaching*, Vol. 3: *Assessment of Student Learning*. Chicago: Higher Learning Commission, 2004.

30. Penn State E-Portfolio site: http://portfolio.psu.edu/about/index.html, accessed on June 27, 2007.

31. K. B. Yancey, "General Patterns and the Future." In B. Cambridge (ed.), *Electronic Portfolios: Emerging Practices in Student, Faculty, and Institutional Learning* (pp. 83–87).Washington, DC: American Association of Higher Education, 2001.

32. Ibid.

33. M. Heath, "Are You Ready to Go Digital? The Pros and Cons of Electronic Portfolio Development" *Library Media Connection*, 23(7), 66–70, 2005.

34. See, for example, S. Lawton & D. Ernesti, "Are Staffers Headed in the Right Direction?" *Nursing Management*, 29(7), 28–30, 1998.

35. B. Filipczak, M. Hequet, C. Lee, M. Picard, & D. Stamps, "360 Degree Feedback: Will the Circle Be Broken?" *Training*, 33(10), 24–25, 1996.

36. E. Jones & T. Pittman, "Toward a General Theory of Strategic Self-Presentation." In J. Suls (ed.), *Psychological Perspectives on the Self* (pp. 231–262), Mahwah, NJ: Erlbaum, 1982; and J. Conger & G. Toegel, "Action Learning and Multi-Rater Feedback as Popular Leadership Development Interventions: Popular But Poorly Deployed." *Journal of Change Management*, 3(4), 332–348, 2003.

37. K. Ellis, "Individual Development Plans: The Building Blocks of Development." *Training*, 41(12), 20–25, 2004.

38. IOMA, "How Arnold & Porter Uses IDPs to Help Associates Plot Their Careers." www.ioma.com/law, Issue 06–11, pp. 1–11, November 2006.

39. R. A. Stringer & R. S. Cheloha, "The Power of a Development Plan." *Human Resource Planning*, 26(4), 10–17, 2003.

40. M. M. Lombardo & R. W. Eichinger, *The Leadership Machine: Architecture to Develop Leaders for Any Future*. Minneapolis: Lominger, 2001.

41. R. L. Dilworth, "Personal Learning Goals," personal correspondence, July 11, 1998.

42. K. M. Nowack, "360-Degree Feedback: The Whole Story." *Training & Development*, 47(1), 69–72, 1993.

43. C. Dellarocas, "The Digitalization of Word of Mouth: Promise and Challenges of Online Feedback Mechanisms." *Management Science*, 49, 1407–1424, 2003; and G. E. Bolton, K. Katok, & A. Ockenfels, "How Effective Are Electronic Reputation Mechanisms? An Experimental Investigation." *Management Science*, 50, 1587–1602, 2004.

44. S. A. Funderburg & P. E. Levy, "The Influence of Individual and Contextual Variables on 360-Degree Feedback System Attitudes." *Group and Organizational Studies*, 22, 210–230, 1997; J. Colquitt, J. LePine, & R. Noe, "Toward an Integrative Theory of Training Motivation: A Meta-Analytic Path Analysis of 20 Years of Research." *Journal of Applied Psychology*, 85, 678–707, 2000; T. J. Maurer, D. Mitchell, & F. G. Barbeite, "Predictors of Attitudes Toward a 360-Degree Feedback System and Involvement in Post-Feedback Management Development Activity." *Journal of Occupational and Organizational Psychology*, 75, 87–107, 2002; and J. W. Smither, M. London, & R. R. Reilly, "Does Performance Improve Following Multi-Source Feedback? A Theoretical Model, Meta-Analysis, and Review of Empirical Findings." *Personnel Psychology*, 58, 33–66, 2005.

45. M. A. Dalton, "Using 360-Degree Feedback Successfully." *Leadership in Action*, 18(1), 2–11, 1998; and L. E. Atwater, J. F. Brett, & A. C. Charles, "Multisource Feedback: Lessons Learned and Implications for Practice." *Human Resource Management*, 46(2), 285–307, 2007.

46. F. Luthans & S. J. Peterson, "360-Degree Feedback with Systematic Coaching: Empirical Analysis Suggests a Winning Combination." *Human Resource Management*, 42, 243–256, 2003; C. F. Seifert, G. Yukl, & R. A. McDonald, "Effects of Multisource Feedback and a Feedback Facilitator on the Influence Behavior of Managers Towards Subordinates." *Journal of Applied Psychology*, 88, 561–569, 2003; and K. W. Smither, M. London, R. Flautt, Y. Vargas, & I. Kucine, "Can Executive Coaches Enhance the Impact of Multi-Source Feedback on Behavior Change? A Quasi-Experimental Field Study." *Personnel Psychology*, 56, 23–44, 2003.

47. T. J. Maurer, D. Mitchell, & F. G. Barbeite, "Predictors of Attitudes Toward a 360-Degree Feedback System and Involvement in Post-Feedback Management Development Activity." *Journal of Occupational and Organizational Psychology*, 75, 87–107, 2002.

48. D. Antonioni, "Designing an Effective 360-Degree Appraisal Feedback Process." *Organizational Dynamics*, 25(2), 24–38, 1996.

49. L. E. Atwater & J. F. Brett, "360-Degree Feedback to Leaders." *Group and Organization Management*, 31(5), 578–600, 2006.

50. M. Buckingham & C. Coffman, *First Break All the Rules*. New York: Simon & Schuster, 1999; and J. Harter, F. Schmidt, & T. Hayes, "Business Unit Level Relationship Between Employee Satisfaction, Engagement, and Business Outcomes: A Meta-Analysis." *Journal of Applied Psychology*, 87, 268–279, 2002.

51. D. P. Shuit, "Former Pepsico Executives Do a 360 in Managing Yum Brands' Workforce." *Workforce Management*, 84(4), 59–60, 2005.

52. B. Kaye & B. Jacobson, "Mentoring: A Group Guide." *Training and Development*, 49(4), 22–27, 1995.

53. A. Brockbank & I. McGill. *Facilitating Reflective Learning Through Mentoring and Coaching*. London: Kogan Page, 2006.

54. R. Witherspoon & R. P. White, "Executive Coaching: What's in It for You?" *Training and Development*, 50(3), 14–15, 1996.

55. MDA Leadership Consulting, "Perform Some Action Learning Magic in your Organization." Retrieved July 19, 2007, from www.mdaleadership.com/Leadership_Actionlearning_Volkerwinter2003.asp.

56. K. Poulsen, "Implementing Successful Mentoring Programs: Career Definition vs. Mentoring Approach." *Industrial and Commercial Training*, 38(5), 251–258, 2006.

57. K. E. Kram, *Mentoring at Work: Developmental Relationships in Organizational Life*. Glenview, IL: Scott, Foresman, 1985.

58. T. D. Allen, M. L. Poteet, & S. M. Burroughs, "The Mentor's Perspective: A Qualitative Inquiry and Future Research Agenda." *Journal of Vocational Behavior*, 51(1), 70–89, 1997.

59. A. Collins, J. S. Brown, & S. E. Newman, "Cognitive Apprenticeship: Teaching the Crafts of Reading, Writing, and Mathematics." In

L. B. Resnick (ed.), *Knowing, Learning, and Instruction: Essays in Honor of Robert Glaser* (pp. 453–492), Hillsdale, NJ: Erlbaum, 1989.

60. T. D. Allen, L. T. Eby, M. L. Poteet, E. Lentz, & L. Lima, "Career Benefits Associated with Mentoring for Protégés: A Meta-Analysis." *Journal of Applied Psychology*, 89, 127–136, 2004.

61. L. Phillips, "Mentors Save First Direct £1m." *People Management*, February 22, p. 12, 2007.

62. S. Glover & M. Wilson, *Unconventional Wisdom: A Brief History of CCL's Pioneering Research and Innovation*. Greensboro, NC: Center for Creative Leadership, 2006.

63. D. P. Young & N. M. Dixon, *Helping Leaders Take Effective Action*. Greensboro, NC: Center for Creative Leadership, 1996.

64. T. D. Allen, M. L. Poteet, & S. M. Burroughs, "The Mentor's Perspective: A Qualitative Inquiry and Future Research Agenda." *Journal of Vocational Behavior*, 51(1), 70–89, 1997.

65. K. Williams, *Mentoring the Next Generation of Nonprofit Leaders: A Practical Guide for Managers*. Washington, DC: AED Center for Leadership Development, 2005.

66. H. Lancaster, "You Might Need a Guide to Lead You Around Career Pitfalls." *Wall Street Journal*, July 30, 1996.

67. R. M. Fulmer, "The Evolving Paradigm of Leadership Development." *Organizational Dynamics*, 25(4), 59–72, 1997.

68. M. McDermott, A. Levenson, & S. Newton, "What Coaching Can and Cannot Do for Your Organization." *Human Resource Planning*, 30(2), 30–37, 2007.

69. M. McDougall & R. S. Beattie, "Peer Mentoring at Work." *Management Learning*, 28, 423–437, 1997.

70. H. Mintzberg & J. R. Gosling, "Reality Programming for MBAs." *Strategy and Business*, 26(1), 28–31, 2002.

71. R. H. Schaffer, "Outside Experts, Internal Learning Opportunities." *Leverage*, 21, 1–4, 1998.

72. L. McDermott, "Wanted: Chief Executive Coach." *Training and Development*, 50(5), 67–70, 1996.

73. C. R. Bell, *Managers as Mentors: Building Partnerships for Learning*. San Francisco: Berrett-Koehler, 2002.

74. Ibid.

75. H. Peters, "Peer Coaching for Executives." *Training & Development*, 50(3), 39–41, 1996.

76. T. D. Allen, M. L. Poteet, & S. M. Burroughs, "The Mentor's Perspective: A Qualitative Inquiry and Future Research Agenda." *Journal of Vocational Behavior*, 51(1), 70–89, 1997.

77. W. Q. Judge & J. Cowell, "The Brave New World of Executive Coaching." *Business Horizons*, 4(4), 71–77, 1997.

78. D. Schön, *The Reflective Practitioner: How Professionals Think in Action*. New York: Basic Books, 1983; and G. McGonagill, "The Coach as Reflective Practitioner: Notes from a Journey without End." In C. Fitzgerald & G. J. Berger (eds.), *Executive Coaching: Practices and Perspectives* (pp. 59–85). Palo Alto, CA: Davies-Black, 2002.

79. D. E. Gray, "Executive Coaching: Towards a Dynamic Alliance of Psychotherapy and Transformative Learning Processes." *Management Learning*, 37(4), 475–497, 2006.

80. M. Newman, "Response to Understanding Transformation Theory." *Adult Education Quarterly*, 44(4), 236–242, 1994.

81. K. Dovey, "The Learning Organization and the Organization of Learning." *Management Learning*, 28, 331–349, 1997.

82. P. G. Hutcheson, "Ten Tips for Coaches." *Training and Development*, 50(3), 15–16, 1996.

83. J. Waldroop & T. Butler, "The Executive as Coach." *Harvard Business Review*, 74(6), 111–117, 1996.

84. K. Williams, F. Kiel, M. Doyle, & L. Sinagra, "Breaking the Boundaries: Leveraging the Personal in Executive Coaching." In C. Fitzgerald & G. J. Berger (eds.), *Executive Coaching: Practices and Perspectives* (pp. 119–133), Palo Alto, CA: Davies-Black, 2002.

85. S. Sherman, "How Tomorrow's Leaders Are Learning Their Stuff." *Fortune*, 132(11), 90–102, 1995.

86. S. L. Elkins, "Transformational Learning in Leadership and Management Positions." *Human Resource Development Quarterly*, 14(2), 351–358, 2003.

87. R. Krim, "Managing to Learn: Action Inquiry in City Hall." In P. Reason (ed.), *Human Inquiry in Action: Developments in New Paradigm Research* (pp. 144–162). Thousand Oaks, CA: Sage, 1988.

88. W. R. Torbert, "Initiating Collaborative Inquiry." In G. Morgan (ed.), *Beyond Method: Strategies for Social Research* (pp. 272–291). Thousand Oaks, CA: Sage, 1983; and W. R. Torbert, *Managing the Corporate Dream: Restructuring for Long-Term Success*. Homewood, IL: Dow Jones-Irwin, 1987.

Chapter Eight

1. See, for example, N.R.F. Maier, "Assets and Liabilities in Group Problem Solving: The Need for an Integrative Function." *Psychological Review*, 74(4), 239–249, 1967; and E. Schein, *Process Consultation*, Vol. 1. Reading, MA: Addison-Wesley, 1967.

2. G. H. Varney, "Guidelines for Entry Level Competencies to the Field." *Academy of Management ODC Newsletter*, 9–11, Winter 1998.

3. I. Cunningham, "Beyond Modernity: Is Postmodernism Relevant to Management Development?" *Management Education and Development*, 21, 207–218, 1990.

4. I. L. Janis, "Groupthink." *Psychology Today*, 5(6), 43–46, 74–76, 1971.

5. Private communication from Kevin Wheeler, November 12, 2006.
6. M. Knowles, *Self-Directed Learning: A Guide for Learners and Teachers*. New York: Cambridge Books, 1975.
7. P. Reason & J. Rowan (eds.), *Human Inquiry: A Sourcebook of New Paradigm Research*. Hoboken, NJ: Wiley, 1981.
8. J. Heron, *Six Category Intervention Analysis. Human Potential Research Project*, University of Surrey, Guildford, U.K., 1989.
9. C. Donaghue, "Toward a Model of Set Adviser Effectiveness." *Journal of European Industrial Training,* 16(21), 20–26, 1992.
10. R. G. Weaver & J. D. Farrell, *Managers as Facilitators*. San Francisco: Berrett-Koehler, 1997.
11. B. W. Tuckman, "Developmental Sequences in Small Groups." *Psychological Bulletin,* 63, 384–399, 1965.
12. P. Hersey & K. H. Blanchard, *Management of Organizational Behavior* (5th ed.). Upper Saddle River, NJ: Prentice Hall, 1988.
13. D. Carew, E. Parisi-Carew, & K. Blanchard, *Group Development and Situational Leadership II*. Escondido, CA: Blanchard Training and Development, 1990.
14. See R. G. Weaver & J. D. Farrell, *Managers as Facilitators*. San Francisco: Berrett-Koehler, 1997.
15. K. Lewin, *Field Theory in Social Science* (D. Cartwright, ed.). New York: HarperCollins, 1951.
16. C. D. Scott & D. T. Jaffe, *Managing Organizational Change*. Los Altos, CA: Crisp Publications, 1989.
17. Ibid.
18. M.F.R. Kets de Vries, "Leadership Group Coaching in Action: The Zen of Creating High Performance Teams." *Academy of Management Executive,* 19(1), 61–76, 2005.
19. R. W. Revans, *The Origin and Growth of Action Learning*. Brickley, U.K.: Chartwell-Bratt, 1982.
20. This case has been adapted from J. A. Raelin, "Action Learning and Action Science: Are They Different?" *Organizational Dynamics,* 26(1), 23–25, 1997.
21. R. Vince & L. Martin, "Inside Action Learning: An Exploration of the Psychology and Politics of the Action Learning Model." *Management Education and Development,* 24, 205–215, 1993; and R. Leitch & C. Day, "Reflective Processes in Action: Mapping Personal and Professional Contexts for Learning and Change." *Journal of In-Service Education,* 27(2), 237–259, 2001.
22. D. Goleman, *Emotional Intelligence: Why It Can Matter More Than IQ* (10th ed.) New York: Bantam Books, 2006.
23. H. Höpfl & S. Linstead, "Learning to Feel and Feeling to Learn: Emotion and Learning in Organizations." *Management Learning,* 28(1), 5–12, 1997.
24. P. Reason, *Participation in Human Inquiry*. Thousand Oaks, CA: Sage, 1994.

25. P. Reason & J. Rowan (eds.), *Human Inquiry: A Sourcebook of New Paradigm Research*. Hoboken, NJ: Wiley, 1981.

26. R. Vince & L. Martin, "Inside Action Learning: An Exploration of the Psychology and Politics of the Action Learning Model." *Management Education and Development*, 24, 205–215, 1993.

27. J. Habermas, *The Theory of Communicative Action*, Vol. 1: *Reason and the Rationalization of Society* (Trans. T. McCarthy). Boston: Beacon Press, 1984.

28. W. J. Gregory & N.R.A. Romm, "Critical Facilitation: Learning Through Intervention in Group Processes." *Management Learning*, 32(4), 453–467, 2001.

29. W. Griffith, "The Reflecting Team as an Alternative Case Teaching Model: A Narrative, Conversational Approach." *Management Learning*, 30, 343–362, 1999.

30. W. Isaacs, *Dialogue: The Art of Thinking Together*. New York: Doubleday, 1999.

31. S. Bell, "Self-Reflection and Vulnerability in Action Research: Bringing Forth New Worlds in our Learning." *Systemic Practice and Action Research*, 11(2), 179–191, 1998.

Chapter Nine

1. T. Hayes, "Conversation with a Change Agent: Al Vicere on ARAMARK." *Human Resource Planning*, 27(2), 5–8, 2004.

2. R. Lessem, "A Biography of Action Learning." In M. Pedler (ed.), *Action Learning in Practice* (2nd ed., pp. 17–30). Aldershot, U.K.: Gower, 1991.

3. L. Beaty, T. Bourner, & P. Frost, "Action Learning: Reflections on Becoming a Set Member." *Management Education and Development*, 24, 350–367, 1993.

4. B. Caie, "Learning in Style: Reflections on an Action Learning MBA Programme." *Journal of Management Development*, 6(2), 19–29, 1987.

5. P. West & R. Choueke, "The Alchemy of Action Learning." *Education and Training*, 45(4), 215–225, 2003.

6. R. F. Poell & F. J. Van der Krogt, "Project-Based Learning in Organizations: Towards a Methodology for Learning in Groups." *Journal of Workplace Learning*, 15(5), 217–228, 2003.

7. Robert Kittrell, former president of Leadership Solutions, personal correspondence, February 14, 2000.

8. G. Morgan & R. Ramirez, "Action Learning: A Holographic Metaphor for Guiding Social Change." *Human Relations*, 37(1), 1–28, 1983.

9. David Ashton, personal correspondence, April 12, 2004.

10. Institute of Management and Administration, "Action Learning at Southern Co. Fills the Talent Pipeline." *IOM's Report on Managing Training and Development*, 2–3, February 2003.

11. P. Marsh & B. Wood, "Pressed for Results: An Action Learning Project in Practice." *Industrial and Commercial Training*, 33(1), 32–36, 2001.

12. T. H. Davenport, D. W. De Long, & M. C. Beers, "Successful Knowledge Management Projects." *Sloan Management Review*, 39(2), 43–57, 1998.

13. J. Clarke, R. Thorpe, L. Anderson, & J. Gold, "It's All Action, It's All Learning: Action Learning in SMEs." *Journal of European Industrial Training*, 30(6), 441–455, 2006.

14. V. M. Tucker & M. W. Taylor, "Action Projects: Common Pitfalls and Ways Around Them." ISOE Working Paper, WP-97/001, The Pennsylvania State University, University Park, 1997.

15. H. T. David, "Action Learning for Police Officers in High Crack Areas." *Action Learning: Research and Practice*, 3(2), 189–196, 2006.

16. I. De Loo & B. Verstegen, "New Thoughts on Action Learning." *Journal of European Industrial Training*, 25(2/3/4), 229–234, 2001.

17. V. M. Tucker & M. W. Taylor, "Action Projects: Common Pitfalls and Ways Around Them." ISOE Working Paper, WP-97/001, The Pennsylvania State University, University Park, 1997.

18. J. Hayes & C. W. Allinson, "Cognitive Style and the Theory and Practice of Individual and Collective Learning in Organizations." *Human Relations*, 51(7), 847–871, 1998.

19. J. Lave, *Cognition in Practice: Mind, Mathematics, and Culture in Everyday Life*. Cambridge, U.K.: Cambridge University Press, 1988.

20. M. J. Tyre & E. von Hippel, "The Situated Nature of Adaptive Learning in Organizations." *Organization Science*, 8(1), 71–81, 1997.

21. J. C. Meister, "Experiential Learning Integrates Action Coaching to Maximize Results." *Chief Learning Officer*, 6(4), 58, 2007.

22. J. A. Raelin, "The Design of the Action Project in Work-Based Learning." *Human Resource Planning*, 22(3), 12–28, 1999.

23. J. S. Kuhn & V. J. Marsick, "Action Learning for Strategic Innovation in Mature Organizations: Key Cognitive, Design, and Contextual Considerations." *Action Learning: Research and Practice*, 2(1), 27–48, 2005.

24. S. Willcocks & P. Milne, "Developing Work-Based Learning for Practice Managers in Primary Care." *Work Based Learning in Primary Care*, 4, 311–321, 2006.

25. See also V. M. Tucker & M. W. Taylor, "Action Projects: Common Pitfalls and Ways Around Them." ISOE Working Paper, WP-97/001, The Pennsylvania State University, University Park, 1997; J. A. Raelin, "The Design of the Action Project in Work-Based Learning." *Human Resource Planning*, 22(3), 12–28, 1999; and O. Zuber-Skerritt, "A Model for Designing Action Learning and Action Research Programs." *Learning Organization*, 9(4), 143–149, 2002.

26. J. A. Raelin, "Don't Bother Putting Leadership into People." *Academy of Management Executive*, 18(3), 131–135, 2004.

27. C. L. Davey, J. A. Powell, & I. Cooper, "Action Learning in a Medium-sized Construction Company." *Building Research and Information*, 30(1), 5–15, 2002.

28. L. Chapman, "Improving Patient Care Through Work-Based Learning." *Nursing Standard*, 20(41), 41–45, 2006.

29. K. Weinstein, *Action Learning: A Journey in Discovery and Development*. New York: HarperCollins, 1995.

30. P.A.C. Smith, "Action Learning and Reflective Practice in Project Environments That Are Related to Leadership Development." *Management Learning*, 32(1), 31–48, 2001.

Chapter Ten

1. See, for example, A. Lewis & W. Marsh, "Action Learning: The Development of Field Managers in the Prudential Assurance Company." *Journal of Management Development*, 6(2), 45–56, 1987.

2. A. Mumford, "Managers Developing Each Other Through Action Learning." *IFAL Journal*, 1, 72–80, 2000.

3. J. S. Wholey, "Using Evaluation to Improve Program Performance." *Bureaucrat*, 20(2), 55–59, 1991.

4. J. A. Raelin, "Whither Management Education: Professional Education, Action Learning, and Beyond." *Management Learning*, 25(2), 301–317, 1994.

5. V. Swallow, "Learning on the Job: Accredited Work Based Learning." *Emergency Nurse*, 8(6), 35–39, 2000.

6. C. Prince, "University Accreditation and the Corporate Learning Agenda." *Journal of Management Development*, 23(3), 256–269, 2004.

7. B. Dewar, R. Tocher, & W. Watson, "Using Work-Based Learning to Enable Practice Development." In T. Shaw & K. Sanders (eds.), *Foundation of Nursing Studies Series*, 2(3), 1–4, 2003.

8. *NHS Cumbria, Lancashire, & Greater Manchester Strategic Health Authority, Accreditation of Prior and Work Based Learning*, Vol. 1. Preston, U.K.: University of Central Lancashire, 2005.

9. E. Miles, "A Scheme for Accreditation of Workplace Learning by Part-time BSc Biomedical Science Students." In *Models and Implementations of Work-Based Learning Conference Proceedings, Work-based Learning Network of the Universities Association Promoting Continuing Education*, November 22–23, 2001.

10. N. M. Dixon, "The Responsibilities of Members in an Organization That Is Learning." *Learning Organization*, 5(4), 161–167, 1998.

11. R. E. Quinn & G. M. Spreitzer, "The Road to Empowerment: Seven Questions Every Leader Should Consider." *Organizational Dynamics*, 26(2), 37–49, 1997.

12. A. Jones & C. Hendry, "The Learning Organization: Adult Learning and Organizational Transformation." *British Journal of Management*, 5(2), 153–162, 1994.

13. D. Schön, *The Reflective Practitioner: How Professionals Think in Action*. New York: Basic Books, 1983, p. 328.

14. See D. Pearce, "Getting Started: An Action Manual." In M. Pedler (ed.), *Action Learning in Practice* (2nd ed.) (pp. 349–366). Aldershot: Gower, 1991.

15. See, for example, C. K. Brancato, *New Corporate Performance Measures*. Report No. 1118–95-RR. New York: Conference Board, 1995.

16. R. E. Wintermantel & K. L. Mattimore, "In the Changing World of Human Resources: Matching Measures to Mission." *Human Resource Management*, 36(3), 337–342, 1997.

17. This example was reported in J. W. Boudreau and P. M. Ramstad, "Measuring Intellectual Capital: Learning from Financial History." *Human Resource Management*, 36(3), 343–356, 1997.

18. T. F. Urban, G. R. Ferris, D. F. Crowe, & R. L. Miller, "Management Training: Justify Costs or Say Goodbye." *Training and Development Journal*, 39(3), 68–71, 1985.

19. U.S. Department of Labor, "Road to High-Performance Workplaces: A Guide to Better Jobs and Better Business Results." Washington, DC: U.S. Department of Labor, 1994.

20. M. Harvey & T. Slaughter, "Assessment and Evaluation in Work Based Learning." Paper presented at the Universities Association for Lifelong Learning Annual Conference, University of Edinburgh, March 2005.

21. K. Islam, "Alternatives for Measuring Learning Success." *Chief Learning Officer*, 32–37, November 2004.

22. J. S. Wholey, "Using Evaluation to Improve Program Performance." *Bureaucrat*, 20(2), 55–59, 1991.

23. T. B. Lawrence, C. Hardy, & N. Phillips, "Institutional Effects of Interorganizational Collaborations: The Emergence of Proto-Institutions." *Academy of Management Journal*, 45(1), 281–290, 2002.

24. J. Burgoyne & R. Stuart, "Implicit Learning Theories as Determinants of the Effect of Management Development Programmes." *Personnel Review*, 6(2), 5–14, 1977.

25. N. Rackham & T. Morgan, *Behaviour Analysis in Training*. New York: McGraw-Hill, 1977.

26. B. Joyce & B. Showers, *Student Achievement Through Staff Development*. London: Longman, 1988.

27. H. Alder, "The Bottom Line." *Training Tomorrow*, 33–34, November 1992.

28. W. B. Brenneman, J. B. Keys, & R. M. Fulmer, "Learning Across a Living Company: The Shell Companies' Experiences." *Organizational Dynamics*,

27(2), 61–69, 1998; and R. M. Fulmer & A. A. Vicere, "Executive Development: An Analysis of Competitive Forces." *Planning Review*, 24(1), 31–36, 1996.

29. J. E. Enderby & D. R. Phelan, "Action Learning Groups as the Foundation for Cultural Change." *Quality Magazine*, 3(1), 42–49, 1994.

30. Leadership in International Management Ltd., *Developing Global Business Leaders Through Action Reflection Learning*. Pennington, NJ: Leadership in International Management Ltd., 1997.

31. IR Holdings, Ltd., "Forum Case Study: Action Learning." Retrieved July 19, 2007, from http://www.forum.com/docs/basic/ActionLearningTeam.pdf.

32. D. L. Kirkpatrick, *Evaluating Training Programs*. Alexandria, VA: American Society for Training and Development, 1975.

33. Center for Creative Leadership, Connected Leadership Project, "Developing Next-Generation Leaders with an Action-Learning Approach." Greensboro, NC: Center for Creative Leadership, 2007.

34. S. Humphries, "Assessing to Learn—Learning to Assess." Cambridge, MA: Society for Organizational Learning. Retrieved July 20, 2007, from http://www.solonline.org/repository/download/index.html?item_id=443220.

35. V. J. Marsick & K. E. Watkins, "Informal and Incidental Learning." *New Directions for Adult and Continuing Education*, 89, 25–34, 2001.

36. See, for example, J. H. Boyett, & H. P. Conn, "Developing White-Collar Performance Measures." *National Productivity Review*, 7, 209–218, 1988; and C. K. Brancato, *New Corporate Performance Measures*. Report No. 1118-95-RR. New York: Conference Board, 1995.

37. H. Willmott, "Critical Management Learning." In J. Burgoyne & M. Reynolds (eds.), *Management Learning: Integrating Perspectives in Theory and Practice* (pp. 161–176). Thousand Oaks, CA: Sage, 1997; V. Fournier & C. Grey, "At the Critical Moment: Conditions and Prospects for Critical Management Studies." *Human Relations*, 53(1), 7–32, 2000; J. Garrick & S. Clegg, "Stressed-Out Knowledge Workers in Performative Times: A Postmodern Take on Project-Based Learning." *Management Learning*, 32(1), 119–134, 2001; and T. Fenwick, "Emancipatory Potential of Action Learning: A Critical Analysis." *Journal of Organizational Change Management*, 16(6), 619–632, 2003.

38. M. Reynolds, "Towards a Critical Management Pedagogy." In J. Burgoyne & M. Reynolds (eds.), *Management Learning: Integrating Perspectives in Theory and Practice* (pp. 312–328). Thousand Oaks, CA: Sage, 1997.

39. P. Allman, *Critical Education Against Global Capitalism: Karl Marx and Revolutionary Critical Education*. Westport, CT: Bergin and Garvey, 2001; and T. Fenwick, "Ethical Dilemmas of Critical Management Education." *Management Learning*, 36(1), 31–48, 2005.

40. C. Johnson & D. P. Spicer, "A Case Study of Action Learning in an MBA Program." *Education and Training*, 48(1), 39–54, 2006.

41. C. Rigg & K. Trehan, "Reflections on Working with Critical Action Learning." *Action Learning: Research and Practice*, 1(2), 149–165, 2004.

42. P. L. Inman & S. Vernon, "Assessing Workplace Learning: New Trends and Possibilities." *New Directions for Adult and Continuing Education*, no. 75, 75–85, Fall 1997.

43. B. F. Blair, M. Millea, & J. Hammer, "Impact of Cooperative Education on Academic Performance and Compensation of Engineering Majors." *Journal of Engineering Education*, 93(4), 333–338, 2004; and S. Dressler & A. Keeling, "Benefits of Cooperative Education for Students." In R. Coll & C. Eames (eds.), *International Handbook for Cooperative Education* (pp. 217–236). Hamilton, New Zealand: Waikato Print, 2004.

44. G. Somers, "How Cooperative Education Affects Recruitment and Retention." *Journal of Cooperative Education*, 25(1), 72–78, 1986.

45. J. W. Wilson, "Assessing Outcomes of Cooperative Education." *Journal of Cooperative Education*, 25(2), 38–45, 1989; S. Dressler & A. Keeling, "Benefits of Cooperative Education for Students." In R. Coll & C. Eames (eds.), *International Handbook for Cooperative Education* (pp. 217–236). Hamilton, New Zealand: Waikato Print, 2004; and J. Eyler & D. E. Giles, *Where Is the Learning in Service-Learning?* San Francisco: Jossey-Bass, 1999.

46. K. Pittenger, "The Role of Cooperative Education in the Career Growth of Engineering Students." *Journal of Cooperative Education*, 28(3), 21–29, 1993; and P. D. Gardner, D. C. Nixon, & G. Motschenbacker, "Starting Salary Outcomes of Cooperative Education Graduates." *Journal of Cooperative Education*, 27(3), 30–41, 1992.

47. A. Bandura, *Social Foundations of Thought and Action: A Social Cognitive Theory*. Englewood Cliffs, NJ: Prentice Hall, 1986.

48. A. Bandura, "Self-Efficacy Mechanism in Human Agency." *American Psychologist*, 37(2), 122–147, 1982; and R. W. Lent & G. Hackett, "Career Self-Efficacy: Empirical Status and Future Directions." *Journal of Vocational Behavior*, 30, 347–382, 1987.

49. M. E. Gist & T. R. Mitchell, "Self-Efficacy: A Theoretical Analysis of Its Determinants and Malleability." *Academy of Management Review*, 17, 183–211, 1992.

50. J. A. Raelin, "Does Action Learning Promote Collaborative Leadership?" *Academy of Management Learning and Education*, 5(2), 152–168, 2006.

51. L. S. Shulman, "Making Differences: A Table of Learning." *Change*, 34(6), 36–44, 2002.

52. J. Piaget, *The Mechanisms of Perception*. New York: Basic Books, 1969.

53. J. Mezirow, "A Critical Theory of Adult Learning and Education." *Adult Education*, 32, 3–24, 1981; D. Boud, R. Keogh, & D. Walker (eds.), *Reflection: Turning Experience into Learning*. London: Kogan Page, 1985; and S. Billett, *Learning in the Workplace*. Crows Nest, Australia: Allen and Unwin, 2001.

54. J. Piaget, *The Mechanisms of Perception*. New York: Basic Books, 1969.

55. B. Teekman, "Exploring Reflective Thinking in Nursing Practice." *Journal of Advanced Nursing*, 31(5), 1125–1135, 2000; and D. Leonard, & W. Swap, "Deep Smarts." *Harvard Business Review*, 82(9), 88–97, 2004.

56. J. A. Raelin, "Individual and Situational Predictors of Successful Outcomes from Action Learning." *Journal of Management Education*, 21(3), 368–394, 1997.

57. C. Johnson, "The Essential Principles of Action Learning." In Electronic Conference, "New Approaches to Management Education and Development (NAMED)." Bradford, U.K.: MCB University Press, 1997.

58. H. Frank, "Action Learning at Work: The Learning Experiences of British Managers in Yorkshire." Unpublished manuscript, 1988.

59. R. E. Nemire & S. M. Meyer, "Educating Students for Practice: Educational Outcomes and Community Experience." *American Journal of Pharmaceutical Education*, 70(1), 1–6, 2006.

60. M. R. Dunlap, "Adjustment and Developmental Outcomes of Students Engaged in Service Learning." *Journal of Experiential Education*, 21(3), 47–53, 1998; and J. S. Kuhn & V. J. Marsick, "Action Learning for Strategic Innovation in Mature Organizations: Key Cognitive, Design, and Contextual Considerations." *Action Learning: Research and Practice*, 2(1), 27–48, 2005.

61. See, for example, A. Lewis & W. Marsh, "Action Learning: The Development of Field Managers in the Prudential Assurance Company." *Journal of Management Development*, 6(2), 45–56, 1987; and K. Weinstein, *Action Learning: A Journey in Discovery and Development*. New York: HarperCollins, 1995.

62. M. Bazerman, *Judgment in Managerial Decision Making* (6th ed.). Hoboken, NJ: Wiley, 2005.

63. A. Kelly, "Measuring Payback from Human Resource Development." *Industrial and Commercial Training*, 25(7), 3–6, 1993.

64. Adapted from W. Kaydos, *Measuring, Managing, and Maximizing Performance*. Portland, OR: Productivity Press, 1991.

65. K. E. Sveiby, *The New Organizational Wealth*. San Francisco: Berrett-Koehler, 1997.

Chapter Eleven

1. American Society for Training and Development, "Caterpillar." *Training and Development*, 60(10), 60, 2005.

 2. D. L. Dotlich & J. L. Noel, *Action Learning: How the World's Top Companies are Re-Creating Their Leaders and Themselves*. San Francisco: Jossey-Bass, 1998.

 3. R. M. Burnside & V. A. Guthrie, *Training for Action: A New Approach Executive Development*. Greensboro, NC: Center for Creative Leadership, 1992.

4. J. Lukinsky, "Reflective Withdrawal Through Journal Writing." In J. Mezirow and Associates (eds.), *Fostering Critical Reflection in Adulthood* (pp. 213–234), San Francisco: Jossey-Bass, 1990.

5. E. Cell, *Learning to Learn from Experience*. Albany: State University of New York, 1984.

6. M. Pedler (ed.), *Action Learning in Practice* (2nd ed.). Aldershot: Gower, 1991.

7. J. L. Noel & R. Charan, "Leadership Development at GE's Crotonville." *Human Resource Management*, 27(4), 433–447, 1988; J. L. Noel & R. Charan, "GE Brings Global Thinking to Light." *Training and Development*, 46(7), 29–33, 1992; and J. Durett, "GE Hones in Leaders at Crotonville." *Training*, 43(5), 25–27, 2006.

8. C. Argyris, *Reasoning, Learning and Action*. San Francisco: Jossey-Bass, 1982.

9. S. Brookfield, "Uncovering Assumptions: The Key to Reflective Practice." *Adult Learning*, 3(4), 13–18, 1992.

10. G. A. Kelly, *The Psychology of Personal Constructs*. New York: Norton, 1955; and D. Deshler, "Metaphors and Values in Higher Education." *Academe*, 71(6), 22–29, 1985.

11. Quoted in J. Raelin, "Stimulating 'Leaderful' Change in a Senior Management Network." *Systems Thinker*, 15(1), 8–10, 2004.

12. Khanya-aicdd, retrieved July 30, 2007, from http://www.khanya-aicdd.org/site_files/index.asp?pid=113.

13. GAN-Net and the Generative Change Community, in particular, is the brain-child of Dr. Steve Waddell. See, for example, S. Waddell, "Realising Global Change: Developing the Tools; Building the Infrastructure." *Journal of Corporate Citizenship*, 26, 69–84, June 2007; S. Waddell, "Large Systems Change CoP: Four Activity Areas Supporting GAN Change Efforts." *Global Action Network Net*, 3(2), 2007; B. Pruitt, "The Generative Change Community: Cases About the Meaning of 'Generative Dialogic Changes Processes,'" *Reflections*, 8(2), 1–5, 2007; and the Web site, http://www.gan-net.net.

14. See, for example, M. L. Jones, "Action Learning as a New Idea." *Journal of Management Development*, 9(5), 29–34, 1990.

15. F. Shipper, R. C. Hoffman, & D. M. Rotondo, "Does the 360 Feedback Process Create Actionable Knowledge Equally Across Cultures?" *Academy of Management Learning and Education*, 6(1), 33–50, 2007.

16. A.W.K. Harzing, "Response Rates in International Mail Surveys: Results of a 22-Country Study." *International Business Review*, 6(6), 641–665, 1997; and C-M. Lau & H. Y. Ngo, "Organization Development and Firm Performance: A Comparison of Multinational and Local Firms." *Journal of International Business Studies*, 32(1), 95–114, 2001.

17. R. K. Yeo, "Learning Institution to Learning Organization: Kudos to Reflective Practitioners." *Journal of European Industrial Training*, 30(5), 396–419, 2006.

18. M. Marquardt, "Using Action Learning with Multicultural Groups." *Performance Improvement Quarterly*, 11(1), 113–128, 1998.

19. L. Yiu & R. Saner, "Use of Action Learning as a Vehicle for Capacity Building in China." *Performance Improvement Quarterly*, 11(1), 129–148, 1998; and L. Yiu, "Cultural Variance of Reflection in Action Learning." Paper presented at the Annual Meeting of the Academy of Management, Atlanta, GA, August 14, 2006.

20. A. Chuaprapaisilp, "Improving Learning from Experience Through the Conduct of Pre- and Post-Clinical Conferences: Action Research in Nursing Education in Thailand." Unpublished doctoral dissertation, University of New South Wales, Australia, 1989.

21. P. Freire, *Pedagogy of the Oppressed*. New York: Seabury Press, 1970.

22. O. Fals-Borda & M. A. Rahman, *Action and Knowledge: Breaking the Monopoly with Participatory Action Research*. New York: Apex Press, 1991.

23. D. L. Dotlich & J. L. Noel, *Action Learning: How the World's Top Companies Are Re-Creating Their Leaders and Themselves*. San Francisco: Jossey-Bass, 1998.

24. N. J. Adler, *International Dimensions of Organizational Behavior*. Cincinnati, OH: South-Western, 2002.

25. J. S. Black & M. Mendenhall, "Cross-Cultural Training Effectiveness: A Review and a Theoretical Framework for Future Research." *Academy of Management Review*, 15(1), 113–136, 1990.

26. H. Axel, "Company Experiences with Global Teams." *Conference Board's HR Executive Review*, 4(2), 1–18, 1996.

27. L. Beamer, "Learning Intercultural Communication Competence." *Journal of Business Communication*, 29(3), 285–303, 1992.

28. K. Smith & D. Berg, "Cross-Cultural Groups at Work." *European Management Journal*, 15(1), 8–15, 1997.

29. Reported in C. M. Solomon, "When Training Doesn't Translate." *Workforce*, 76(3), 40–44, 1997.

30. T. Hayes, "Conversation with a Change Agent: Al Vicere on ARAMARK." *Human Resource Planning*, 27(2), 5–8, 2004.

31. This case was generously provided by Ernie Turner, President of LIM, Leadership in International Management, Ltd. For more information on the Action Reflection Learning approach referred to, see I. Rimanoczy & E. Turner, *Action Reflection Learning: Solving Real Business Problems by Connecting Earning with Learning*. Mountain View, CA: Davies-Black, 2008.

Index